MORE PRAISE FOR *THE MOBILE REVOLUTION*

"A comprehensive account of the market and service evolution of mobile communications… illustrated with real-world experiences of mobile players."
Thomas Geitner, Chief Technology Officer, Vodafone Group Plc

"A comprehensive and authoritative summary of the new era of mobile communication."
Sean Maloney, Executive Vice President, GM Mobility Group, Intel Corporation

"An exciting exploration of what's turning out to be the most transformative technology of the twenty-first century. Less a tale of tech than a story of our own evolution, and the near-supernatural new things we can do. A mind-bending read."
Geoffrey Frost, Chief Marketing Officer, Motorola Inc

"Combines the evolution of the global mobile ecosystem with strategic and tactical insights. A book all those involved in today's content businesses would benefit from reading."
Pete Downton, Director of Business Development and Strategic Partnership, Warner Music International

"Understanding the technology that enables more mobile products and services to exist is only a small part of the mobile revolution. But as The Mobile Revolution *points out, what really matters is understanding people's ever-changing demands and expectations."*
Dave McCaughan, Executive Vice President, Director of Strategic Planning, McCannErickson, Japan

"Exciting insights into the future of mobile; all in a global context. A fundamental resource for anyone interested in the next stage of communications evolution."
Barry Peters, Director, Emerging Media and Relationship Marketing, Carat Interactive

"A time machine – effortlessly taking the reader back into intricate details of so many interwoven plays of technology, marketing, design and visionary achievement that created the mobile revolution we know today."
Frank Nuovo, Chief Designer of Nokia's mobile phones

THE MOBILE REVOLUTION

THE MAKING OF MOBILE SERVICES WORLDWIDE

DAN STEINBOCK

KOGAN PAGE

London and Philadelphia

Publisher's note

Every possible effort has been made to ensure that the information contained in this book is accurate at the time of going to press, and the publishers and authors cannot accept responsibility for any errors or omissions, however caused. No responsibility for loss or damage occasioned to any person acting, or refraining from action, as a result of the material in this publication can be accepted by the editor, the publisher or any of the authors.

First published in Great Britain and the United States in 2005 by Kogan Page Limited.
Paperback edition 2007
Reprinted 2007

120 Pentonville Road
London N1 9JN
United Kingdom
www.kogan-page.co.uk

525 South 4th Street, #241
Philadelphia PA 19147
USA

© Dan Steinbock, 2005

ISBN-10   0 7494 4850 4
ISBN-13   978 0 7494 4850 9

British Library Cataloguing-in-Publication Data

A CIP record for this book is available from the British Library.

Library of Congress Cataloging-in-Publication Data

Steinbock, Dan.
   The mobile revolution : the making of mobile services worldwide / Dan
Steinbock.
      p. cm.
   Includes bibliographical references and index.
   ISBN 0-7494-4296-4
   1. Wireless communication systems. 2. Mobile communication systems. 3.
Telecommunication. 4. Internet. I. Title.
HE9713.S728 2005
384.3'3–dc22

                          2005004338

Typeset by Saxon Graphics Ltd, Derby
Printed and bound in Great Britain by Bell & Bain, Glasgow

Contents

Figures

Tables

Boxes

Acknowledgements

As I was researching *The Mobile Revolution*, I nicknamed it 'The Great Software Monster', as Nokia's struggling executives once termed the GSM project. Fascinating subject, but a lot of work. I've written most of the book in downtown Manhattan, Shanghai and Pudong, London, Helsinki and Hong Kong.

The experiences of the leading mobile pioneers – vendors, operators, Hollywood studios, media companies, music publishers and record companies, marketers and advertisers, as well as global brands – are not just important, but make a fascinating story. I am indebted to some 80 senior executives across the world. In addition to these interviewees who so generously gave their time and thoughts, I owe an additional debt to their assistants, secretaries, PR agencies and spokespersons because often they were the ones who made these interviews happen.

In particular, I would like to extend my sincere thanks to Anssi Vanjoki, executive vice president of Nokia Multimedia, the marketer who globalized Nokia's brand in just a few years and is now one of the visionaries of mobile multimedia; Geoffrey Frost, chief marketing officer of Motorola, Nike's former brand wizard who created the great Michael Jordan and Tiger Woods campaigns and is now 'Moto-morphing' the mobile world; Sean Maloney, executive vice president of Intel, the technology and marketing guru who is mobilizing Intel for a new era; Dr Paul E Jacobs, group president of Qualcomm, the pioneer of the core technology of the 3G era (CDMA), and a tireless promoter of the BREW platform; Bert Nordberg, senior vice president of the LM Ericsson, the veteran Swedish leader of infrastructure equipment; and Ed Suwanjindar, lead product manager at Microsoft's mobile devices who has persuasively advocated the adoption and use of smart phones worldwide. Among operators, I am deeply grateful to Takeshi Natsuno, managing director of multimedia services at NTT DoCoMo in Tokyo, an ingenious marketer and an industry visionary who has played a critical role with i-mode, the most successful mobile online service worldwide; Thomas Geitner, chief technology officer of Vodafone, who played such an important role in the birth of Vodafone Live! and was willing to tell the story; and Richard Brennan, executive vice president of global brand marketing at Orange SA, the Australian brand thinker who simplified the clumsy telecom speak to us mortals and probably knows more about European marketing than the Europeans themselves. I owe gratitude to Sung Min Ha, head of strategic planning at SK Telecom, who gave his time to talk about the experiences of the Korean broadband powerhouse which is now a legendary trendsetter worldwide, and Paul Palmieri, Verizon Wireless's multimedia chief, who has played a key role in the arrival of mobile multimedia in the United States.

I was also privileged to talk with all major Hollywood studios and would like to express my gratitude particularly to Larry Shapiro, executive vice president of business development at the Walt Disney Internet Group, the pioneering mobile content player worldwide, which is testing future services with NTT DoCoMo in Japan, and Rio Caraeff, vice president of wireless services at Sony Pictures, the entertainment studio and consumer electronics innovator, which is mobilizing its array of entertainment properties. I'm deeply grateful to Mitch Lazar, vice president of the wireless properties at Turner Broadcasting System International, who took the time to illustrate the rapid evolution of CNN's mobile properties worldwide. I'm grateful to Doug Dyer, vice president of wireless at Warner Bros. Online, the eloquent advocate of WB entertainment properties worldwide; John Smelzer, vice president of business development at Fox Sports Interactive Media which, along with News Corp's many subsidiaries in Europe and Asia, is pioneering mobile sports; Paul Jelinek, vice president of new business development at Nickelodeon Online, which along with MTV plays a critical role in the mobile future, due to its powerful hold of tweens in America and elsewhere; and Bruce Gersh, vice president of business development at ABC Entertainment, who has contributed to the fusion of mobility and broadcasting.

Among music publishers and record companies, I would like to single out Pete Downton, heading wireless activities at Warner Music International, the advocate and pioneer of mobile music; Jonathan Channon, senior vice president of EMI Music Publishing, who signed with Nokia what is said to have been the first ringtone deal ever; Richard Conlon, vice president of marketing and business development at BMI, who, in the United States, has played an important role in mobile music rights; Jeremy Laws, executive director of media licensing at Universal's Consumer Products, who guided the author through the labyrinth of media licensing business; Christa Haussler, vice president of new technology at BMG Entertainment, the sober common-sense technologist who's impressed by results rather than new mousetraps; and Keith Jopling, director of market research at IFPI (International Federation of the Phonographic Industry), who was most helpful with industry research and studies.

For years now, newspaper publishers have been exploring opportunities to mobilize their products and services. A couple of years ago I interviewed Neil Budde, the former founding editor and publisher of the Wall Street Journal Online, for a study on the internet, subscription model and strategic success. Now I had a chance to interview him again, along with Jessica Perry, vice president, and Richard Tumble, director, of business development at Dow Jones Interactive Publishing, on the mobilization of the Wall Street Journal Interactive. In the Silicon Alley of New York City, Martin A Nisenholtz, CEO of New York Times Digital, is the highly regarded pioneer of electronic publishing. He gave his time generously to talk about the mobilization of 'all news fit to print'. I was also able to interview Randall Maxwell, the knowledgeable head of Yahoo Asia's wireless services (formerly MTV's point man in Asia). And during a Finnair flight, somewhere between Helsinki and New York City, I met Anders Stenbäck, who, along with Eero Korhonen and Jarkko Kyttänen, serves in the development team of Helsingin Sanomat, the leading Finnish daily and a mobile pioneer.

Usually when people talk about mobile multimedia, they tend to think of consumer services only. But during the past few years, there has been a rising momentum in mobile enterprise solutions. I was privileged to interview executives in all leading mobile ES players, including Douglas Dedo, marketing manager of Microsoft's Windows Mobile and a highly regarded industry thinker, and also such industry veterans and visionaries as Cindy Patterson, vice president of enterprise data sales at Verizon Wireless; Mary McDowell, senior vice president of enterprise solutions at Nokia; Kurt Sillen, vice president of mobility world at Ericsson; Letina Conelly, director of strategy at IBM's pervasive computing; and Deborah Conrad, vice president of solutions market development at Intel.

Among mobile marketers, I spent hours with sharp visionaries, such as Mike Windsor, CEO of Ogilvy Interactive Worldwide, the veteran of interactive marketing worldwide; Martin Copus, managing director of 12snap UK, a pioneer of mobile marketing; Pamir Geleben, director of corporate development at Flytxt, a trendsetting industry thinker; David Turchetti, CEO of 21 Communications in Shanghai, who is pioneering US mass marketers' mobile campaigns with tens of millions of Chinese consumers; Ami Hasan, partner at Hasan & Partners, a Finnish brand wizard; Brian Levin, CEO of Mobliss, and the mobile pioneer behind the combo of texting and broadcasting (read: the role of SMS in the success of *American Idol*); Dr Michael Birkel, group CEO of 12snap; and Dave McCaughan, director of strategic planning at McCann-Ericsson Asia-Pacific, a market researcher who offered fresh, even surprising, data on mobile behaviour in Asian nations.

Additionally, I was privileged to interview some of the most highly regarded industry veterans, including Martin Cooper, the former Motorola R&D chief who developed the first cell phone, and Rob Glaser, CEO and chairman of the famed RealNetworks and the trendsetting player behind mobile streaming. I had the pleasure to talk a couple of times with Frank Nuovo, vice president and chief designer of Nokia Mobile Phones, whose work has set industry standards across the world and who is now widely copied from Europe to Asia and to the United States. Then there was Juha Putkiranta, senior vice president of imaging business at Nokia, who has been pioneering the camera phones business. Similarly, Ilkka Raiskinen, senior vice president of Nokia's entertainment and media, and industry veteran, has been in charge of the extraordinary effort to mobilize online games, through his work with N-Gage. I also had the opportunity to debate mobile marketing and media with Lauri Kivinen, formerly chief of Nokia's corporate communications and now the company's EU point man, who has seen so intimately the rise of mobility since the late 1990s; Tapio Hedman, vice president of communications and a highly-regarded veteran at Nokia Mobile Phones, and many other Nokians, including Christian From, Nancy Sobota and Kirsi Harra-Vauhkonen.

I would also like to thank those numerous interviewees who wish to remain anonymous and who represent industry practitioners in Finland and Sweden, Germany, the UK, Hong Kong and China, Korea and Singapore.

Due to the limitation of space, I deeply regret that it has been impossible to incorporate all the interviews fully. As a result, half of the interviews have been framed as boxes, and the remaining half have been deployed as quotations or as context.

I am indebted to Cara Anselmo, who did great work in reviewing a seemingly massive pile of manuscript pages. I am grateful to research assistants from Baruch College who transcribed hours of interviews. Also, the completion of *The Mobile Revolution* would not have been possible without the support of a number of people at Kogan Page, Europe's leading independent publisher, including Pauline Goodwin, Stephen Lustig, Martha Fumagalli, Heather Langridge and Suzanne Mursell in London and Keith Ashfield in the United States. However, I take responsibility for the conclusions of the book, which are mine alone.

Most intimately, I am grateful to my family, my father, mother and brother in Helsinki, Finland, especially during these difficult times when life feels so precious and fragile. And I would like to thank Donna. When I started the book, she was my best friend; now she's my wife. I am privileged to have her in my life.

Dan Steinbock
New York City

Acronyms

1G	first generation (analog cellular)
2G	second generation (digital cellular)
2.5G	enhanced digital cellular
3G	third generation (multimedia cellular)
4G	fourth generation (broadband cellular)
AMPS	advanced mobile phone system
ARPU	average revenue per user
ATM	automated teller machine
C2P	content-to-person
CDMA	code-division multiple access
CEO	chief executive officer
CIO	chief information officer
CRM	customer relationship management
DMB	digital multimedia broadcasting
DVB-H	digital video broadcast – handheld
DRM	digital rights management
ERP	enterprise resource planning
ES	enterprise solutions
EV-DO	EVolution, Data Only, a '3G' standard
FCC	Federal Communications Commission (US)
FDI	foreign direct investment
GSM	Global System for Mobile
IC	NTT DoCoMo's contactless smart card (FeliCa IC)
IM	instant messaging
IMTS	improved mobile telephone service
IP	internet protocol
IP Datacast	combination of digital broadcast and internet protocol

ISP	internet service provider
IT	information technology
ITU	International Telecommunication Union
LAN	local area network
LBS	location-based services
MMS	multimedia messaging service
MRP	material requirement planning
MRP-II	manufacturing resource planning
MTS	Mobile Telephone Service
MVNO	mobile virtual network operator
NMT	Nordic Mobile Telephony
OEM	original equipment manufacturers
OMA	Open Mobile Alliance
P2P	person-to-person
PDA	personal digital assistant
PDC	personal digital cellular (Japan)
PIM	Personal Information Manager
PMR	private mobile system
PTT	postal, telephone and telegraph office
PVR	personal video recorder
R&D	research and development
RFID	radio frequency identification
ROI	return on investment
RTT	real-time technology
SCM	supply chain management
SIM	subscriber identity module card
SIP	Session Initiation Protocol
SMS	short message service
SSL	Secure Sockets Layer
SWIS	'See What I See'
TCO	total cost of ownership
UMTS	Universal Mobile Telecommunications System
VoIP	voice over internet protocol
VPN	virtual private network
WAN	wide area network
WAP	wireless application protocol
WCDMA	wideband code division multiple access
Wi-Fi	wireless fidelity, high-speed WLAN technology (IEEE 802.11 standard)
WiMax	higher-speed WLAN technology (IEEE 802.16 standard)
WLAN	wireless local area network

Introduction

'We're moving away from the business of ears to the business of eyes.'

Move over Bill Gates, stand aside Steve Jobs, said the industry pundits after CeBIT 1998, the famous trade conference. They'd just seen Nokia's Communicator 9110, a mobile phone with dazzling capabilities, but what really intrigued them was the unforgettable line by Anssi Vanjoki, Nokia's legendary brand chief.

Two to three years later, we met and talked about the coming revolution in mobile services. I was intrigued by the vision, but even more by the way. *How* are we moving from ears to eyes?

That's how *The Mobile Revolution* began.

FROM TECHNOLOGY INNOVATION...

In the past, mobility was driven by technology change. With increasing penetration, the momentum is now on usage. Tomorrow, it will be on mobile content. Yet the frameworks we deploy to understand industry change originate from technologists, not from marketers.

According to conventional industry wisdom, technology-based innovations are part of a continuum of change. Each wave of innovation is typically illustrated with the S-curve, a graph of the relationship between time (the effort put into improving a product or process) and performance (the return on the investment). Each wave of innovation is characterized by a continuous curve. Successive waves are characterized by discontinuities between these curves (see Figure 0.1).

Take the mobile business, for instance. In addition to the costly 3G licence auctions and public efforts to tax operators to the point of bankruptcy, conven-

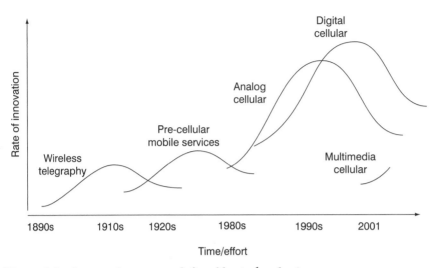

Figure 0.1 Innovation waves defined by technologies

tional wisdom tends to emphasize the role of technologies and performance capabilities. Yet the evolution of mobile communications has been the function of technology *and* marketing innovation. Successive waves of innovation are not autonomous and independent, but cumulative and dependent, building on the previous waves.

In this scenario, the rate of innovation is also defined in terms of S-curves depicting increasing performance capabilities, but these curves are shaped by *markets*, as much as they are shaped by product, process and service competition. Technology-based S-curves can be depicted individually and separately, in terms of time and performance capabilities. However, markets and services must be understood in terms of penetration and usage. While the technological preconditions of this curve may comprise successive waves of technology innovation, the overall market-based (penetration) curve has evolved over decades, up to the explosion of the mass markets and globalization in the 1990s (see Figure 0.2).

Technologies make markets possible; product and service competition makes or breaks markets. As trivial as it sounds, this is still downplayed in technology-intensive industries, often with costly consequences.

... TO MARKETING INNOVATION

According to the conventional view, successive waves of innovation are triggered by emerging technologies. In this scenario, markets are only an afterthought, and services are identified with products, as if the two were identical (which they certainly are not). Instead of technologies and products only, it is time also to spotlight markets and services, and to give credit where it is due. If we truly want to

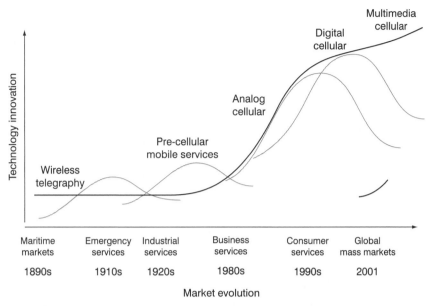

Where technologists see disruptive technologies, marketers often see incrementally evolving market penetration and usage. Disruptive *technology* innovation does not automatically translate to disruptive *market* innovation.

Figure 0.2 Innovation waves defined by markets

understand the transition from the ears to the eyes, we must understand better the shift from technology innovation to marketing innovation.

From the late 19th century to the present, mobile leaders have not been companies that have excelled in technology innovation alone. Rather, the winners have excelled in technology innovation *and* marketing innovation. The history of mobility, like the evolutionary trajectories of so many other industries, is littered by failures when companies have got right only one side of the equation.

When companies have been successful in technology development but failed in market pioneering, new technologies have led to new products, processes and services, but these have failed to create new markets. The WAP debacle is a textbook example. At the end of the 1990s, the leading European mobile vendors and operators developed Wireless Application Protocol as an open international standard for applications using wireless communication. Despite great R&D and investment, it was essentially branded technology rather than branded services. In saturated markets driven by sophisticated consumers, such creations are doomed.

Conversely, when companies have been successful in market development but failed in technology development, old offerings have been provided for new and changing markets. Unwilling to cannibalize its successful products and services, Motorola in the early 1990s delayed digital transition so long that it fell behind rivals and had to spend years in a futile catch-up game.

During the past century, the mobile industry has gone through successive waves of innovation. Technology has not made markets. It is the interplay of technology and marketing that has resulted in new products, processes and services. However, the last ones – services – are a relatively recent phenomenon.

MOBILE SERVICES WORLDWIDE

Pioneered by Guglielmo Marconi, wireless telegraphy created the first customers and business models in the mobile industry, particularly in the maritime sector. Over time, it led to AM communications, which was pioneered by police departments in the United States, and FM communications, which provided a substantial military advantage to US defence forces during the Second World War.

After the war years, these technologies led to the pioneering of mobile industrial services and the development of the first consumer test markets. However, there was only one (and very primitive) service, really: voice – and this defined the mobile services for the next half a century.

The cellular concept was discovered as early as 1947 at the Bell Labs, but commercialization followed only in the 1980s with analog cellular networks. These services appealed primarily to automobile drivers and corporate markets. Starting in the early 1990s, digital transition made possible consumer mass markets, which have been rapidly specializing and globalizing ever since.

As voice services were coupled with short message services (SMS), subscribers got a rudimentary idea of new mobile services. Since 2001, worldwide mobile markets have witnessed the first transition to the multimedia cellular, known as UMTS (Universal Mobile Telecommunications System) in Europe and 3G in the United States. These, however, were preceded by NTT DoCoMo's service innovation in Japan.

As software applications began to drive mobile communications, the world's leading IT enablers, from Microsoft to Intel, entered the business, with aggressive efforts to 'mobilize' broadband technologies. The transition from voice communications to data communications enables advanced mobile services, which have already triggered the entry of the world's largest content providers, including Hollywood studios.

In the past, voice drove mobility. Yesterday, software was the key driver, but as mobile subscribers, we couldn't care less about data; we're attracted by new services and compelling content.

THE STRUCTURE OF THE BOOK

In this book, the perspective of marketing innovation is applied to the mobile business, particularly the changing mobile markets, service pioneers, mobile consumer services and business services, as well as strategy. Unlike existing works on the subject, this book is not only based on extensive review of theoretical frameworks and empirical industry competition, but also supported by in-depth interviews with some 80 senior executives from among the world's leading mobile vendors, operators, IT enablers, media and entertainment conglomerates, consumer electronics concerns, mobile developers and brand marketers. The inside stories illustrate pioneer successes (and in some cases failures) in the massive transition from voice to data – that is, in mobile service innovation.

The first part provides context on the changing markets. In Chapter 1, market innovation is explored in worldwide context, by lead markets, and the world's leading mobile vendors and operators. Until the late 1980s, the market leadership belonged to the United States. After the mid-1990s, Nordic countries captured leadership, while industry momentum has shifted to the Asia-Pacific, in relation to both service innovation (Japan, Korea) and massive growth markets (China, India). Mobile globalization is exemplified by the pioneer experiences of SK Telecom, Ericsson, Ogilvy Interactive Worldwide, and pioneering mobile marketing service providers such as 21 Communications in China.

Chapter 2 focuses on mobile innovation, which parallels four historical marketing approaches (product, selling, marketing and customer concept). Particular attention is dedicated to the transition from voice to data, and the adoption of new broadband technologies, before the 3G implementation. This chapter develops the notion of the dominant design from products and processes to services, while focusing on the unique characteristics of the mobile service experience. Interviews with the senior executives of Motorola, Nokia, Orange, Intel and Qualcomm illustrate these developments.

Chapter 3 focuses on mobile service pioneers. It tells the inside story of NTT DoCoMo's service innovation, which, along with SK Telecom's success in Korea, has captured imagination worldwide. It also examines the inside story of Vodafone's service innovation in Europe (Vodafone Live!), the rise of rivals, and the story of the leading US operator, Verizon Wireless and its service innovation (Get It Now). These events are narrated by key insiders at NTT DoCoMo, Vodafone and Verizon Wireless.

Part II explores the rapid expansion of mobile consumer services worldwide. Chapter 4 illustrates the basic service categories that the pioneers created, from rich voice and messaging to personalized content and mobile portals. It also provides an overview of significant shifts in content evolution, and an in-depth look at the experiences of content providers, such as Wall Street Journal Interactive, New York Times, and Yahoo Asia.

Chapter 5 examines the evolution of the service portfolios that these pioneers have created and currently manage, while assessing the future prospects. Starting with the pioneering of NTT DoCoMo, it focuses on dynamic mobile content, from multimedia messaging services to mobile phone television. It also explores the genesis of ringtones and mobile music. These trendsetting industry experiences are coupled with inside stories of the groundbreaking Nokia–EMI deal, licensing revolution in the United States

(BMI), mobile streaming (RealNetworks), integration of mobile music (Warner Music, BMG), and the rise of mobile sports (Fox).

Chapter 6 examines the efforts at mobile media and entertainment. It illustrates the emerging value chain, including the nascent business models, and digital rights management. These pioneering efforts are explored in greater detail with three in-depth cases: the rise of mobile news worldwide (CNN and Turner Broadcasting), the evolution of mobile games (and the creation of Nokia's N-Gage), and the expansion of mobile entertainment (Disney Mobile). The interviews with senior executives are coupled with the experiences of Universal (mobile media licensing), Sony and Warner Bros (mobile entertainment and games), and ABC (mobility and interactive broadcasting).

Chapter 7 focuses on the design and transformation of mobile devices (or 'the devices formerly known as cellphones', as Motorola's marketing chief Geoffrey Frost likes to call them). Starting with the dual role of the handset (physical form factor, emotional expression), it explores the evolution of the mobile design, from Motorola's 'brick' to Nokia's segmentation. It pays particular attention to the pressures of commodification and differentiation, and the evolution of segmentation (by technology, lifestyle, functionality, and experience). It also includes a section on the rise of wearable phones (including mobile devices that operate via bone conduction!). This chapter is illustrated with in-depth interviews with key senior executives at Nokia, Motorola and Microsoft.

Part III focuses on mobile business services and the role of mobility in strategy. Chapter 8 focuses on the nascent field of mobile marketing. It provides an overview of the emerging industry, mobile marketing campaigns, and the adoption of mobile innovations. It includes the inside story on the success of SMS and *American Idol*, and the rise of mobile Nickelodeon and MTV. It features in-depth interviews with several trendsetting marketing service providers and industry observers, including 12 Snap, Mobliss, Flytxt, as well as McCann-Ericsson, Carat Interactive and Hasan & Partners.

Chapter 9 focuses on mobile business services, solutions and markets. It examines the evolution of mobile business services, the shift from the internet to mobilization, and the service categories in the business sector. It also provides a view of the enterprise solution providers in the mobile space, the role of the large customers particularly in the United States, and the rise of employee usage profiles. It is augmented by the experiences of trendsetting industry leaders: Microsoft, Nokia, Ericsson, Vodafone, Verizon Wireless, Intel, IBM and many others.

Chapter 10 examines the challenge of mobility in competitive strategy. Starting with an analysis of distorted market signals, it explores mobility in relation to competitive advantage (firm value chains) and competitive strategy (industry attractiveness). Focusing on the role of business models and competition, as well as mobile opportunities, it provides numerous examples of the adoption of mobility in value chains and industry forces.

The book at hand is about those winning companies that have excelled in technology innovation and marketing innovation. It tells the story of the making of mobile markets and services worldwide.

The Mobile Revolution is the road map of mobile service revolution.

Part 1

Market transformation

1

Globalization

In 1998, there were some 200 million mobile customers worldwide. Toward the end of 2004, the figure had climbed to some 1.6 billion. By 2006, it is expected to be close to 2.6 billion. Since the late 1990s, the industry has been characterized by increasing globalization, worldwide market evolution, regional differentiation and great new growth markets, particularly in China and India. Mobile expansion is taking off worldwide.

GLOBALIZATION OF MARKETS

In the mid-1980s, Kenichi Ohmae argued that worldwide industry leaders had to maintain a strong position in the key developed markets: the United States, Western Europe and Japan.

> This Triad is where the major markets are; it is where the competitive threat comes from; it is where new technologies will originate... The prime objective of every corporation must be to become a true insider in all three regions.
>
> (Ohmae, 1985: 27, 121)

From Marconi's wireless telegraphy in the 1890s to the analog cellular in the 1980s, the centre of wireless innovation was in the United States. In the 1990s, Euro-Nordic innovation overtook industry leadership. By the end of the decade, industry leadership migrated to Western Europe, service innovation shifted to Japan and Korea, and volume growth to China and India (see Figure 1.1). Today, mobile innovation is spread across the 'Triad Plus': the developed markets of Western Europe, North America and the Asia–Pacific.[1]

Figure 1.1 Regional evolution: most populous country markets (1984–2003)

Industry competition

Until the 1980s, a single network operator, typically the national telecom monopoly, was the wireless value system in most developed country markets. In the United States, 'Ma Bell' controlled the industry value chain, from manufacturing to sales and service. Today, leading companies compete and cooperate with global strategies in a worldwide theatre, engaging in a game of 'global chess'.

In the 1980s, vendors and operators that enjoyed a large-scale home base had a natural comparative advantage. A decade later, industry players that were able to create scale through globalization leveraged their competitive advantage. In the past, the key players globalized to respond to competition;

today, they must globalize to compete. In the past, they grew global over time; today, many are born global (Steinbock, 2002).

Specialization and globalization

Today, specialization and globalization of value activities is an inherent part of the business. In the 1980s, the markets were still domestic; in the 1990s, they became regional. Today, the business is driven by the specialization of the industry chain, where individual value activities are rapidly globalizing. This value system is complex, including contractors, equipment manufacturers, consumer electronics, platforms, enablers, content aggregators, retailers, network operators and service providers. Each layer is dominated by industry giants with worldwide scale and scope (see Figure 1.2).

Convergence of mobility and the internet

With the convergence of mobility and the internet, the opposition between European-based mobile leaders and US-based IT leaders has been magnified by evolutionary differences. Mobile leaders are transitioning from voice to data, IT leaders from data to voice. The former have stressed vertical coordination, the latter horizontalization. With intensifying convergence, even industry leaders have hedged their bets. Nokia, for instance, promotes vertical coordination (with a major stake in Symbian), while preparing for horizontalization (the launch of Series 60) and teaming with Intel and Symbian to develop handset templates (despite heavy reliance on Texas Instruments for such chips). Meanwhile, Asian-based consumer electronics giants, which tend to operate in maturing markets, are busy embracing mobile multimedia. The traditional players (Sony, Matsushita) rely on innovation strategies, whereas emerging

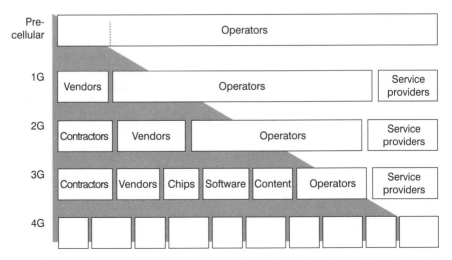

In the past, a single national telecom operator used to dominate the entire mobile value system. Today, the system is specialized and globalized (grey colour) across business and geographic segments

Figure 1.2 Industry globalization: industry value system (not to scale)

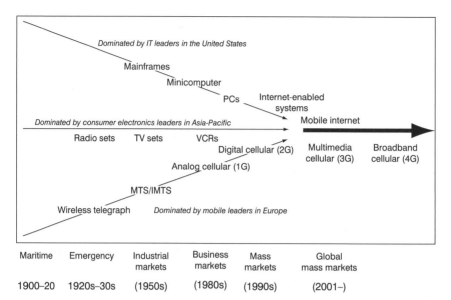

Figure 1.3 of diagram labels:

Dominated by IT leaders in the United States

Mainframes

Minicomputer

PCs   Internet-enabled systems

Dominated by consumer electronics leaders in Asia-Pacific   Mobile internet

Radio sets   TV sets   VCRs

Digital cellular (2G)   Multimedia cellular (3G)   Broadband cellular (4G)

Analog cellular (1G)

MTS/IMTS

Wireless telegraph   Dominated by mobile leaders in Europe

Maritime	Emergency	Industrial markets	Business markets	Mass markets	Global mass markets
1900–20	1920s–30s	(1950s)	(1980s)	(1990s)	(2001–)

Figure 1.3 Triple convergence: US information technology, European mobile communications, Asian consumer electronics

challengers (Chinese electronics suppliers) employ cost advantage; still others (Samsung and other Korean manufacturers) have used both (see Figure 1.3).

With the transition to data, new services require content-driven business models. As a result, the sector has prompted the entry of the world's leading media and entertainment businesses in the developed markets.

Leading operators and vendors

The worldwide evolution of operators and vendors – until recently the two key strategic groups in mobile communications – reflects these competitive realities. At the dawn of the cellular revolution, Nordic countries were the pioneers. Through most of the 1980s, US operators and vendors dominated the business. In the late 1990s, European GSM (Global System for Mobile) players captured leadership. Toward the end of the decade, the growth momentum shifted to Asia, via innovation (Japan, Korea) and scale (China, India). During the past two decades, small-country pioneers have been replaced by large-country followers. At the same time, the scale and scope of operations have escalated dramatically. The winning companies of the future will be neither national nor uniformly global. They will be primarily US, Western European, and Asian firms whose strategic advantages are increasingly specialized and globalized (see Table 1.1).

Today, the bargaining power of the traditional mobile players (primarily European-based vendors and operators) over the value system is eroding as a result of increasing specialization, the entry of the US-based IT leaders (Microsoft, Intel), the rise of service innovators (NTT DoCoMo, SK Telecom), scale players (China Mobile), and the outsourcing of manufacturing

Table 1.1 The world's leading mobile operators (1983–2002)

1991

Rank	Operator	Standard	Country	Subs.
1	AT&T Wireless	AMPS	USA	1,656,100
2	Mobility Canada	AMPS	Canada	1,501,800
3	SBC	AMPS	USA	1,229,000
4	GTE	AMPS	USA	1,032,700
5	BellSouth Mobility	AMPS	USA	812,500
6	NTT DoCoMo	NTT	Japan	772,100
7	Bell Atlantic Mobile	AMPS	USA	764,500
8	Vodafone	TACS	UK	690,000
9	AirTouch	AMPS	USA	626,500
10	Telia Mobitel	NMT	Sweden	568,180
11	BT Cellnet	TACS	UK	535,000
12	T-Mobile	C-450	Germany	532,250
13	Alltel	AMPS	USA	530,000
14	Telecom Italia Mobile	TACS	Italy	493,140
15	Ameritech	AMPS	USA	404,000

Mid-2002

Rank	Operator	Standard	Country	Subs.
1	Vodafone (U.K.)	GSM	UK	101,000,000
2	China Mobile Comm.	GSM	China	89,000,000
3	China Mobile (HK), Ltd.	GSM	China	76,397,000
4	T-Mobile International	GSM	Germany	66,900,000
5	NTT DoCoMo		Japan	40,951,000
6	Orange	GSM	UK	39,300,000
7	China Unicom	GSM	China	31,000,000
8	Telefónica Moviles	GSM	Spain	30,800,000
9	SK Telecom		Korea	30,268,000
10	Verizon Wireless	TDMA	USA	29,600,000
11	America Movil		Mexico	29,000,000
12	TIM	GSM	Italy	24,100,000
13	Cingular Wireless		USA	22,000,000
14	AT&T Wireless Services		USA	21,400,000
15	mmO2 PLC	GSM	UK	17,240,000

In 1991, right before the 2G era, 9 of the leading 15 operators worldwide were located in the United States. Two out of three relied on the US standard or its derivatives. The leading four operators had 1.2–1.7 million subscribers. In 2002, the number of US-based operators had fallen to just three, whereas European operators had increased to six, and Asian players to five (three were Chinese). Two out of three operators relied on GSM. The leading operators *each* had 66–100 million subscribers.

Source: Industry data.

capabilities to cost-efficient Asian producers – from Japanese consumer electronics leaders (Sony and Matsushita, Nintendo) to Korean tech conglomerates (Samsung), emerging Chinese electronics giants (Ningbo Bird, TCL), as well as agile contractors and sub-contractors. As the competitive intensity is still escalating, the rules of the competition are changing (see Box 1.1).

Markets and strategy

From the business standpoint, globalization can be assessed in terms of lead markets, critical country markets, as well as maturing and emerging markets.

Lead markets

Not all markets are equal. The goal is to invade and win over those markets that are truly valuable for an effective global strategy. The lead market is the geographic market or country that, in one way or another, is ahead of the rest of the world in its development. That is where new developments tend to set trends for other markets to follow. It serves a bellwether function (Jeannet and Hennessey, 1998: 254). In the mobile business, such a market may lead others in terms of technological development (innovation), perceived quality (differentiation), volume and integration (cost structure), or combinations of all three.

With ever increasing penetration and saturation, market rivalry today is about scale. It is dominated by developed economies, which are characterized by high income and slowing growth (large Western European nations, Japan and the United States), and developing economies, which are characterized by low income and rapid growth (China, India, and others). Big is beautiful.

Critical country markets

Regional markets represent highly aggregated measures for market development, from the standpoint of an individual company. For business purposes, all markets have to be examined on a country-by-country basis, and in some cases on a region-by-region basis (take, for instance, the extraordinary diversity of China's mobile marketplace). The leading vendors, operators, contractors, IT houses and content providers are seldom concerned with all country markets. They focus their resources on the critical country markets. These are markets that a company 'must win' if it seeks global leadership. In practice, the largest such markets are North America (United States, Canada), the four to five top European economies, and certain key nations in the Asia–Pacific (particularly Japan, China, India) (see Figure 1.4).[2]

To individual companies, a target nation may be a lead market, but not strategic – just as it may also be of substantial strategic significance, but not a bellwether market.

Box 1.1 'IT'S A DIFFERENT MARKET NOW'

Salesperson is the best title you can have at Ericsson, says Bert Nordberg, senior vice president of Ericsson's sales and marketing. But what bothers him is that the sales profession does not enjoy the status it should have within the company. 'I haven't found many people in Stockholm, if any, who have the title salesperson on their business card,' he says. 'It just doesn't seem to be a title anyone wants. People call themselves business managers or they work in marketing, but they are not salespeople. But what's the point of having a flawless supply chain if our order books aren't full?'

Operators coping

Ericsson is the world's leading maker of wireless telecom infrastructure equipment. Network operators and service providers use Ericsson's antennas, transmitters and other wireless infrastructure gear to build and expand networks. In the early 1990s, the market transitioned to digital cellular; now to multimedia cellular. What has changed?

'It is a totally different market today,' says Bert Nordberg. 'Now operators face competition within the industry, but also threat from other industries that they have taken some time to handle. Some industries are pushing the client–server way of doing things. Others are pushing technology and intelligence into the client, whereas operators would like to control the entire network.'

Intense competition

'Competition is more intense, due to convergence. It's an interesting time. Now things are really happening. In the past, everything remained the same. Today, industry forces are in flux. There are so many angles for attacks.'

In the mobile value chain, infrastructure providers deal with massive economies of scale and scope. Some operators have signalled eagerness to backward integrate. 'Some of them might be willing to tighten the value chain,' Nordberg thinks. 'But some want to get into the content, as well.'

'They want to do solutions for everybody. They don't want others to interfere with their enterprise relationships, which they like. If you take a look at the marketplace, the enterprise is a very, very good customer for the operator. There are so many solutions in the enterprise space today that operators can't own the customer relationship. They don't have integration capabilities. I am a heavy enterprise user myself. On the terminal side, I've seen so many different gadgets. The industry has to take the enterprise market more seriously.'

How does Wi-Fi complicate the equation?

'Wi-Fi is a wonderful standard for offices and home, but it's not mobility. In the long term, I also can't see the business case. I think people want to use mobile communications and move seamlessly from one place to another. I don't think people care for 3G or Wi-Fi. They'd just like to have the best connected solution. Ultimately, you won't need Wi-Fi.'

Source: the author's interview with Bert Nordberg, SVP, Group Function Sales and Marketing, Telefonaktiebolaget LM Ericsson, 7 April 2004.

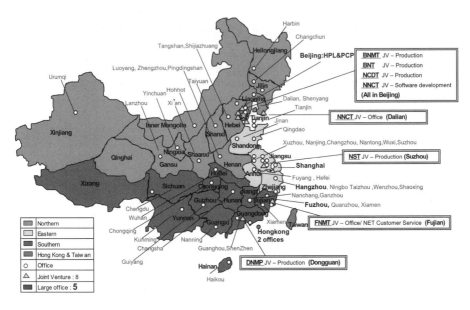

Source: Karjalainen

Figure 1.4   China's mobile marketplace: Nokia's presence (autumn 2003)

Maturing and emerging markets

Because of scale economies, size matters, but it does not automatically translate to strategic importance. Many emerging markets (Brazil) and transitional economies (Russia) provide great potential scale economies but, until recently, have lacked adequate technology infrastructure or institutional stability, or both. In the early 2000s, the mobile world is not a single oyster, but split into two quite different marketplaces. In the developed markets, high-growth years are behind, penetration is saturating, rivals are consolidating, and competition is about replacement demand and value. In the undeveloped markets, high-growth years have barely begun, penetration is low, rivals are often fragmented, and competition is about original demand and volume.

In the developed economies, the handset market is evolving into a maturing consumer electronics segment, with a huge user population who periodically upgrade their devices to take advantage of new offerings. As replacements drive growth, users migrate from entry-level to mid-range handsets, thus creating new demand for handsets with increasing functionality and features. This migration is predicated on the availability of new and attractive handsets with colour screens, multimedia content access and cameras. In the developing economies, digital cellular and prepaid markets are still growing rapidly and gaining new, first-time users.

Over time, these differences between maturing and emerging markets will dissolve. With mobile voice and data, the strategic objectives of vendors, operators and other strategic groups reflect these preconditions. With mobile data, they seek to accelerate the adoption of mobile multimedia services in mature markets, while leapfrogging directly to mobile internet in emerging markets. With mobile voice, many are driving voice from fixed to mobile in mature markets, while speeding up mobile penetration in emerging markets.

WORLDWIDE MARKET EVOLUTION

Since the early 1990s, the mobile revolution has proceeded rapidly in North America, Western Europe, and in key parts of the Asia–Pacific.

Domestic markets: US leadership (1980s)

In the pre-cellular era, mobile markets were small and primarily domestic. In worldwide terms, the growth took off only in the latter half of the 1980s. The pent-up demand came as a surprise to many firms, which had to struggle to keep up with rapid growth. The pre-cellular era peaked in 1983, the first year of analog cellular, but the momentum followed a year later, when it was introduced in the United States. In retrospect, these years illustrate the inevitable shift from small, technologically advanced mobile markets to large-scale regional markets.

In 1983, there were some half a dozen lead country markets in the mobile business:

- North America: the United States;
- Western Europe: the Nordic countries (Sweden, Norway, Denmark, Finland);
- Japan.

Regional markets: European leadership (1990s)

Initially, market innovation proceeded from pioneer countries and high-end niche consumer segments to large-scale country and business markets. Starting with the 2G era in 1992, increasing globalization has made size critical as market momentum has shifted towards large-scale markets. In these competitive circumstances, small market pioneers, particularly the Nordic countries, have struggled to remain R&D leaders for the global players. At the same time, they have lost their function as market leaders.

In 1992, the worldwide lead markets consisted of the following:

- North America: the United States and Canada;
- Western Europe: the UK, Germany, Italy, and France;
- Japan and Pacific Rim, including Australia.

Global markets: triad plus leadership (2000s–present)

For all the talk of globalization, global leadership usually means leading in about a dozen strategic markets. In 2003, the world population was about 6.3 billion. Only 1.2 billion people lived in developed nations, with some 5.1 billion in less developed nations (3.8 billion excluding China). The 10 most populous mobile markets had 846 million subscribers. Considering developing economies, a great untapped and underserved subscriber population existed worldwide.

In 2003, the world's most populous country markets in key regions included the following:

- North America: the United States and Canada;
- Western Europe: Germany, Italy, the UK, France and Spain;
- Asia–Pacific: China, India, Japan, Korea and Taiwan;
- Eastern Europe: Russia and Poland;
- Latin America: Brazil, Mexico;
- Middle East: Saudi Arabia, Israel and Iran;
- Africa: South Africa, Morocco and Egypt.

If a company seeks global presence today, it must be well positioned worldwide.

REGIONAL MARKET EVOLUTION

North America

Until the early 1990s, North America was the centre of mobile innovation worldwide. The United States had the most competitive markets; the most sophisticated vendors, operators and customers, and the most advanced products, processes and services. The analog cellular peaked only in the mid-1990s, when Motorola and many other industry players enjoyed record profits.

The United States lost its regional innovation leadership due to delays in the digital transition. Even as different standards fragmented the US market, the nation remained the most populous worldwide – until mid-August 2001, when China overtook the United States as the largest market, in terms of the number of mobile subscribers. Today, the United States remains the most lucrative country market per capita, whereas China enjoys the most massive population base but lower returns.

Western Europe

In 1983, the tiny Nordic countries still accounted for 99.5 per cent of the entire Western European marketplace. But large European countries soon caught up, and the share of the UK peaked at 37 per cent in 1989. With the digital transition, momentum in the mobile markets returned to Western Europe, particularly Nordic countries. The marketplace comprised large countries (Germany, the UK, France, Italy), emerging markets (Spain), and several small country markets. After the mid-1990s, the British lost market leadership to Italy, which lost it to Germany. By 2000, the four Nordic markets accounted for less than 7 per cent, while the top four Western European markets had more than 61 per cent of the total marketplace (see Box 1.2). With two substantial emerging mobile markets (Spain and Turkey), the top six markets had 77 per cent of the aggregate market.

Eastern Europe

Until the end of the Cold War, mobile business thrived only on the western side of the Berlin Wall. The unification of Germany precipitated the painful reintegration of Europe. In the long term, the largest, most stable and technologically progressive Eastern European countries were expected to evolve into new emerging markets. At the turn of the 1990s, Hungary (more than 80 per cent), Slovenia (20 per cent), and later Croatia dominated these early years of 'mobilization' in the former Socialist Europe. At the end of the decade, size surpassed pioneership. The key countries – Poland, the Czech Republic, Russia, Hungary and Romania – had almost 69 per cent of the entire Eastern European market.

Asia–Pacific

In the 1980s, the Asian market *was* Japan. Like Nordic leadership in Western Europe, this superiority was not sustainable. In 1991, Japan still had almost half of the entire Asia–Pacific market, against Australia, Taiwan, Hong Kong, Korea, Thailand and Malaysia. After China initiated its great opening and reforms, foreign direct investment took off. In 1991 China's mobile penetration still barely exceeded 1 per cent, but its share of the Asia–Pacific market had climbed to 14 per cent. The digital GSM provided an immense growth momentum in China.

At the end of 2000, China had overtaken Japan as the leading country market in the Asia–Pacific, just as it would soon leave behind the United States as the leading country market worldwide. It also had one-third of the regional market share, against Japan (more than 26 per cent), Korea (12 per cent) and Thailand. These four market leaders accounted for 80 per cent of the total market and were the lead markets of the region. In Japan, NTT DoCoMo pioneered the first content services and 3G markets. In Korea, operators such as SK Telecom (see Box 1.3), and vendors, such as Samsung, had a similar role in CDMA-based services and markets. India held significant future potential, but the country's wireless penetration was very low until the late 1990s.

Box 1.2   THE GREAT REVERSAL: SCANNING MARKETS WORLDWIDE

'Historically advertising is about pushing things on people. We must rethink businesses, whether it's the phone or Blackberry. Everything is changing. Today, we should think about what the customers want – not about how to push things on them.'

As CEO of OgilvyInteractive Worldwide, Mike Windsor is responsible for Ogilvy's interactive resources in 42 markets around the world. As chief executive of Anderson & Lembke, he built the largest integrated advertising and interactive agency on the West Coast, winning 90 per cent of Microsoft's interactive advertising and a majority of its traditional advertising. At OgilvyInteractive, he oversees the Motorola account.

'The interactive marketing world requires fast decisions,' says Windsor. 'The ability to adapt quickly and a willingness to leap repeatedly into the unknown... skills that I honed jumping out of perfectly good airplanes with parachutes that didn't always open.'

Worldwide marketing challenge

'With mobility, much of innovation occurs outside the United States. Most of the developing world can bypass fixed phone systems. Adoption rates in some places, for instance in Mexico and Latin America, have been faster than in the United States.

'In the United States, we didn't really need the mobile. There were phones set up everywhere and calls were cheap. In Europe and Asia SMS was very popular, especially among teens because it was an inexpensive way to communicate. In the United States, cellular phones were cheap. People use them less for SMS, more for voice calls.'

While the leading marketing service providers and ad agency networks have worldwide operations, they are often headquartered in the United States.

'In the past it was fairly easy to pick up the trends, we could almost predict the timing. With mobility, developments are much more disorganized. So we try to keep an eye in each market to find out what is going on. For the first time, we might actually want to bring to New York something that is going on in Spain. That didn't happen in the past. In mobility, Europeans are far ahead North America. Rather than reinvent things here, we must start tapping into those resources.

'A lot of innovations come from the smaller markets anyway. First, smaller budgets require more ingenuity and ways to adopt in certain new technology. Second, small markets mostly have the buyers, so it's easier to make money. We are going to see a lot of innovations picked up first in small markets. But small markets mean lower consumer demand.

'In the Japanese market, i-mode came so fast into everyone's hands that people didn't feel need for computers. They could get on the web and do more than in many Japanese websites. Consumer behaviour is fundamentally different in Japan. They can get people to pay for games. You can make money with relatively inexpensive subscriptions. We have a successful program for Nestlé where people can pull down menus on their hand-helds and get recipes and shopping lists. I thought it would be a huge failure, but it turned out to be a major success. It's a different culture. That behaviour is not for the rest of the world.'

Mobile innovation

'There are some sexy things coming up when your phone can recognize a billboard that you're passing, while downloading information and coupons. The computer is much better in terms of richness, details and quick information. Surfing on the mobile is not particularly fun. If I want something specific, it's great, but to look for something is a nightmare. The web is very simple and its ease of use enables a good relationship. The phone is ultimate convenience because I have it all the time. It's available when I need it.

'It's already pretty nice to see on the handset if my plane is delayed or when it's arriving. If I could pick and choose, I wouldn't mind if there was some sponsorship. But I don't want to turn on my phone and then have to delete 10 advertising messages.

'In Europe, marketers use SMS in more innovative ways. One of my favourite mobile case studies is the Cadbury campaign in the UK. They used SMS for promotion. Cadbury Schweppes came up with the idea and hired Flytxt to do the campaign. They had instant access to data and greater success in terms of participants and the number of candy bars sold. The campaign provided good benefits because it was real time and measurable.

'In Korea, television-style mobile capabilities are already up for sale. People may use it more for video clips than for watching TV. It is an extremely good delivery mechanism, especially if demand is linked with the ability to pinpoint location. If you can get people to opt in to things they want, it has great potential.'

Splintering media channels

'Eventually, this business is not about technology but about branding,' says Windsor. 'The screen will never be huge and it won't be a better medium. Marketing and brand building is just about touch points, about how many places I intersect with the brand and how many of those are positive or negative, and what's my sum total feeling at the end of the day.

'Digitization is a matter of splintering media on a bigger scale. In the past, you had four television channels. With cable, you had 50. With digital, you've got 100. There are so many media outlets that it's hard to reach people unless you have a very diverse marketing programme. Technology just adds to the fragmentation and drives it.'

Clueless big media

'As the world gets more complex and the gadgets into people's hands, we have to think of more ways to capture attention.

'My problem is getting people who think about 30-second television commercials and still have direct mail programmes to know that there are better ways to do stuff. The big media companies hate this because their models are built on the notion of 'Give us your money and we will negotiate really low rates within the top 20 properties.' As you get to 500 properties, it's a pretty intensive amount of work and smaller dollars per outlet.

'Media companies don't have a model that allows them to make money in this world. So they are kicking and screaming. If the media companies are not going to drive mobile business, independent companies will spring up to optimize your budget across the media marketing platform, or we are going to have to do it ourselves or we may have to get a new channel planner. Right now it's a big hurdle.'

Source: the author's interview with Mike Windsor, CEO, Ogilvy Interactive Worldwide, 19 May 2004.

Box 1.3   THE SK TELECOM SUCCESS STORY: TRANSLATING TECHNOLOGY PIONEERSHIP TO SERVICE INNOVATION

'We have established Wireless Internet as our premier growth engine,' says Sung Min Ha, head of strategic planning at SK Telecom. 'Through June, we're also offering a multimedia messaging service that enables customers to send and receive a variety of multimedia content such as streaming video, audio and text via their cellular phone.'

As long ago as November 2002, the carrier launched 'June', an advanced multimedia service aiming to fulfil market demand for 3G services and offering video on demand, music on demand, videophones, internet use and TV broadcasting. By June 2003, the service had experienced explosive growth, garnering about 1.7 million subscribers. At the same time, the carrier increased its data revenue from 10 per cent to almost 16 per cent of the total.

'We're looking at new business models,' says Ha. 'We're exploring strategic partnerships with local companies. We work to offer a broader service based on our technological expertise.'

Strategic leadership through technology pioneership

As the leading wireless communication services provider in South Korea, SK Telecom serves 18 million cellular users (54 per cent market share), nearly 16 million of which have data-capable phones. After launching the world's first CDMA (Code-Division Multiple Access) cellular service, it has introduced the world's first commercial 2.5G service, CDMA (2000 1X) and 3G CDMA (2000 1xEV-DO) services.

In addition to June, Moneta and other services, SK Telecom has been developing a chip-based mobile banking service, 'M-Bank', in cooperation with several banks. It was introduced in March 2004. SK Telecom launched a satellite for digital multimedia broadcasting (DMB) service in March 2005 and is planning to launch the commercial service in May 2005.

'SK Telecom is committed to becoming a major global player in information and communication,' says Ha. The carrier's CDMA activities are spreading throughout Asia, including the Korean, Chinese and Japanese markets, which comprise more than a quarter of the world's mobile phone subscribers. 'Network engineering is the foundation for the information communication industry. We are pioneering new markets and exporting our knowledge base in these areas. We have a global vision.'

Service leadership through technology pioneership

'We want to continue revolutionizing the telecom industry and develop new business models that combine telecom with finance, media, commerce and entertainment. This strategy enables us to ride on the crest of the emerging communication wave.'

SK Telecom's product and service strategy emulates its broader objectives in strategy and innovation. 'Our strategy is to enhance the technical capabilities of our wireless networks, and we seek to improve data transmission rates and service quality, which enables us to offer a greater variety of services,' says Ha. 'We also aim to provide a range of new wireless data and internet services and to increase revenue from these services. Third, we seek to retain and capitalize on the loyalty of our large subscriber base. And finally, we're positioning ourselves to be a leader in new wireless technologies.'

SK Telecom seeks strategic leadership through technology pioneership. The carrier must find ways to translate its technology edge into more sustainable strategic advantage. That is not an enviable job.

Source: the author's interview with Sung Min Ha, head of Strategic Planning Divisional Group, SK Telecom, 17 May 2004.

Latin America

By the mid-1980s, Mexico enjoyed superior regional leadership (60 per cent), but small countries, such as Puerto Rico and Anguilla, had greater penetration than even Chile or Brazil. By 2000, market-share leadership was captured by large regional economies, particularly Brazil (36 per cent), after extensive privatization. It was followed by Mexico (23 per cent), Argentina, Venezuela and Chile. In the absence of macroeconomic and institutional stability, the penetration of substantial country markets was 1–3 per cent, including Colombia, Peru, Paraguay, Uruguay and Panama. The top four country markets in the region (Brazil, Mexico, Argentina and Venezuela) had a 77 per cent share of the aggregate marketplace. In fact, only two country markets – Brazil and Mexico – accounted for some 58 per cent of the Latin America's share.

Middle East

Saudi Arabia played a significant but brief role in mobile evolution around the mid-1980s, when Ericsson pioneered the Saudi Kingdom's network. Along with Oman, Kuwait and the United Arab Emirates (UAE) had an important role in the region. At the end of the 1990s, Israel dominated the Middle Eastern market (42 per cent) against UAE (14 per cent), Saudi Arabia (12 per cent) and Iran (less than 10 per cent). Because of its small population base, Israel's leadership has been eroding since the mid-1990s, as large Arab countries have struggled to embrace modernization.

Africa

Mobile business arrived in Africa through two entry points: the North African Maghreb countries, located closer to the advanced Western European GSM markets, and South Africa, the regional economic centre. In 1985, Tunisia still 'owned' the African market. Soon thereafter, South Africa and certain Maghreb countries in the north overtook the market leadership. At the end of 2000, South Africa still held almost half of the market, against Morocco (18 per cent) and Egypt (14 per cent). All other country markets had less than 5 per cent of the market. In this region, these three countries accounted for almost 80 per cent of the market. Otherwise, the market remained highly fragmented.

GREAT NEW GROWTH MARKETS

China's market revolution: trading technology for access

At the end of July 2001, China had 120.6 million mobile phone users compared with 120.1 million in the United States. Amidst the US tech consolidation and Europe's 3G birth pains, China's rapid growth kept the mobile business humming. Chinese operators signed more than 5 million new subscribers per month. For almost a quarter of a century, leading mobile vendors, operators and IT enablers have traded access for R&D and foreign direct investment (FDI). Eager to bring in new investors, China's special economic zones (SEZs) in the coastal provinces and urban centres have provided preferential conditions to foreign investment. Investments by mobile vendors mirror advancements in the general investment environment, but also represent typical developed-country FDI.

In the late 1980s, the powerful Ministry of Posts and Telecommunications (MPT) still served as China's national PTT and was responsible for policy and regulation. Competitive conditions intensified in 1994, when China's government set up China Unicom as the first competitor of China Telecom. Until the reforms of the late 1990s, mobile communications was perceived as a luxury service, which justified high tariffs. With the reforms, the Chinese government separated industry regulation from business activities. Volumes soared, costs declined and the first price wars began.

Operators

Between 1995 and 2000, service revenues of Chinese operators nearly tripled from US $15 billion to almost US $45 billion. The top four operators possessed barely 7 per cent of the total market. Between 2003 and 2008, the number of mobile subscribers in China will grow from 269 million to 498 million, reaching a penetration rate of 38 per cent. Commercial 3G deployments will begin in 2005, and 3G subscribers will grow to 118 million by 2008. Through 2008, China Mobile will still hold the leading position in the mobile market in terms of its large subscriber base and operation experience (see Box 1.4). China Unicom will maintain its position as the second largest carrier during this time, and 2003 and 2004 will see it improve its market share in line with the expansion of its CDMA network. With the entrance of new carriers, both will see an erosion of their market share due to increased competition (In-Stat/MDR, 2004a).

Vendors

Between 1979 and 2001, global mobile vendors provided a powerful lift to China's mobile communications through exports, FDI, presence, instruction and training. During the past few years, Chinese vendors have upset the global supply chain. Formerly dominated by international brands such as Nokia, Motorola and Siemens, the mobile handset market saw Chinese vendors gain a 55 per cent share by mid-2003. Chinese handset vendors achieved their rapid growth in three basic ways: by focusing on production rather than technical strengths, continually launching new models, and committing resources to their sales and marketing channels. Among the Chinese handset vendors, the top nine vendors controlled 95 per cent of the local market. The three leading local vendors were Ningbo Bird, TCL and Konka.

Box 1.4   PIONEERING MOBILE MARKETS IN CHINA

'Some 80 per cent of the campaigns we do in China have never been done anywhere else in the world,' says David Turchetti, CEO of 21 Communications, who has been positioning his company for growth within the fast-moving markets of Asia. 'The vast majority of the clients that we've worked with – including KFC, Dell, Estée Lauder, and so on – have not done mobile marketing anywhere in the world. We're pioneering and there is no standard really.'

Mobile opportunities in China

'By 2002 we had already built up our infrastructure with China Mobile and China Unicom, identifying the opportunity in mobile. Since foreign companies were not permitted to do business with these two operators, we had to acquire a local player and find a way to control that company through certain legal structures,' recalls Turchetti. 'So the first step is to establish a domestic company that you can work through as a foreign player. Once that's done, that company needs to have the necessary licences and permits. The licences are highly coveted in China. The whole process takes one to two years. Once the legal structure and the licences are in place, you can bring your business plan to a provincial operator, not China Mobile or China Unicom, but to Shanghai Mobile or Shanghai Unicom or Guangdong Mobile. You have to sell your plan to the operators. They are only interested in companies they are convinced will generate revenue and scale for them. That's how we got started and now we have revenue sharing agreements with the operators.

'China Mobile takes 15 per cent of the revenues and gives 85 per cent to the service provider. China Unicom has a sliding scale, so your best-case scenario is that the service provider gets 88 per cent but it can slide all the way from 60 per cent to 88 depending on your volume. Regionally and globally speaking, the Chinese operators are quite generous on a revenue-sharing percentage basis. However, the bad debt ratio or the uncollected payments from the operators can be quite significant or maybe higher than the regional averages. You may get a higher percentage of the revenues, but, there can often be quite a discrepancy between what you record on your platform and what the operator actually pays you.'

Scale, scale, scale

The one defining difference between campaigns in Europe and China is scale. 'Scale is enormous in China, it's the biggest mobile market in the world, with nearly 300 million subscribers. What's even more significant is that nearly all of them are data users. They send and receive SMS, which is very different from European and especially US markets, where perhaps just 10 per cent of subscribers use data. The Chinese mobile user is also much more savvy and accustomed to mobile marketing.

'We reach millions of people,' says Turchetti. 'It correlates directly to the amount of media that the brand or the media company wants to make available to promote the campaign. If a client just wants to do a beta campaign where they're just experimenting with mobile and they don't want to really invest, it can be quite small. If we put something on national TV, that's where the numbers really start to pick up. With PNG on Hunan Satellite TV, we did a campaign that was a live beauty pageant vote using SMS. In a matter of minutes, it generated 50,000 votes, instant turnaround!

'Chinese people are, generally speaking, more comfortable using their phone as a data medium than, for example, North Americans,' says Turchetti. 'My guess is that above 80 per cent use the mobile for SMS. Of course the teens are the pioneers.

'The mobile phone is often the first phone that a person or family ever had in the rural areas where they're hopscotching over wired telephony directly to wireless, especially with the inexpensive wireless service being offered by China Telecom. Since they're not PC users, their first experience with the internet will be over the phone.'

Chinese mobile subscribers

'Chinese people are like people in the rest of the world,' says Turchetti about content preferences. 'They want their sports, they want their music, they want their entertainment, stock information, weather, the stuff that we want in real time anywhere in the world. They want games, pictures and ring tones.

'In terms of marketing, the Chinese are very discount oriented, they love a good offer of free product or special discount. In Europe the subscribers are probably more focused on the fun, novel, celebrity type promotions. In China it's really, 'How much off can you give me on a product, can you offer a free trial?' That works really well in China, sometimes too well. You can have a mob of people showing up at a store!

'They are crazy about PC and online games. We run the biggest PC gaming community on mobile phones in China to support players of games like Counter Strike, Diablo and War Craft and others, and they absolutely have a huge number of teens that sign up for game tips on their phones of how to play these games better.

'In Chinese television and radio, it's easier to come across mobile marketing or mobile media, mobile interactive campaigns. People like to express their opinions over the phone and send messages to the DJs or the VJs. Polls are common, people love competitions, and entertainment alerts are used as means of attracting groups of people to different points of sale.'

China's lead

'Many campaigns that we're doing in China have never been done elsewhere in the world,' says Turchetti. 'It's the brand's first mobile experience worldwide. The marketing industry is being pioneered in China for the whole world. 'We're just starting to work with Dell in China. KFC in China was the first to ever do anything on the phone. Estée Lauder wanted to attract a younger generation of consumers to the product.

'In China we're leading and the whole world is looking. In the past, marketing agencies have been dominated by executives from America and Hong Kong. Now, for the first time ever, the Chinese are coming back and saying to the industry, 'You're two to three years behind...'.

'In the United States, mobile marketing is still in its infancy compared to what's going on in China.'

Source: the author's interview with David Turchetti, CEO, 21 Communications, 30 April 2004.

China's domestic vendors learn or buy quickly from Japanese, South Korean and Taiwanese partners to keep up to date with new handset functionality. They use European design houses to ensure their handsets have the right 'look'. By 2003, the Chinese mobile phone market amounted to more than 250 million subscribers. Of these, 94 per cent had GSM, and 6 per cent CDMA phones. There were close to 50 brands in the market (21 international, 26 local), and a whopping 803 models (701 GSM models, 102 CDMA models). The continent-sized marketplace was characterized by a culturally diverse population, highly variable geography, dozens of languages and dialects. In addition to great urban mobile centres (Beijing, Shanghai, Guangzhou, Shenzhen), there were close to 170 cities with more than 1 million people. Each formed a diverse market in its own right. The 'new Chinese consumers' were information-hungry, well-informed and highly value-conscious.[3]

Of the 10 most populous markets worldwide, China – a single nation – represents an entire third of the population. With over 330 million mobile subscribers, more than 4 million new subscribers added every month and a penetration rate of some 25 per cent in 2004, China is the largest cellular market in the world and a potential hotbed of 3G activities. It is also an intensely competitive market.

'Price wars are a big headache for us. As the first player in the mobile communications market – the 'Lao Da' as we call it in the industry – we still occupy 70 per cent of this market,' acknowledges Lu Xiangdong, who has been China Mobile's executive director and vice president since early 2003. 'However, new entrants into this market are always trying to rapidly expand market share and they use price wars as the simplest method to achieve this. When the six mobile operators of China and Hong Kong enter into a price war, the fight goes so far and so low that no one is able to make any profits.' Even the world's largest operator cannot avoid price competition. In China, these battles are common. 'If we do not match the competitors' pricing, our customers start to complain. If we do cut our prices, our products become valueless. The solution therefore is to increase the quality of our service and products as rapidly as possible so that we can raise the profile of our brand' (Gilmore and Dumont, 2003: 35–49).

India: learning by outsourcing

Between 1995 and 2000, the annual growth of India's cellular subscribers exceeded 115 per cent. In China, the comparable figure was 88 per cent. China had 1.3 billion inhabitants, India more than 1.1 billion. That translated to a compound annual rate of 53 per cent – double China's 26 per cent rate. With more than 34 million subscribers in mid-2004, India is expected to have in excess of 150 million over the next five years. The drivers of this explosive growth stem from economic expansion, regulatory reforms, pent-up demand, and low penetration (3 per cent) (Strother, 2004).

Despite India's mobile growth, China has driven the wireless business, even though more than 2 million new Indian subscribers were being created monthly. Paradoxically, India's democratic leaders have been slower to adopt new public policy than China's communist reformers.

India, the world's largest democracy, is the seventh largest country in the world and the fifth largest economy in terms of purchasing power parity. The nation possesses a rich and diverse culture, geography and climate, and natural resources. But until the early 1990s, the economy was characterized by a highly regulated business environment, a pervasive licence system and high tariff barriers. Sweeping reforms changed the course of the Indian economy. With economic freedom, the government's policies have been geared towards promoting domestic and foreign private investment. Like China in the early 1990s, India stood at the beginning of its cellular explosion. The country has thriving IT clusters, and operators are more inspired by innovation and differentiation opportunities than classic Western telecom models. In many places, landline telephony does not exist, which indicates substantial potential demand for data services, particularly internet access and low-cost voice service.

Operators

In 2003, India's annual GDP growth amounted to 8.1 per cent. While its mobile market puts it on pace to become 'the next China', the marketplace has unique characteristics of its own. Most operators had very aggressive growth plans. Two dozen provided mobile service in India's 19 telecom regions and four metro areas (Delhi, Mumbai, Chennai and Calcutta). Some 80 per cent of the subscribers are pre-paid. The four leading operators – Reliance, Bharti, BSNL and Hutchison – accounted for almost 70 per cent of total subscribers (over 24 million). Average revenue per user amounted to US $11, but it was expected to decline as growth among less affluent subscribers kicked in. Over time, new data services were expected to boost ARPU slightly. Three out of four subscribers used GSM phones, while CDMA had only a fourth of the market. Unlike the US market, many Indian operators offer both CDMA and GSM service. Although early in its CDMA launch, Reliance was experimenting with mobile entertainment, including Qualcomm's Brew platform. As the operator created a wireless zone dedicated to a Hindu holiday, the first eight hours witnessed 10 million hits and 2 million downloads (Marek, 2003).

Vendors

Mobile leaders had been assessing investment opportunities in India since the end of the 1990s. In January 2001, Qualcomm invested US $200 million to acquire a 4 per cent stake in Reliance Communications. Three years later, Nokia announced a new research centre in Mumbai. It will serve as Nokia's premier CDMA research hub in the Asia–Pacific.

Despite great advances in economy and technology, as well as a growing middle class, India's high-tech prowess is recent and thin. The entire IT industry employs fewer than one million people, compared with 40 million registered unemployed (Waldman, 2004). With an economic growth rate of 6 per cent in the past 20 years, India is becoming a robust market, with a younger and more educated population. While around 300 million Indians still live on less than $1 a day, only an estimated 659,000 households have computers. In the spring of 2004, this socioeconomic gap led to the extraordinary election defeat of the Hindu-nationalist-led government, which had delivered the country to a new era of prosperity. Still, peaceful political transition, continuing growth prospects, regulators' moderation and relative regional calm indicate that, for now, the opportunities in India far outweigh the potential threats.

Future growth markets

After the hypergrowth years of the 1990s and severe stagnation around 2001–3, worldwide wireless subscriber growth is experiencing robust expansion. Through 2007, GSM markets are expected to see steady growth, with expanding worldwide footprint and as a result of customer migration from older technologies. But another reversal is behind the door. Starting around 2008–9, GSM growth will begin to decline as operators move subscribers to WCDMA. The worldwide wireless market will grow to more than 2.5 billion subscribers. European subscriber growth will continue to slow, and it will stall in Scandinavia (the world's first fully mature wireless market) and Western Europe. While China continues to lead the world in overall subscriber growth, the percentage growth leaders continue to be found in other parts of Asia, particularly the Southern Asia region, which includes India. As growth in China begins to slow, India can be expected to pick up the slack, and will be a significant engine of global subscriber growth (In-Stat/MDR, 2004b).

TOWARD THE NEXT 'NEXT BIG' MARKET

Driving the boom in many emerging countries is the explosion in prepaid service that has already made cell phones available to millions of low-income users in Europe, once excluded by monthly payments and credit checks. In Latin America, for instance, the number of subscribers has tripled from fewer than 40 million in 1999 to 118 million in May 2004, turning one in five Latin Americans into a cellphone user and making it a US $20.4 billion market. While in 1995 fewer than 2 per cent of people in most Latin American countries had cellphones, the introduction of prepaid service has sent use skyrocketing, to 29 per cent in Venezuela and 48 per cent in Chile. Despite the contraction of its economy, Venezuela has Latin America's second highest rate of cellphone use, after Chile. However, economic powerhouses like Mexico and Brazil have the largest number of subscribers (Ellsworth, 2004).

Along with the emerging markets, transitional economies, particularly Russia, have exhibited extraordinary mobile growth in the past few years. The Russian mobile phone market grew to 187 million handsets in 2003, according to IDC, 88 per cent more than in 2002. The Russian companies selling cellular phones earned a record US $2.4 billion. Siemens had 23 per cent share of the market while Motorola trailed by only one percentage point.

By July 2004, the Russian market of mobile subscribers grew to more than 53 million. In just one month, mobile operators added 3 million new names into their books, while cellular penetration reached 36.6 per cent. Driven by Moscow, the operator industry was highly concentrated. With some 47 million subscribers, the three leading players – MTS, VimpelCom and MegaFon – dominated an estimated 85–90 per cent of the total marketplace. No other rival had more than 3 per cent of the market. The number of mobile subscribers was expected to grow to 56–60 million in 2004. That meant subscriber growth of more than 1 million per month, but also a slowdown in the pace of growth from 100 per cent in the past two years to 60 per cent. By the same token, the average revenue per user (ARPU) was expected to go down.[4]

Ideally, the next 'next big markets' should have a large population, rising per capita income and relatively low penetration. Both China and India have more than 1 billion inhabitants, while per capita income is relatively high in advanced urban centres. In comparison with China and India, the potential next 'next big markets' are not quite as impressive, despite explosive growth. No other nation can boast comparable scale. By 2004, Brazil, Mexico and Thailand had relatively strong indicators, even if each country market penetration was close to 30 per cent. Between 1998 and 2003, Nigeria and Egypt demonstrated the greatest growth (175 and 130 per cent, respectively), but failed with other indicators (see Table 1.2).

New challenges

Conventional wisdom says that companies from the periphery of the global market cannot compete against established global giants from Europe, Japan and the United States. Companies from developing countries have entered the game too late; they don't have the resources. In 2003, mobile vendors discovered that conventional wisdom no longer holds.

In 1992 Motorola still dominated the mobile business with its mass marketing strategy. Nokia captured the leadership with segmentation. By the end of the decade, both Nokia and Motorola were taken aback by the challenge posed by the sudden emergence from homegrown Chinese handset brands. In the 1990s, Chinese vendors had no market share; in 2001, it was less than 10 per cent; in 2003, in excess of 50 per cent.

The problem for most aspiring multinationals from peripheral countries is that they enter the global marketplace in low-margin businesses at the bottom of the value curve, and they stay there. But it doesn't have to be that way (Bartlett and Ghoshal, 2000). Increasing evidence demonstrates that emerging multinationals may enjoy global success when they treat global competition as

Table 1.2   The next 'next big markets'

Economy	Population 2003	GNI/capita 2003	Cellular mobile subscribers				
			(k) 1998	(k) 2003	CAGR 1998–03	Per 100 2003	Of tel. subs. 2003
1 China	1,288.4	4,990	23.9	269.0	62	21.4	50.6
2 India	1,064.4	2,880	1.2	26.2	85	2.5	34.8
3 United States	291.0	37,500	69.2	158.7	18	54.3	46.6
4 Indonesia	214.5	3,210	1.1	11.7	82	5.5	60.2
5 Brazil	176.6	7,480	7.4	46.4	45	26.4	54.4
6 Pakistan	148.4	2,060	0.2	2.6	66	1.8	39.7
7 Russia	143.4	8,950	0.8	17.6	120	12.0	33.2
8 Bangladesh	138.1	1,870	0.1	1.4	79	1.0	64.8
9 Nigeria	135.6	900	0.0	3.1	175	2.6	78.7
10 Japan	127.2	28,620	47.3	86.7	13	68.0	54.9
11 Mexico	102.3	8,950	3.3	25.9	67	25.5	63.4
12 Germany	82.6	27,400	13.9	64.8	36	78.5	54.4
13 Philippines	81.5	4,640	1.7	15.2	72	19.1	82.1
14 Vietnam	81.3	2,490	0.2	2.7	65	3.4	38.4
15 Turkey	70.7	6,690	3.5	27.9	51	40.8	59.6
16 Ethiopia	68.6	710	–	0.1	–	0.1	18.4
17 Egypt	67.6	3,940	0.1	5.8	130	8.5	39.9
18 Iran	66.4	7,190	0.4	3.4	54	5.1	18.8
19 Thailand	62.0	7,450	2.0	16.1	69	26.0	71.3
20 France	59.7	27,460	11.2	41.7	30	69.6	55.1

Sources: Population and GNI/capita from World Bank; other indicators from ITU.

an opportunity to build capabilities and move into more profitable segments of their industry – and that, due to their massive homegrown scale, Chinese challengers may enjoy scale advantages that match global strategic advantages.

Like aspiring multinationals on their path to globalization, the new Chinese brands have broken out of the mind-set that they were unable to compete successfully as global industry leaders. They have adopted strategies that made being a late mover a source of competitive advantage. And they had leaders who drove them relentlessly up the value curve.

A 'sea of people' strategy

At the dawn of the millennium, Chinese companies focused on building distribution networks that took them even into small cities where foreign rivals seldom ventured, an approach called by pioneer Ningbo Bird a 'sea of people' strategy. The Chinese companies also pushed clever advertising campaigns and developed product designs that appealed to local consumers, with an affection for such features as 'clamshell' handsets that fold open or models encrusted with fake gems and multicoloured lights. The rise of the Chinese brands was eased by outsourcing production to Taiwanese and South Korean electronics manufacturers while gradually building their manufacturing resources.

Even in 2001, Nokia's mobile phone sales operation in China hardly extended beyond a handful of the biggest cities. In some cases, sales staff convened in the backrooms of local Kentucky Fried Chicken. But the days of relying entirely on third-party national distributors and the power of the Nokia brand in China are long gone. Foreign manufacturers have halted the rising market share of Chinese challengers to 38 per cent, while expanding their grip on sales of the most lucrative models. With foreign brands taking the Chinese market almost for granted, the Chinese companies were able to exploit the weaknesses. Their 'sea of people' approach was hugely successful, but limited. 'The things they did were short term and copy-able,' says Colin Giles, the chief of Nokia's China operations. 'We think we are now as competitive as any Chinese company in distribution' (Dickie, 2004).

The Empire Strikes Back

In 2004, Nokia had people in more than 300 Chinese cities as part of a retooled sales distribution system that reached deep into the world's most populous telecoms market. In design, Nokia moved to adjust to local tastes, introducing clamshell phones. In downtown Beijing, the R&D centre developed China-targeted phones. For instance, the 6108 came with a stylus and touch pad to make it easier for consumers to write text messages in Chinese characters. Nokia could also push advanced phones with high-definition cameras and other functions difficult for local rivals to match. As one of the main beneficiaries, its shipments outstripped those of Motorola, which used to dominate the Chinese market.

The struggle for the world's most populous marketplace, however, is a marathon that has barely begun, as reflected by the challenges of the impending 3G networks, products and services in China. It is also far too soon to write off the local competition. While some smaller Chinese producers are unlikely to survive, leading local companies will endure the 'hard times' of recent months. The top players, Ningbo Bird and TCL and a handful of other companies, are expected to continue to grow over the long term and to become very large global handset makers.

2

Innovation

While the first chapter explored *where* new markets have been developed in the mobile business, this one will examine *how* they evolve. The story of technology innovation is fairly well known, but that of marketing innovation is not. People do not buy things; they buy solutions to problems. That is where marketing imagination comes into the picture. 'In the factory we make cosmetics,' Charles Revson used to say. 'In the store, we sell hope' (Levitt, 1986: 127–28). Mobile communications is no exception. With its network of manufacturing facilities worldwide, Nokia makes handsets, but 'connecting people' is what it sells. Innovation is not just about technology innovation; it is also about marketing innovation – the differentiation of new products and services, of customers, markets and geographic segments.

WAVES OF INNOVATION

Mobile evolution comprises four broad eras: wireless telegraphy, the pre-cellular era, the cellular era, and the mobile era. Through successive waves of mobile innovation, functionalities have been upgraded substantially, particularly with analog, digital, multimedia cellular and broadband platforms (Figure 2.1). Technology innovation is a critical part of the story, but it is not the full story. Industry leaders are those companies that have been successful in technology and market innovation. Historically, many of the winners have capitalized on the transition points between successive waves of innovation.[1]

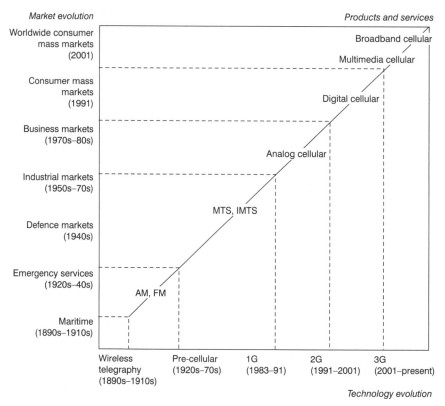

Figure 2.1 From Marconi to 4G: technology and market evolution

Technology innovation

The pre-cellular origins

In 1895, Marconi transmitted wireless signals across a distance of more than a mile, an event that many consider the birth of radio. In the early 1920s, wireless innovation was dominated by conventional amplitude modulation (AM) techniques. These were followed by frequency modulation (FM) techniques. Through the war years, popular developments in radio and the wireless were constrained by military pursuits. In 1945, the US Federal Communications Commission (FCC) began to explore spectrum allocations for a variety of uses. The birth of the cellular concept was soon followed by the electronics revolution. 'Integrated circuits,' wrote Dr Gordon Moore, Intel's future chairman, 'will lead to such wonders as home computers, automatic controls for automobiles, and personal portable communications equipment' (Moore, 1965).

The 1G era: analog cellular

Launched in the early 1980s, the nascent first generation (1G) networks relied on analog transmission for voice communication. The underlying concepts originated from two key standards – the Nordic NMT and the US AMPS. In 1983, at the peak of the pre-cellular era, NTT's proprietary system in Japan held a fourth of the worldwide market. By 1991, the US standard ruled in North America, the largest and most advanced market representing more than half of worldwide demand. A derivative of the US AMPS, the British standard, dominated two-fifths of Western Europe, as did the Nordic standard. In Asia–Pacific, the Japanese system enjoyed a significant position.

The 2G era: digital cellular

In the early 1990s, the European Commission made GSM mandatory in Europe. Due to the lower-power operation, the digital GSM networks enabled smaller and lighter handsets with greater security and longer battery life. Regional wireless leaders – Nordic vendors Ericsson and Nokia and a new generation of competitive operators, including Vodafone – seized the standard to leverage their domestic advantages in foreign markets. Meanwhile, the United States was swept by a decade of licensing turmoil. By the year 2000, Western Europe had almost two-fifths of the worldwide market. Even in the Asia–Pacific, GSM held 57 per cent of the regional market.

The 3G era: multimedia cellular

Before the transition from voice to data, mobile evolution was often depicted as a linear progression from analog to digital to multimedia to broadband cellular: 1G, 2G, 3G and 4G. The competitive realities were less orderly. Initially, the goal was to achieve a single global standard for the 3G era (UMTS), but now the European GSM was challenged by the US-based Qualcomm's more efficient technology CDMA. Still, GSM guided the evolution of platforms until the internet concept emerged as a new dominant paradigm. At the end of the 1990s – after a slate of trade war threats, behind-the-scenes political intrigues, and efforts at transatlantic business dialogue – regional differences led to a single flexible standard. The first adoption of the 3G platform, however, did not coincide with the transition from voice to data. In Japan, NTT DoCoMo pioneered the data transition in 1999 – two years before the first 3G implementation.

Toward the 4G era: rise of wireless broadband

With each subsequent cellular platform, the core technologies have substantially increased spectrum capacity. During the past decade, mobile industry leaders have aggressively pushed new high-speed wireless networks (Figure 2.2). Eager to enter the wireless business, IT enablers such as Microsoft and Intel have been particularly innovative in the wireless broadband space, not least because of delays in 3G implementation.

'For the last twenty-five years we talked about putting a computer on every desk and in every home, that was our mission,' said Steve Ballmer, Microsoft's president and CEO in 2000. 'Now we talk about empowering people, through great software, any time, any place, and on any device' (Register, 2000). At

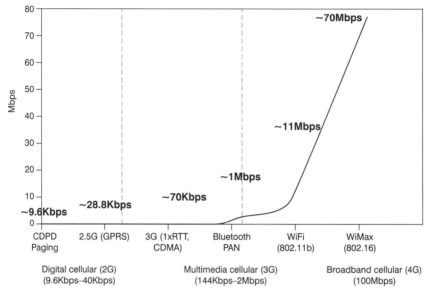

Source: Industry Data.

Figure 2.2 Expansion of wireless bandwidth

about the same time, Microsoft made its great commitment to escalate invest-ments in R&D, in order to bring telephony and PC scenarios together. Later, in the famous International Telecommunication Union (ITU) speech, Bill Gates, chairman and chief software architect of Microsoft, portrayed software as the great enabler of the broadband future (Gates, 2003).

With its marketing muscle, Intel has played the key role building demand for Wi-Fi chips in laptops and other devices, followed by more powerful alter-natives, including WiMax, ZigBee, UWP and Mobile-Fi (see Box 2.1). The mobile industry has a new growth engine, broadband wireless, says Sean Maloney, Intel's executive vice president:

> It will be disruptive for certain kinds of business models. Broadband wireless will reduce capital and operating expenses. Vertical industries like construction and retail are going to be changed by broadband wireless. People will no longer have to seek for information. Information will seek for them.[2]

NTT DoCoMo began to implement 3G mass markets in 2001, but the R&D activities were initiated back in the late 1980s. In 2005, most of the world had yet to adopt 3G and the high-speed data services it makes possible, but in Japan 3G cellular was a reality. With increasing competition, DoCoMo was already working on 4G networks, although it did not expect to introduce 4G service before 2010 (Rocks, 2004).

Box 2.1   DISRUPTIVE POTENTIAL OF BROADBAND WIRELESS

At Intel since 1982, Sean Maloney's career reflects the coming together of technology and marketing, as well as globalization. It began in the chipmaker's European head-quarters in the UK, in engineering and marketing for Intel Europe. Maloney spent the early 1990s as technical assistant to Dr Andrew S Grove, Intel's legendary chairman and chief executive. After the mid-1990s, he moved to Hong Kong to manage Intel's sales and marketing activities in the Asia–Pacific and took over Intel's worldwide sales organization in 1998.

Since 2001, Maloney has served as executive vice president and head of Intel Communications Group (ICG). As third in command, his task is to turn around the combined operations, which in 2003 lost US $858 million on US $4 billion in revenues. After the success of Wi-Fi, his next great hope is for WiMax, which could transform telecom markets.

The new growth engine

'The new growth engine is broadband wireless. During the 1990s internet boom, the business restructured around internet applications. Most companies deployed web for customers or transactions. In the next five to ten years, something similar will happen with mobility and mobile access to the web. You're going to get major re-engineering in the retail industry around mobile data applications. It's going to happen in healthcare and in education, which is already well underway. It's going to happen industry after industry.

'The result is enormous growth traffic over the network. The networks have to carry more and more traffic without increasing their capital expenditures or their operating expenditures, and that means that they're going to have to get very, very lean and efficient.

'At the same time, the equipment manufacturers, including Intel, must every one to two years deliver equipment at the same price. That will cause everybody to readjust the way they do things. The whole industry faces a future which potentially is more like the airline industry – very large traffic volume and low margin.'

Disruptive potential

'Broadband wireless is going to be disruptive for certain kinds of business models,' Maloney warns. But for many retailers, it could boost sales and increase customer satisfaction.

'Hyundai in Korea is one of my favourite examples. Right now, if you go to any of the big US stores, they have your shopping history already, but it's at the terminal, often only accessible through some clumsy interface. What Hyundai has done in its stores is to give all the store assistants PDAs [personal digital assistants]. So when you come in the door, the guy says, "Good morning. What's your phone number?" and you give your number, he says, "Oh, hi, You bought so-and-so here last week…" The PDA will automatically suggest what you want to buy today. So, by giving all the assistants PDAs, they become personal shoppers. You don't have to check out, because he's got your credit card detail there, so he just ticks off that you've got it, and you walk out the door. The experience is smoother, and the store has the opportunity to get you to buy more stuff.'

Source: the author's interview with Sean Maloney, EVP, general manager, Intel Communications Group, Intel Corp, 31 April 2004.

Sustaining and disruptive innovation

Successive waves of innovation are characterized by alternating periods of incremental and drastic change. In the first case – with sustaining innovation – the emphasis is *within* a given wave of innovation. In the second case – with disruptive innovation – it is *between* two waves of innovation; one wave of innovation leads to another, while subverting the very base of competition.[3]

Historically, mobile innovation has been characterized by both sustaining and disruptive innovation. Periods of sustaining innovation have been relatively long; periods of disruptive innovation have been relatively few. The latter have been accompanied by significant changes in products and processes.

In the late 1990s, many expected a comparable logic to prevail with the transition from voice to data, but competitive realities proved more complicated. European mobile players initiated the move from 2G to 3G *networks*; US IT enablers launched alternative broadband wireless *platforms*; and in Japan, NTT DoCoMo pioneered *service* innovation.

MARKET INNOVATION

From Marconi to the post-war era, marketing activities were rudimentary in the mobile business. Sophistication accelerated only after the launch of the first true consumer segments in the late 1980s.

Evolution of consumer markets

Marconi's wireless telegraphy pioneered the first phase of the industry, first with governments and national telecom monopolies. In shipping, one of the clients was the Royal Navy, which ordered 32 wireless sets for a total cost of £6,000 with an annual royalty payment of £3,200 (Garrard, 1998: ch 1). That was the business model: an initial payment for equipment and an ongoing revenue flow. Central to Marconi's strategy, it was replicated with the French government and shipping firms worldwide.

AM communications: mobs versus cops

The first version of a truly mobile radio telephone may have been developed by the Bell Laboratories in 1924. However, AT&T and other telecom monopolies were unwilling to develop markets which they thought would cannibalize their lucrative revenue base. Because of this 'marketing myopia', wireless AM communications first emerged in the US police departments, which were coping with the Prohibition and the gangsters' high-powered cars.

The Second World War and FM communications

In the early 1930s, Edwin M Armstrong, a brilliant electrical engineer and inventor, introduced a wide-band FM system that promised great advances in size, cost, performance and reliability. But commercial applications had to wait for a more peaceful era. After a trip to Germany, Paul Galvin, the legendary founder of Motorola, was convinced that the impressive autobahns 'have not been built just for autos, they are war roads'. Galvin prodded the defence forces to recognize the military potential of the wireless:

> I wonder how many of you realize the importance of radio as a deciding factor in who is going to win the war? What is it that gives the vicious efficiency to vehicles of destruction in modern mechanized warfare? It is radio. What is today revolutionizing aircraft, naval, and anti-aircraft tactics and strategy? It is radio and radar. It is our job – the industry's job – to deliver these precious and important instruments.
>
> (Petrakis, 1965: 159)

With the 35-pound backpack and a range of 10 miles or more, *Walkie-Talkies* were deployed throughout Europe and the Pacific, and provided critical radio links at Anzio, Guadalcanal, Iwo Jima and in Normandy.

First civilian applications

As servicemen returned from the war, surplus military radio equipment, particularly the Motorola *Handie-Talkie*, entered civilian life as taxi dispatch radios. Industry practitioners saw the moment in almost evangelical terms. As one Motorolan summed up the pitch to taxicab owners:

> Radio would be the answer to the cab companies' prayers. Telephone line charges for cab stands would disappear. Income per cab would soar. They would no longer be tied to a fixed cab location or be forced to cruise the high customer areas.
>
> (Quoted in Brown 1992: 66)

In the late 1940s, mobility entered a new era – that of *commercialization*.

Industrial services

Between 1940 and 1948, the number of wireless users in the United States soared from a few thousand to 86,000. The FCC began to explore spectrum allocations for a wide variety of uses in industrial services, such as police and fire departments, forestry, utilities and transportation. The typical wireless user was not a consumer, but a dispatch employee in a private mobile system (PMR). Similarly, the Cold War contributed to the growth of two-way radio by increasing investment in civil defence and general emergency preparedness.

First consumer services

In June 1946, in St Louis, Missouri, AT&T and Southwestern Bell introduced the first US commercial mobile radio-telephone service to private customers (Mobile Telephone Service, MTS). Through incremental advancements, the MTS of 1946 evolved into the Improved MTS (IMTS), in the early 1960s. Waiting lists proliferated and systems became oversubscribed. By 1976, only 545 subscribers in New York City had Bell System mobiles, while 3,700 remained on a waiting list. More than 20 million people had only 12 available channels (Gibson, 1987: 8)!

If market innovation is the objective, marketing mix (the 'four Ps', or product, price, place and promotion) is the tactic. Historically, *marketing* innovation in mobility has proceeded through a sequence of four phases (product, selling, marketing and customer concept). Each phase has posed different requirements to the marketing mix.[4]

Product concept: nascent markets

In the 1970s, marketing mix continued to be driven by the classic product concept. In most country markets, the national telecom monopoly was the channel, setting the price and dominating the products. Except for Nordic markets, pricing was not affordable and involved few choices. Relative to contemporary offerings, products were heavy, quality was poor, and technology was primitive. Driven by product quality and performance, this concept pioneered the customer base. It ruled as long as markets were regulated, competition was minimal, and consumer penetration was low.

The 'bricks' are coming!

In 1973, Motorola launched its first hand-held portable phone in New York. The DynaTAC was 56.2 cubic inches in size, and 38.4 ounces (1,089 g) in weight. Developed by Dr Martin Cooper, who set up a base station in New York, it was the first working prototype of a cellular telephone. The tests and experiments set the stage for Motorola's first cellular phone – the legendary 'brick' (see Box 2.2).

Market skimming

In the United States, early mobile telephone services were considered premium services. Affordable pricing was not the objective. Many national telecom organizations favoured setting high prices to 'skim' the markets. Tariff-setting was a matter of adjusting age-old price structures to reflect the effects of inflation. In Northern Europe, however, the objective was price parity between fixed and mobile phone services. That boosted rapid penetration and expansion of services.

Monopoly distribution

In the absence of competition, the national telecom monopoly was the only distribution channel. There was little need or incentive for the single service provider to differentiate itself, segment the market, target specific niches, or market different price options and discounts to customers.

Box 2.2　THE FIRST CALL

On 3 April 1973, Dr Martin Cooper was on his way to a press conference in the Manhattan Hilton. Motorola had installed a base station to handle the first public demonstration of a phone call over the cellular network. It was trying to persuade the FCC to allocate frequency space to private companies for use in the emerging technology of cellular communications.

AT&T's research arm, Bell Laboratories, had introduced the idea of cellular communications in 1947 and wanted the first system to be limited to car phones. While Bell Labs was still using 30 lb units in the trunks of cars, Motorola packed the whole thing into a 2 lb unit. It was a great breakthrough, with Motorola, the David of the wireless business challenging Ma Bell, the telecom monopoly Goliath. Dr Cooper, Motorola's then chief of R&D, wanted people to be able to carry their phones with them – anytime and anywhere.

Standing on a street nearby, he decided to try a private call before the press conference. He picked up the DynaTAC handset, pushed the 'off hook' button, which connected him with the base station on the roof of the Burlington Consolidated Tower (now the Alliance Capital Building) and into the land-line system. To the bewilderment of the New Yorkers who were passing by, he dialled the number and held the phone to his ear.

'The first call I made was to Joel Engel,' Cooper said. Engel was the Bell Labs head of research. 'I think they were a little bit annoyed,' he says, with a gentle smile. 'They thought it was impertinent for a company like Motorola to go after them.'

A few months later, the cover of *Popular Science* magazine featured Motorola's mobile, which it called a 'new type of computerized, walkie-talkie-size portable'. The only service it could offer was voice communication. But at the time, that alone was extraordinary. Since telephone was still synonymous with fixed lines, the mere idea of unplugging the cord was disruptive.

The 'look and feel' of the cell phone

The portable remains the dominant design of the mobile phone. But how did the Motorolans come up with it? What kind of variables went into that design?

'I decided that the way to show the world that the cellular phone was practical was to design one,' recalls Dr Cooper. 'I had to make a real cellular phone that worked and could serve as a personal telephone. The technology to do that was all over the place.' For all practical purposes, the physical form factor emulated the conventional (fixed-line) phone. But a portable would be more complicated. 'Now what kind of box did you put it in?' I asked Rudy Krolopp who ran the design group. He got very excited about the challenge and held a contest. I ended up taking the team out to dinner and each designer got up and presented the concept of what a future telephone should look like.

'Some of the models looked remarkably similar to the phones that exist today. Kyocera has announced the keyboard that flies out from underneath the phone and sure enough, one of the guys actually created a version of such a phone. I thought it was nicer than what they have come up with today. There was also a fold-up phone. But for practical reasons, we ended up selecting another. With the simpler phone, there was less chance that something would break during demonstration.

'We picked a phone that was functional in appearance. It was a single unit that did not have any collapsible parts to break and was attractive in appearance. The designer came up with a unit that was three or four inches tall and maybe three-quarters of an inch wide. We handed that model to the engineers and told them to squeeze all the parts in there. By the time they were finished, it had grown to the size of a brick!'

From DynaTAC to StarTAC

'The model that we started with in 1973 survived for about 15 years,' recalls Dr Cooper, the father of the first cellular phone. And while Motorola did expand its portfolio, most models emulated the original 'brick'. 'I'd like to think that designs should be fresh but the world liked the brick and just took it and made it smaller. The biggest departure was the StarTAC at Motorola, the first cell phone and the world just copied that. Motorola tried to patent it, but that effort was not successful. It also tried to produce one that twists around. Kyocera made one that slides underneath, but the clamshell approach was seminal in the mid-1980s. The primary issue for most people remains a design that is comfortable to carry around.

'Motorola achieved the number one position in the world. The Nokians were refracted to the marketplace and created phones that appealed to different sections of the market. There is no question about that. Take, for instance, the shell that you can put on a phone so that you can have different colours. It sounds so trivial, but it was crucial to Nokia's success.

'Motorola was arrogant enough to think that the digital phase would arrive more slowly than it did. They just were not ready. They did not have all the models ready and they also allowed the ability to quickly respond in the market to deteriorate. Also, they never really understood the user interface. Only recently have the Motorola phones become easy to use, like Nokia's. The combination of the poor user interface and the inability to have sufficient amount of models to cover every single area in this space was Motorola's downfall. You have to be responsive to the marketplace. You cannot let your market position make you arrogant.'

Something similar happened to Nokia in 2004, when it lost market share, not least because of the lack of clamshell models. 'But how does one determine what people's taste will be?' says Cooper. 'They lost touch with the changes in the marketplace. It's a tough job. I've always had a clamshell phone since Motorola's StarTAC. For some reason, most people gravitate towards it. Functionally there is little advantage to the clamshell over candy-bars, the kind of form factor that Nokia has used.'

Source: the author's interview with Martin Cooper, executive chairman and co-founder, ArrayComm Inc, 29 April 2004.

Sales over marketing

Given the monopoly, few operators had a functional marketing department. The Nordic players had a 'public service' mission, but this had little to do with marketing services, as they are known today. Tariffs ensured that the service was targeted for the high-end markets.

Selling concept: business markets

Through the 1980s and until the early 1990s, the United States held leadership in the wireless industry. Most country markets remained regulated. National telecom monopolies were still the only game in many markets. Emphasizing selling and promotional tools, the selling concept left little room for market pull. At first the buyers were emergency services, then cellular phones appeared in cars, in corporate markets, and finally in some high-end consumer segments. Sales orientation reigned over marketing. Penetration grew fastest in deregulated markets, from the United Kingdom to Nordic countries. Markets were still primarily domestic in scope. The marketing mix followed car phones to business markets.

Mass marketing: Motorola's DynaTAC

After 15 to 20 years and US $150–200 million in development, Motorola launched the world's first commercial cellular portable phone. 'Consumers were so impressed by the concept of being always accessible with a portable phone that waiting lists for the DynaTAC 8000X were in the thousands, despite the initial $3,995 retail price,' recalls Rudy Krolopp, of the original Motorola design team. 'In 1983, the notion of simply making wireless phone calls was revolutionary ' (Motorola, 2003). The portable was 35 cubic inches in size and 30 ounces (869 g) in weight. As the vendor saw it, its attractiveness was based on four drivers: size, weight, cost and battery life.

Market skimming

In the early 1980s, connection and subscription fees remained relatively high, and price strategies were crafted to optimally ration the scarce spectrum. Many national telecoms still favoured setting high prices to 'skim' the market, which, in mobility, ensured low penetration and low sales growth (OECD, 1999: ch 5). With more competitive public policies later in the decade, pricing instruments began to shift toward market penetration strategies.

Distribution rivalry

Promotion of channel competition evolved first in the most competitive markets, particularly in the UK, the United States, and to a lesser degree in the Nordic country markets. Competition was vital for the development of competitor differentiation, market segmentation, niche targeting and price options.

Marketing over sales: toys for yuppies

Starting in the UK and the United States, the shift toward competition and market-driven operators was reflected in the first major marketing campaigns, including Ericsson's Harry Hotline campaign in Sweden. It featured a free spirit, who owed his freedom to the ability to travel the world and stay in touch with his Ericsson HotLine wireless (Meurling and Jeans, 1997: 38). In the late 1980s, this yuppie fantasy for the business markets was one of the many campaigns that established the image of the mobile phone as a yuppie toy. In these advanced markets, the campaigns emulated the previous high-end car phone campaigns. From the developed markets, the idea diffused into other markets through a ripple effect.

Marketing concept: consumer markets

Penetration was still very low (less than 10 per cent) even in the most advanced mobile markets. In 1993, the number of cellular users was only around 20 million; today it is more than 1.3 billion. The shift from selling to marketing coincided with the transition from regulated to more competitive and developed markets (Levitt, 1960: 45–56). Prices began to fall and bargaining power shifted. In the 1990s, the cell phone became affordable in consumer mass markets, and business grew global. Emerging with the digital transition, the marketing concept was typical of more competitive mobile markets. Selling focused on the needs of the seller; marketing, on the needs of the buyer.

Segmentation

Through the 1980s, Nordic vendors still benchmarked and imitated Motorola's product strategies and portfolios. With digital cellular in the 1990s, the mobile business shifted from Motorola's singular design to Nokia's segmentation, which established an array of basic categories, each of which morphed into multiple segments (Figure 2.3). In the past, platform products emerged in business markets and then trickled down to the low-end consumer markets. Now, products first evolved in consumer segments.

Penetration pricing

In the past, the absence of competition and fear of product cannibalization had kept differentiation and volume low. With digital transition, leading operators and vendors seized market-penetration pricing. With vendors, higher sales volume resulted in lower unit costs. To increase their share, operators offered lower monthly fees and higher usage fee plans. 'Flexible talk plans' enabled price premiums.

Channel specialization

Promotion of competition led to the proliferation, consolidation and segmentation of channels. At the end of the 1990s, even the leading mobile vendors and operators struggled to attract and retain end-users – often through a confusing melange of marketing channels. As operators consolidated, increasing bargaining power made them bolder, and they began to exert more pricing pressure on vendors, dictating specifications and boosting branding.

Differentiation and branding

In order to reach the mass consumer markets, marketers had to get rid of the yuppie image. As the rivals' product technology and service quality became homogeneous, brand emerged as a competitive base of differentiation. Because vendors globalized their activities before operators, they were the first to use global branding, but operators were followed in footprints, as evidenced by the story of Orange SA (see Box 2.3). Among the GSM manufacturers, Nokia, a latecomer, was the first to create a 'single, unified approach' across the Triad regions.

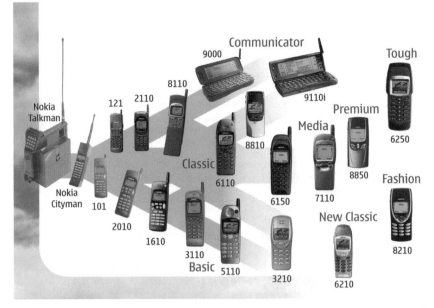

In addition to the Communicator product family, Nokia covered several target groups, which were illustrated by the names of the product categories: Classic, Expression, Premium, Tough, Media and Fashion

Source: Nokia Corp.

Figure 2.3   Evolution of mobile phone categories and segments (Nokia 2003)

Customer concept: service markets

Emerging with the convergence of the internet and mobility toward the end of the 1990s, the customer concept is typical to developed, competitive mobile markets. The marketing concept reflects customer *segments*, whereas the customer concept focuses on *individual* customers, by shaping personalized offers, services and messages. Products and services are under escalating price pressure. These drivers began to accelerate with the shift from first-time buyers to replacement purchases, and from niche markets to high volumes. Despite variation in timing, the sequence has been fairly similar in developed markets.

From original demand to replacements

The transition from original demand to replacements evolved first in the Nordic markets, then in Western Europe and finally worldwide. In Finland, the most advanced country market of the period, the number of replacements exceeded new sales in the middle of 1998. Regional trends mimicked pioneer developments. In Western Europe, the number of replacements exceeded those of new sales in mid-2000 (Steinbock, 2003a). This made the job of the

Box 2.3   DIFFERENTIATING IN A CROWDED MARKET

'When we launched in 1994, we were entering a market where there were already three aggressive competitors. However, we knew that if we delivered for customer needs, we could really differentiate and create an experience that would be very different.'

Richard Brennan is the executive vice president of global branding at Orange SA, which grew and internationalized with the rise of the digital cellular.

Clear identity

While excelling in operational effectiveness, Orange built a strong and clear identity to set itself apart, with simple Talk Plans that offered real value for money, per second billing, Caller ID, itemized billing free of charge, and direct customer relationships. After establishing these innovations in the trendsetting UK marketplace, it extended and leveraged them internationally. In 1994, Orange had 379,000 subscribers. Today, with the integration of parent France Telecom's mobile operations, it has 44.5 million subscribers in 20 countries

'We spent a lot of time developing products and services that we thought would be quite unique in the market but also really gave great customer benefit. We focused on having an expert quality network and customer services.'

Positioning the brand around 'Orange'

'We had to find a brand positioning and strategy that was very different from the competition. The competition was using very "techy" names like Cellnet, One-to-One which all put them in the same category. We had to establish a new category.

'In the 1990s most companies named their services the way they did because they were brought up on an engineering pedigree. They never had a marketing heritage. Orange decided to have both technology and marketing people to really communicate the benefits to customers.

'The next part was to come up with a brand and brand image. We did a lot of research on different names and different positionings. "Orange" kept coming through as being unique and differentiated. The advertising featured no phones and made no reference to technology. We relied on imagery that gave an optimistic view of the future in an innovative way.'

Next level: personalization

'We have started to take things to the next level by personalizing a lot of what we do in communications, instead of a one size fits all. Customers can access and utilize a service that is relevant to them, via "My Orange" for instance. When you first sign on to Orange World, it will ask what you are interested in. The next time you come to the site, it will deliver these interests for you.

'It is this concept of keeping things simple, personal and compelling that keeps visitors visiting and using more features. The key is to have your feet on the ground, the tangible elements that are a consistent experience wherever you use Orange.'

Source: the author's interview with Richard Brennan, EVP, global brand marketing and products, Orange SA, 12 May 2004.

marketer far more challenging, well *before* the 3G introduction. Until the end of the 1980s, mobility was driven by low volume and high cost. During the 1990s, this trend was reversed. If the customer already had a relatively satisfactory and affordable mobile device and service plan, the incentives for migration were lower and the demand for added value was higher.

Relationship marketing

With maturing and replacement markets, vendors and operators are focusing on strong brands and items. Promotional and advertising activities are increasingly driven by efforts at rapid diffusion and deeper customer relationships. With customer orientation, all industry players seek to differentiate customers in terms of their needs and value to the company. They interact with mobile subscribers and users, trying to customize products, services and messages to each customer. All struggle for profitable growth by capturing a larger share of each customer's expenditures, boosting customer loyalty, and focusing on customer lifetime value.

Pricing

In the 1990s, the growth markets went hand in hand with penetration pricing. As competition intensified, downward price pressure became the rule in advanced markets. With data transition, the leading companies priced to match their rivals or best market competitors. As the growth has lingered, industry rivals have engaged in price cuts and, more often than not, price wars. Among vendors, even Nokia initiated substantial price cuts in the spring of 2004, seeking to recapture its share in mid-range models. In developing economies, promotional pricing has been favoured. In developed markets, discriminatory pricing reigns.

Distribution

In growth markets, rivals engaged in intensive distribution. In maturing markets, they went selective, phasing out unprofitable outlets. As vendors and operators were coupled with IT enablers, content producers and other new strategic groups, the marketing channels were becoming tight and left less space for new entrants and challengers. For instance, Nokia's sales and distribution channels included operators, distributors and independent retailers. With the proliferation of rivals (operators, providers and independent wholesale/retail chains), operators have used market-share strategies, thus heavily subsidizing handset costs.

With increasing price competition, commodification haunts the mobile business. Industry rivals seek to diversify brands and basic offerings. In growth markets, competitors heighten brand differences and benefits, while encouraging brand switching. In maturing markets, they reduce advertising to the level needed to retain hard-core loyal users, while reducing promotion to the minimal level.

MOBILE SERVICE INNOVATION

Dynamics of mobile service innovation

In the past, the dynamics of innovation has focused on products and processes in a wide variety of industries, including typewriters, automobiles, televisions and television tubes, transistors, electronic calculators, the integrated circuit, Winchester disk drives, supercomputers and so forth (Utterback, 1994: ch 2). Today, innovation has to do increasingly with services, or more precisely, hybrids: combinations of product, process and service innovation.

Product

In the absence of standards or uniform product expectations, early participants experiment in new industries. In mobile communications, these periods of fermenting activity have been seen with every successive wave of technology and market innovation, from Marconi's efforts to extend the coverage of wireless telegraphy to Intel's development of wireless broadband. The flurry of radical product innovation eventually ends with the emergence of a 'dominant design'. As the bases on which product innovation can take place become fewer, the focus of R&D narrows to incremental innovations on existing features. Users develop loyalties and preferences, and the marketing mix leads to greater standardization. In analog cellular, this phase was seen in the late 1980s; with digital cellular, toward the end of the 1990s. Something similar happened with marketing innovation. In the late 1980s, Ericsson's Harry Hotline campaign targeted business professionals, while positioning the cell phone as a 'yuppie tool'. In the 1990s, digital cellular penetrated mass consumer markets, after marketers had redefined and repositioned the cell phone in the marketplace.

Process

During the formative period of a new product technology, the processes employed to manufacture it tend to be inefficient and based on skilled labour and general-purpose machinery and tools. As product features are agreed to by producers and customers, and as markets expand, there is a major shift from product to process innovation, and greater reliance on specialized and expensive equipment, while late movers may face excess capacity. Around 2000 and 2002, many European-based vendors divested or joint-ventured their manufacturing capabilities to Asian-based producers and contractors. As Intel's Sean Maloney comments:

> In a period of intense innovation, it's important to be disciplined and focused on operational execution. Most people can strategically figure out what's to be done. We can all say the world is going to go wireless. The trick is to get there... You have to get the product functioning, working, and out the door in time. As the winners get bigger, the losers lose more. Success and failure are much starker than they used to be.[5]

Service

Product and process innovation are interdependent. As the rate of product innovation decreases, the rate of process innovation tends to accelerate. But there is more to the story. Product and process innovation give rise to service innovation. Following product and process innovation, operators and service providers engaged in a flurry of service innovation in the 1980s. Digitization improved the basic voice service, but it did not lead to new services in the 1990s, except for the SMS. The true change came only at the end of the decade, with NTT DoCoMo's service innovation. As the dominant design evolves for service innovation, it defines the 'look and feel' of mobile services.

Dominant design

The notion of dominant design is often used interchangeably with that of dominant product design. In reality, product, process and service innovation each in turn give rise to a dominant design. The design tends to embody the requirements of many classes of users of a particular product, process or service, even if it may not match the needs of a particular class to the same extent as a customized design.[6] There is thus a triple shift from product innovation to process and service innovation. Each of these three elements is autonomous and yet interdependent (Figure 2.4).

Service has been an inherent part of the mobile business system for decades. But it was all about voice – a service that was barely and rarely differentiated – until the development of SMS in the 1990s and the mobile internet services at the end of the decade.

Each new wave of innovation is characterized by a peak in the number of competing firms around the institution of the dominant design, with a decline thereafter. In the mobile business, the 1980s analog cellular attracted many new entrants. The barriers of entry and production volumes were still very low, due to the low penetration. In the early 1990s, the annual volume of handset units, for instance, was less than 2 million. By the end of the 1990s, the unit volume amounted to 120 million; by 2006, it will exceed 600 million.

In the past, technology innovation boosted market penetration. Today, advanced markets are saturated. In such circumstances, usage is more likely to be boosted by marketing innovation that focuses on services.

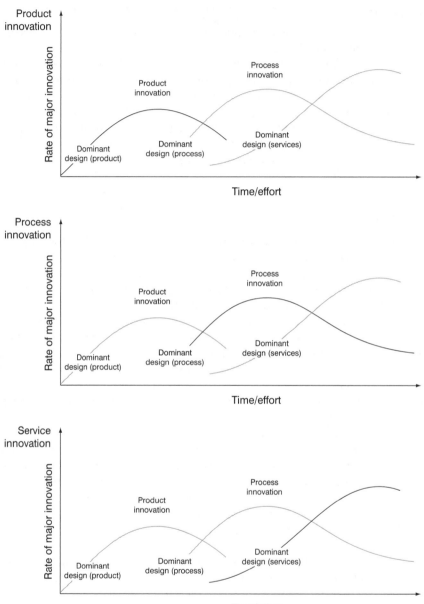

Figure 2.4 Product, process and service innovation in the mobile business

UNIQUE CHARACTERISTICS OF MOBILE SERVICES

Services dominate most developed economies, representing close to 80 per cent of the US gross domestic product. They drive globalization. In the early 1970s, the service sector accounted for only a quarter of the stock of foreign direct investment worldwide; by 2002, it had risen to about 60 per cent or an estimated US $4 trillion (UNCTAD, 2004). With deregulation and liberalization, telecommunications, and particularly mobile services, have contributed to this massive shift toward services worldwide. Yet they have rarely been explored as services. Through the 1970s and early 1980s, researchers studied the difference between goods and services. Thereafter, research has focused on the consequent managerial and marketing implications (Swartz and Iacobucci, 2000: 1–5).

Services have unique characteristics that distinguish them from products and processes, and that may significantly affect the design of marketing programmes: intangibility, inseparability, variability and perishability (Kotler, 2003: ch 12).

Intangibility

Unlike products, services cannot be sensed or touched before they are purchased. The service-buying decision is more complex than the more tangible product-buying decision. It is one thing to test the latest model by Nokia or Samsung; it is quite a different thing to test the most recent service portfolio by NTT DoCoMo or Vodafone. Companies often speed up service development to deter competition, even if it may be relatively easy for competitors to copy or imitate their services.[7] It is more difficult to protect services than products, because they can more easily be copied or imitated. To reduce uncertainty, buyers look for evidence of the service quality. The service provider's task is often seen as to make the intangible tangible (Figure 2.5) (Levitt, 1981).

Inseparability

Physical goods may be manufactured, put into inventory, distributed and consumed later. Since services are typically produced and consumed simultaneously, both provider and customer shape the outcome.[8] The mobile service experience can be crafted, especially as much of the customer support is automatic. If the provider neglects its role in the co-creation of the service, the experience – the 'moment of truth' – will fail the end-user, as the WAP debacle demonstrated.

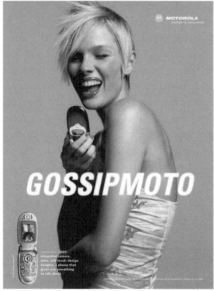

'Intelligence Everywhere' (Motorola)

Where product marketers try to add abstract ideas, service marketers seek for physical evidence and imagery to abstract offers. For instance, equipment manufacturers try to find ways to couple their products with technological, lifestyle, functional or experiential ideas.

Motorola's 'Intelligence Everywhere' campaign has rendered the tangible more intangible by linking the mobile device with more abstract ideas. Conversely, as mobile players aspire to make intangible more tangible, they seek new ways of doing so.

Source: Frost (2003).

Figure 2.5 Making the intangible tangible

And of course that phone you're carrying is really more than just a phone. It probably gives you voice recognition technology, significant memory and storage capabilities, text messaging and remote e-mail, and the ability to establish an 'always on' connection to the internet – among other intelligent features. It's really 'the device formerly known as the cell phone'.

What if things could respond to you personally and even anticipate your needs? ATMs that recognize you on sight. Rental-car buses that sense who you are from your PDA, check for your reservation in their computer and take you straight to your car, which then guides you to your hotel. Or hotels that could sense your presence the moment you walk in the door and put your registration information onto your PDA – which would become your wireless key.

Source: 'Intelligence Everywhere', Motorola Inc, 2004.

Figure 2.5   continued

Variability

Pure services depend on people who provide them, and when and where they are provided. They are highly variable (or 'heterogeneous', as some authors call them). This is not the case with pure products. As a result, standardization of service delivery is not as simple as with physical products. The positive news is that, unlike tangible products, intangible services allow greater opportunity for differentiation, including customization.[9] In mobile services, it is the experience of the overall service portfolio – rich voice, mobile internet, messaging and personalized content – that is critical.

Perishability

Unlike tangible products, services cannot be stored or inventoried. Services are produced when they are consumed. Typically, perishability is not a problem when demand is steady, but fluctuating demand may cause problems, as mobile operators and service providers have found in peak or crisis situations. Take, for instance, the morning of 11 September 2001 in New York City, when the mobile networks collapsed due to usage overload and destruction of equipment at more than 14 cell sites. A notable exception was text messaging. Often, perishability necessitates further new services to fill the gap created by peaks and valleys in demand.

THE SERVICES MARKETING MIX

Until the mid-1990s or so, the traditional marketing mix did capture most circumstances in the wireless because these comprised only voice services, which were 'product-like'. With the emergence of mobile services, service portfolios and content services, the classic mix remains necessary, but is no longer sufficient to capture the special circumstances. Recently, product competition has been turning into service rivalry in most industries (Webster, 1994; Grönroos, 1997).

Today, services marketing and management – particularly mobile service marketing and management – is coping with three great challenges. How can it surpass the traditional manufacturing-based model? How can it manage the contact staff and more generally human resources management in service businesses? How can it deal with the new hybrids of products and services?[10] In addition to the product, price, place and promotion considerations that permeate any marketing effort, a service firm needs to manage the personnel and customers who are involved in the service experience, the physical aspects of the service, and the process by which the service is created and delivered. The traditional marketing mix must be augmented by these 'three new Ps'.

Moreover, many forms of customer service are today being delivered with the help of technology. Much of this technology-delivered service is initiated and performed by the consumer and involves no direct or indirect contact with representatives of the service provider. The internet and mobile environments in which customers deliver their own services are prime examples of the trend. In contrast to traditional 'dumb' markets, which were relatively static, fixed and basically information-poor, smart markets are dynamic, turbulent and information-rich (Barnes, 2000; Glazer, 2000). The distinction applies particularly well to the transition from voice communications to data communications in the mobile industry. Still, the promise of mobility comes with a trade-off. As human interaction is removed from the provision of the service, it is accompanied by an environment where the responsibility for service provision rests with the customer, not with the service provider.

In addition to substantial efforts to make the intangible service aspects more tangible in customer perceptions, pioneer mobile service marketers are coping with these challenges through service innovation that underscores ease-of-use and simple design (see Chapters 3 to 6), and a determined focus on service experience and experiential marketing (see Chapters 7 and 8). These efforts permeate business service marketing and strategic considerations, as well (see Chapters 9 and 10).

A TOTAL SERVICE PORTFOLIO

Since the mobile service experience has both tangible and intangible aspects, it can be considered a service hybrid. In the 1980s, voice was the only service; with the 1990s, it was coupled with SMS. Today, the mobile service portfolio comprises rich voice, the internet, messaging and personalized content. Service marketers often emphasize that services should not be associated with products because, in effect, they differ from physical goods and thereby require different strategies.[11] Mobile services too have unique characteristics. In mobile services, the total service portfolio comprises the generic, expected, augmented and potential services (Figure 2.6) (Levitt, 1980).

Generic services

Dominant design provides only the generic service portfolio. With mobility, it comprises those basic services – voice, mobile internet, a set of content services – that are now taken to provide the basic 'look and feel' of wireless services. No subscriber of i-mode pays for the generic product; all expect their service plan to incorporate the generic product.

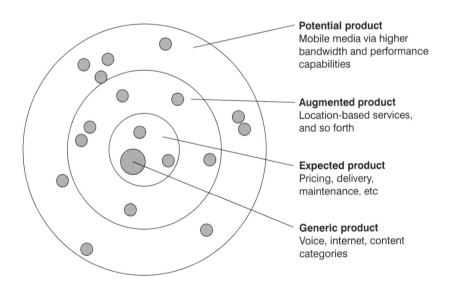

Potential product
Mobile media via higher bandwidth and performance capabilities

Augmented product
Location-based services, and so forth

Expected product
Pricing, delivery, maintenance, etc

Generic product
Voice, internet, content categories

The dots inside each concentric circle represent specific attributes. For instance, inside the expected product are service conditions, maintenance, post-purchase services and so forth.

Figure 2.6 Total service portfolio

Expected services

The expected services reflect the customer's minimal expectations. While these may vary widely by customers, services and regions, every subscriber has some expectations that exceed the generic product itself. With multimedia services, for instance, customers expect that the plan is priced 'right', that the speed is 'right', that the support is 'right', and so forth. These expectations also vary across services, segments and regions. As the customers expect more than just the generic product, the different instruments by which competing providers seek to fulfil these expectations distinguish their offerings from one another.

Augmented services

Expectations change over time. And in innovation-driven rivalry, they can shift relatively rapidly. In Japan, NTT DoCoMo has stimulated usage and thereby revenue generation via traffic. Such augmentations are a means of product differentiation, while educating the subscriber about what it is reasonable to expect from the service provider.

Potential services

In mobility, the potential services comprise everything potentially feasible to attract and hold customers. With mobile services, this refers to the shift from (multimedia) service innovation, which is still confined by bandwidth and performance capabilities, to (broadband) mobile media, which are permeated by pervasive and ubiquitous mobile computing.

NEW SERVICE DEVELOPMENT

The transition from voice to data is the result of the interplay of technology and market innovation, which, along with new products and processes, is resulting in new services (see Box 2.4). Most new-to-the-world services may well be rare in a service environment. Many are versions of existing services or copies of competitors' products. For most practical purposes, 'new' can be understood as a service that, *from the customer's perspective*, represents a change. Thus 'new' is considered a change that affects or is noticeable to the customer (Figure 2.7).

Disruptive services

Focusing on new services, only those that are perceived as truly new services in new markets may be considered new-to-the-world services.[12]

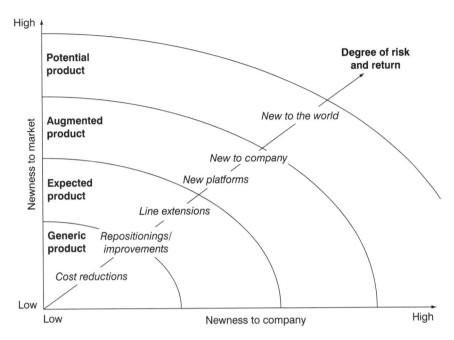

Figure 2.7 New service development

New-to-the-world service

These services are new to the company and to the marketplace. They typically build on a major innovation. They are the rarest of all new services, and carry the highest risk, but also the greatest potential rewards, from the first television broadcast service to the first automated teller machine (ATM). In mobility, these correspond to those new post-SMS services that are emerging with the transition from voice to data.

Sustaining services

However, most new services are incremental revisions of existing services. These sustaining services can be more or less influential; they are certainly more common than disruptive services. They also carry less risk and lower potential reward. This category includes an array of familiar examples, including:

- *New service line.* New to the company, but not to the marketplace. By the same token, risk remains higher than with existing services but lower than with new services. Think of the new services by FreeMove Alliance to challenge Vodafone in Europe, or Vodafone Japan's new services to confront NTT DoCoMo's i-mode and FOMA.

Box 2.4   TOWARD THE FUTURE

'Mobility reverses the roles of the customer and the provider,' says Anssi Vanjoki. In the early 1990s, he turned Nokia's brand global in just a few years. Now, as executive vice president and general manager, he heads a business group that is responsible for offering devices and content for bringing mobile multimedia to consumers, including images, games, music.

From consumers to prosumers

In the past, markets were driven by production and supply; today, they are driven by consumption and demand. From Vanjoki's standpoint, mobility is now completing this massive shift, which has substantial consequences, especially in customization and pull-driven marketing. 'Power is shifting toward demand,' says Vanjoki. 'As consumers, what we all want to have is customization, tailoring, something that's "made just for me". That's what consumers want to see, even to the degree that terms such as prosumer have been introduced. This is a challenge to any medium which allows for immaterial stuff to be digitized. Other materials need to be tagged so that they can be marketed through digital means with the mobile.

'Permissions marketing is predicated on the idea that I am the target of marketing,' says Vanjoki. 'I am the one who decides whether I want to be "sensitized" to marketing. I make the choices. I am ready to acknowledge that I'm interested in this and that. I have an incentive to do so because now I shall receive what I want to receive.

'Conversely, the arrangement also benefits the marketer because he/she will learn more about my profile over time and also how to approach me, whether it's via advertising or promotion, or something else. Mobility enables the creation and main-tenance of the customer relationship better than any other medium. Think about a retail store. They can sell something only when I am in the store. But those are brief moments. What about the times when I'm not in the store? Well, if I'm the retailer's customer and the retailer knows that I happen to like such-and-such Norwegian salmon, then they can deliver information on their product and I can purchase it,' says Vanjoki, and he smiles. 'You see, I really like the salmon.'

When your life goes mobile

'Life goes mobile' is Nokia's slogan in the consumer markets. But actually, what does it mean? In Finland and other pioneer markets, most consumers were using GSM phones already in the mid-1990s. Ultimately, it is the large country markets that will define the future of mobility.

'It's all about penetration,' says Vanjoki. 'The more familiar the device is to masses of people, the more they know about the devices and services, the more it can be utilized. When you get high penetration, other things follow.'

As voice transitions to data, convergence moves to the next phase. 'In the advanced markets, the camera phones have enabled large screens and these devices will create a strong foothold. At the same time, they will provide a powerful boost to conver-gence. Today the PC is still the "eye to the internet". With increasing mobile pene-tration, it becomes the secondary eye. The first one will be the mobile device. Unlike the PC, that's with me all the time.

'With the mobile device, I can signal to others that I'm available, online, with my presence. This experience used to be dictated by the PC. Now the internet becomes available via mobile multimedia. That's something new altogether.'

Corporations follow mass consumers, who follow young demographics, which are most familiar with mobile devices. In the long run, Vanjoki argues, these devices 'will be both a substitute and complementary, both'. 'Take the PC experience,' says Vanjoki. 'You may spend a few hours with your PC. After all, you have a big screen, and beautiful audio and video capabilities. As you're doing it, that's the only activity you're doing. The difference with the mobile is that when you're living an online life, you can choose to become active when something comes to you via your permission, or when you decide to do something quick.

'It's a different experience than an hour-long browsing. Moreover, some mobile experiences may take longer. Take for instance a chat, while you're travelling on the train or on a bus, for an hour or whatever. Instead of just sleeping or feeling dull, you can participate in chat or browse.'

Brave new sensory experience

For years now, Vanjoki has argued that multimedia services will grow, and that this growth will take off relatively fast because they serve the same needs that fuelled the explosive growth of digital handsets and text messaging in the 1990s.

'We are driven by our sensory perceptions,' he says. 'In the past, this experience was still impoverished. Today, it's not. We can now provide new capabilities, which generate a more inclusive virtual and sensory experience. And it's this experience that allows us to share intimate moments, thoughts and feelings.

'With your mobile device, you have a life that's online. You're represented by the context in the network, you have a network personality. As the internet protocol is permeating all systems, you can access the network from any terminal, from traditional phones, PCs, or mobile devices. This allows us to have a network personality to represent us in this network of networks. It is now evolving into a kind of extension of our own personality, even if it is not as versatile as our actual identity.'

This vision of future has elements of *Star Trek*. But unlike the TV show, it is not fictional, but based on potential multimedia applications. 'In the future, we can reflect images onto larger surfaces, or employ virtual optics. It's a bit like the Viewmasters we used to play with. You can peek into a small hole that magically opens up into a great visual experience. Or like those *Star Trek* ideas about ionizing matter through radio waves. Perhaps one day that, too, will become a reality.'

Source: the author's interviews with Anssi Vanjoki, EVP, Nokia Mobile Phones, June 2003 and 23 March 2004.

● *Addition to existing service line.* This is new to the company, but fits into existing service lines. This may well be the most common type of 'new' service: for instance, incremental additions to the Get It Now package by Verizon Wireless.

- *Improvements to existing services.* These are new to the company, but actually a replacement or just an update of an existing service offering. They comprise the incremental revisions of existing mobile services (differentiation advantage) or cost-driven modifications to services that often are not visible to customers (cost advantage).

A good portfolio has an appropriate mix of new services to ensure that existing markets are protected while new opportunities are developed.[13]

3

Service pioneers

Toward the end of the 1990s, the leading European vendors and operators pioneered branded technology, without appropriate services. As WAP (Wireless Application Protocol) flopped in Europe, NTT DoCoMo launched the i-mode service in Japan. With its ingenious business model, the operator provided branded services that captured the imagination of the Japanese consumers. After explosive growth, i-mode has served as the benchmark service as progenitors – Vodafone Live!, FreeMove Alliance, Get It Now by Verizon Wireless, and many others – have emerged worldwide (Figure 3.1).

SERVICE INNOVATION

Since its launch in February 1999, i-mode soon became an integral part of the business and personal lives of more than 43 million customers. In 2000, NTT DoCoMo made headlines all over the world and was seen as the 'most important company to watch in the coming huge battle for the mobile Internet market' (Rohwer 2000). It demonstrated how to end the decline of the average revenue per user (ARPU) with successful data services.[1] By summer 2004, i-mode users in Japan got easy access to more than 81,000 internet sites, with specialized services such as e-mail, online shopping and banking, ticket reservations and restaurant advice. Users can access sites from anywhere in Japan at relatively low rates, because their charges are based on the volume of data transmitted, not the amount of time spent connected.

Due to the foresight of its senior executives, NTT DoCoMo created i-mode at a time when the Japanese market for mobile phones was reaching maturity. At NTT DoCoMo, the foresight belonged to Kouji Ohboshi.[2]

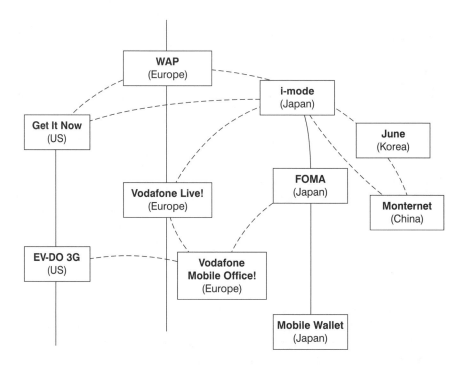

Figure 3.1 Evolution of content services

Origins of i-mode

Like most leading mobile operators worldwide, NTT DoCoMo originated from a national telecom monopoly. Formed in 1952 by the Japanese Ministry of Communications to rebuild Japan's war-ravaged phone system, Nippon Telegraph and Telephone (NTT) enjoyed a monopoly on phone services for more than four decades. NTT first went into mobile communications with a maritime phone service in 1959. In mobility, it was the Asian pioneer. Until the 1990s, the wireless unit was focused on technology innovation, not marketing innovation. It had great ambitions, but a small subscriber base. In 1993, the operator introduced a digital mobile service based on Personal Digital Cellular (PDC).[3] Some time before, NTT sent Kouji Ohboshi to run the then-unprofitable wireless unit.

Two S-curves: crisis over complacency

The year 1996 was the first of three years when mobile phone services in Japan acquired 10 million new subscribers annually. Explosive growth marked the start of the first S-curve. As the number of subscribers surged upward, operating revenues from transmission fees grew dramatically. This was the same S-curve that Nordic operators, the pioneers of digital cellular, had seen a while before, and the one that AT&T would witness later. It was the result of a volume increase, but Ohboshi understood that it was inherently unsustainable. Once the consumers who wanted to use mobile phones had been signed up, the growth momentum would be over. Forty million subscribers had been signed up. That left 20 million more, extrapolating from the 60 million fixed-line phone subscribers in Japan.

Something else happened that year. Young subscribers, who had earlier been so adept with pagers, got attracted to text mail. They were creating a new mobile culture, which migrated from pagers to cell-phone mail, to e-mail on mobile phones. In a document entitled 'Shifting from volume to value', Ohboshi argued that the days of subscriber-driven growth were fading away. The future belonged to data-driven growth (Figure 3.2).[4] If nothing was done, the growth rate would flatten and the operator's revenues would decline. The result would be a zero-sum game, comparable to the price wars of the US long-distance carriers. Ohboshi saw a way out. Why engage in a war of attrition over a limited pool of subscribers, if you could create an entirely new market and trigger a new growth phase?

By 1999, the number of subscribers was growing dramatically, with the expansion of the market scale. DoCoMo was generating some 60 per cent (¥500 billion) of the recurring profit of the NTT Group. Since there was no sense of crisis, Ohboshi created one, by cannibalizing the revenue flows. As voice communications would be coupled with data communications, revenues from data would grow, even if the number of subscribers did not. That would herald the arrival of the second S-curve, the value growth curve. The first curve was all about volume. The second would be all about value. The first enabled voice traffic. The second would instigate data traffic. It would be known as i-mode – which would lead to content-driven growth.

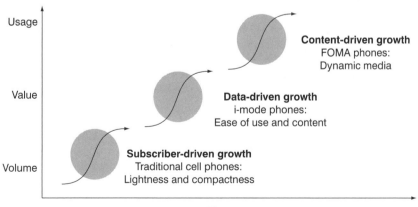

Figure 3.2 The origins of i-mode

THE BIRTH OF I-MODE

Keiichi Enoki met Kouji Ohboshi at two in the afternoon on Wednesday 1 August 1997, in the president's office on the tenth floor of the NTT DoCoMo headquarters in Toranomon, Tokyo. 'We're going to start up a mobile multi-media business based on cell phones!' said Ohboshi, and handed him a report from McKinsey & Co. 'This sounds like a cool business... we have a good chance of success,' was the gut reaction of Enoki, director of gateway business. 'What about some staff?' he asked. 'Bring together whomever you like,' Ohboshi replied (Natsuno, 2000: 1–7).

Enoki needed outsiders. He hired Mari Matsunaga, editor-in-chief of *Torabayu*, a job-search magazine for women, and Takeshi Natsuno, an IT and marketing specialist who had studied in the United States and served as a chief at an internet start-up. After several months of brainstorming, the trio targeted wireless internet access as the next big thing. DoCoMo engineers built a 'packet-switched' network alongside their existing digital cellular network. But all these technologies were available before the DoCoMo. The team was after an innovative business model. Where is our market, they asked? What is the product concept? What technologies will make it a reality? What should be the fee structure? What about content? What about marketing? And continuous growth?

The first news conference at DoCoMo, in February 1999, brought in barely seven journalists, whereas the second attracted more than 500. The news momentum was in Western Europe, where the creators of WAP were branding technology. That was the last thing the founders of i-mode wanted to do. i-mode was positioned carefully to avoid high-tech jargon. In marketing, the word 'internet' was not even mentioned. i-mode was branded as an extension of existing mobile services. As Takeshi Natsuno noted:

> We did not say, 'Internet access from your mobile phone'. Nor did we use internet terminology. Our advertising was mum about terms like the web, access, browser, gateway... Suppose we had decided to focus on the technology. 'We deliver banking from mobile phones, via the internet; our highly secure service, using Secure Sockets Layer (SSL) technology...' Most people hearing that would think, 'Internet? SSL? What on earth is that? It's too high tech for me,' and flee. There was a good reason for our choice of non-technical language in our marketing.[5]

i-mode appealed to the users because it was affordable, easy to use, added value to lifestyle, and contributed to productivity.

Business model

With i-mode, content providers concentrate on developing information, while NTT DoCoMo takes care of all billing on their behalf. Subscribers are attracted by the constantly updated, interesting, relevant and convenient content. The successful business model has been explained by three broad drivers: technology, easy-to-use interface and cooperation.

Technology

i-mode's enabling technology is compatible, efficient, versatile and open. But the service's competitive advantage was elsewhere. 'The WAP promoters did not make a clear distinction between the network layer and the application layer,' says Takeshi Natsuno. 'Network evolution does not automatically translate to application and service evolution.' Applications and services are not identical, although the terms are often used interchangeably.[6]

'Many people keep talking about the differences of the networks, such as 1G, 2G, 3G, 4G, 5G and what not,' says Natsuno on the drivers of i-mode success. 'In reality, from the marketing viewpoint, it is the subscribers, the users who count. The transition from 2G to 3G is less important than the transition from voice application to data application. When we launched the i-mode service, we were using the 2G platform because it was not necessary to have a 3G platform. From the standpoint of the end-user, the critical change was the transition from voice to data. It was far more important than the transition from 2G to 3G.'

Easy to use interface

In addition to the voice capability, i-mode provides mobile phone users with a whole new range of capabilities, with easy dialling and simple web access from their mobile phones, which keeps them connected to the internet at all times. The i-menu is the users' gateway to the internet, enabling easy access to more than 4,200 Japanese and English-language websites. With one-touch simplicity, it offers 'Web to', 'Phone to', and 'Mail to' functions which add convenience. E-mail, one of i-mode's most successful applications, enables users to send messages with the push of a button and receive messages automatically, at low cost.

As *Business Week* reported in early 2000: 'There are a few things a Japanese teenage girl doesn't leave home without: her six-inch platform shoes, some touch-up toner for her hair color of the day, and her i-mode phone. With i-mode, users are always connected – as long as they can receive a signal and their batteries are charged. Through this persistent link, subscribers get a full panoply of Web-based goodies: e-mail and chat, games, online horoscopes, calendars, and customized news bulletins' (Kunii with Baker, 2000).

Customization

In Japan, NTT DoCoMo determines specifications, which are vital because they allow operators to differentiate. According to Natsuno:

> If the European operators want to do things differently, if they want to do something about their profitability, if they want to achieve growth, then my recommendation is customization, customization and customization. If every player has the same type of phone, or the phone with the same colour, the same style,

that makes things impossible for the operator. But by having some customization, operators can have some differentiation, just like the Vodafone guys are now doing in Europe.

Cooperation

To attract content producers, Natsuno first opted for the big nationwide banks, which would inspire everyone else to follow. It was a shrewd move:

> In our model, the partnerships were critical. My tactic was first to approach the nationwide banks. Why? Because banks are the most conservative businesses and enormously influential. If I could make one say yes, other industries would follow. That was my plan when I headed to Sumitomo Bank, which the others looked to for leadership and which had an advanced computer system. Sumitomo, Sakura and Sanwa banks were the first three to participate in i-mode. As the three big banks got on board, others lined up to follow them. At the beginning, we had 67 corporations as partners in providing content, but 21 were banks.

Coordinating and optimizing the entire i-mode value chain, NTT DoCoMo collaborates closely with equipment manufacturers, content providers and other industry participants.[7] Internationally, it is a unique business model because it is predicated on the ability of a single operator to coordinate the full industry value chain (Figure 3.3). To Natsuno, this is an 'ecosystem model that generates high added value'. In the system, the relationship between subscribers and content providers is especially important because, from the subscriber's point of view, it is the content that gives the service value.

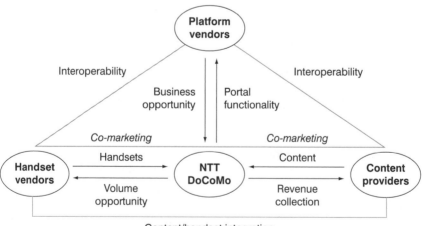

The total value chain management is made possible by a well-balanced mobile multimedia ecosystem of partners in which the operator plays a central coordination role.

Figure 3.3 Origins of i-mode: the collaboration concept

To bring subscribers and attractive content together, however, requires the technological underpinnings for the system, easy-to-understand marketing, and a good business model (Natsuno, 2002: 3–4).

Content quality control
All content is continually updated, kept as comprehensive as possible and designed for maximum clarity and attractiveness. Content in the i-menu must be authorized by NTT DoCoMo. Other content providers offer services through their own sites in response to demand, thus attracting more subscribers.

A simple, affordable pricing system
i-mode customers pay a low monthly fee, low variable data fees, and flat monthly fees for subscribed content sites. They receive a single consolidated bill for all their mobile phone activities. NTT DoCoMo charges a 9 per cent commission for the clearinghouse billing system service, which means that content providers receive more than 90 per cent of the revenue flow. To NTT DoCoMo, thriving content means traffic and volume, while to content providers the revenue sharing ratio has been a magnificent incentive, as evidenced by Disney and many others (see Box 3.1).

In Japan, NTT DoCoMo has had close to 60 per cent of the marketplace, though competitive intensity has accelerated. In most developed markets, the market share of the leading operators is significantly lower, which makes the business model harder to replicate elsewhere.[8]

Globalization efforts

DoCoMo's i-mode is not easily exportable. First of all, the Japanese operator employs proprietary standards.[9] Even more importantly, i-mode is a business model; it is not a system. There is no easy 'translation' of the business model from one country to another country, or set of countries. In the past few years, the i-mode service has been launched in several European countries, with each country offering its own unique content and terminals. This trend began with the launch of i-mode services in 2002 with E-Plus of Germany, KPN Mobile in the Netherlands, BASE in Belgium, and Bouygues Telecom in France, and a subsidiary of Far EastTone in Taiwan. The following years witnessed new launches in Spain, Italy and Greece, and relationship building in the United States.

Seeking to emulate i-mode in Japan, the European i-mode services drew from a number of official i-mode sites (300+) that provide rich voice, mobile internet services, messaging and personalized content. Unlike the Japanese i-mode services, the marketing message has not conveyed the depth and diversity of these services. i-mode has struggled for subscribers in Europe. Ultimately, Natsuno believes that most content categories that work well in Japan will work well worldwide:

I've already developed i-mode services outside Japan. There are almost no differences in terms of tendencies and nationalities. Wherever you are, Japan or Germany, character downloads are a big thing. People like to play games, and so forth. So I can't see too many differences by nationality.

Box 3.1   DISNEY AND DOCOMO'S PIONEERSHIP

In service innovation, it was Disney's cooperation with NTT DoCoMo that allowed the Hollywood studio to thrive when most content providers were still experimenting and burning cash in the mobile business. 'If it weren't for DoCoMo no one would be doing anything,' says Larry Shapiro, executive vice president of business development and operations for the Walt Disney Internet Group (WDIG). 'Everyone would still be struggling with what's the right business model, technology, devices and so forth. Part of the issue is that carriers haven't copied DoCoMo to some extent. I don't know why, especially when you see the success of that model, where a carrier is basically wide open to content development.'

Attractiveness through simplicity

'We spent a large amount of time and commitment to marketing services in Japan,' says Shapiro. 'We are one of the top four or five items when you turn on your DoCoMo phone. Other carriers have been more concerned with managing the process and providing their own editorial oversight over the process. With DoCoMo, it's a competitive market to get on that front screen, so you rely on your marketing and content.

'Anyone can build content; it's a question of how anyone can *find* your content. That's the important thing. In other markets, it's been the carriers determining the placement and screen navigation. They have not followed the simplicity of the DoCoMo model. That's really a shame. If it weren't for DoCoMo, there wouldn't be any content in the United States.'

First Tokyo and Seoul, then LA and New York City

According to the standard argument, the Japanese marketplace is the test laboratory for new content. Some successes are universal, whereas some are 'too Japanese' to export – which is a code term for 'too technology-oriented', 'too miniscule' and a few other arguments as questionable. Shapiro frames the argument in a different way. 'Right now it's a brand issue rather than a content issue,' he says. 'In Japan, our brand is very strong in certain demographics, particularly young women, approximately ages 19–26. In this demographic, our niche brand isn't as strong here in the United States. So it's hard to make that comparison.

'We have a variety of content in Japan that we purposely haven't taken over here, including screensavers, wallpapers and ring tones, games and characters that simply won't perform here. That's one of the benefits of our market position. We can try a lot of stuff in Japan and we'll do the same in Korea. As the US market will evolve pretty quickly, we think we are well positioned on the point of applications.'

Source: the author's interview with Larry Shapiro, EVP, Business Development and Operations, The Walt Disney Internet Group, 12 April 2004.

Some four to five years ago many especially in northern Europe said that Japanese people are somehow different, that Japanese love to download ring tones and games. The suggestion was that this phenomenon was a Japanese curiosity. That's not a good explanation. Maybe it was more of an excuse because those services have taken off in all advanced markets. They're not that different from the internet services, which do not differ much from country to country. Take, for example, the web communities, banking transactions, pornography. These categories have proved similar in one country after another.

SERVICE PORTFOLIO

Evolution of content

It is the internet that provided the conceptual basis for i-mode. 'When we created the i-mode service, I could not predict in advance the content port-folio,' acknowledges Natsuno. 'But from the beginning, I had this idea that we should simulate all internet communities that would provide attractive content to our platform. Those goals led to our official content portfolio.'

Today, i-mode offers a tremendous amount and diversity of content through more than 81,000 internet sites, with new websites being created all the time. A growing number of English sites offer highly convenient instant access to mobile online entertainment, information, database and transactions (see Table 3.1). The service portfolio as a whole and each individual category is dynamic. 'The basic categories of i-mode – information, entertainment, database, and transactions – have been changing over time,' says Natsuno. 'In the early days of the i-mode service, we created these categories because using them it was easier to migrate these categories of content to mobile. For instance, entertainment content is doing very well. With information, things aren't that different. News are thriving as well. Some two to three million people are paying for just to see the headline news from the major newspaper company.'

The early years reflect subtle shifts in content provision. 'The first year of the i-mode service was more about information content and testing the cate-gories,' Natsuno recalls. 'Thereafter entertainment providers began to provide customized content for the mobile. As a result, the entertainment content started to grow rapidly. That was the second year. By the third year, the free internet content began to gain more ground.'

Some content trends surprised even the i-mode creators. The most popular i-mode menu content has been ringing tones/standby screens (37 per cent of subscribers). With the i-mode service, the role of mobile devices has grown more important to their users, not just as something they own, but as some-thing they are, a reflection of their identity. In addition to ring tones/standby screens, the second most popular category has been entertainment (22 per cent of mova subscribers). Games/horoscopes came third (17 per cent) and

Table 3.1 i-mode service variety (ca 2004)

1. Entertainment

Character download; horoscope; fortune telling; karaoke information; hit songs; FM radio information; download ringing tones; club event information.

- 3D Homerun King. A 3D baseball game lets subscribers hit home runs.
- Pokemon Hiroba. With the favourite Pokemon on the display screen, the subscriber can enjoy Pokemon melodies.
- Disney Sports. Soccer, skateboarding and other games featuring Disney characters.
- Hallmark. With Hallmark designs, subtle emotions may touch someone's heart.
- Star Wars Mobile. Downloadable wallpapers and ring tones, and access to the Star Wars database.
- Dwango Seven. A dynamic fighter pilot game with high-quality graphics.
- Gigno Art Paradise. Scrollable virtual art museum, updated weekly and available as standby screens.
- MTV Mobile. Ticket reservations, programming information, music events and more.
- Sim City. Subscribers can play mayor of their own city.

2. Information

News updates; weather forecasts; sports news; stock quotes; business; technology news; town information; horse racing information, etc.

- CNN. Up-to-the-minute news and information from around the world.
- Weathernews. Standby screens provide automatic weather updates.
- iMapFan. Maps and local information on restaurants, hotels and more.
- Bloomberg. Market information and business news updated every 20 minutes.

3. Database

Telephone directory; search; restaurant guide; dictionary service; cooking recipes, etc.

- Zagat. Zagat restaurant reviews searchable by popularity, location and more.
- Ekitan Navi. Train schedule and fare information.

4. Transaction

Money transfer; balance check; security trading; ticket reservation; airline reservation; seat availability; credit card information; book sales, etc.

- Northwest Airlines. Flight schedule, prices, promotions, mileage program and the NWA phone.
- Amazon.co.jp. The online store allowing searches for books, CDs, DVDs, and videos, and supporting reservations for the latest releases.
- Citibank. Transfer payments and check balances safely and easily from your mobile phone.
- Kabu.com Securities. Stock data and charts updated at user-specified intervals.
- Tower Mobile. Search music by artist, view charts of different genres, and receive updates on new releases.

Source: Company reports.

information only fourth (12 per cent), followed by transactions (7 per cent) and database (5 per cent).

The great usage shift

The shift from voice to data has meant substantial shifts in usage patterns. As mobility tends to reflect the user's lifestyle, it is subject to substantial seasonality involving predictable and uncontrollable variations in demand over time.[10]. Some 55 per cent of subscribers access i-mode portal sites, while the rest spend their time with independent (non-i-mode) websites. With FOMA 3G, 60 per cent spend their time with independent websites, and the rest with i-mode portal sites (see Table 3.2). The trend may reflect the usage patterns of younger early adopters (more than 41 million subscribers had access to i-mode in 2004, whereas only 5 million could access FOMA 3G at the same time) rather than the user base as a whole. With content categories, this emphasis on early adopters may account for differences (FOMA users were less interested in entertainment and information, more interested in games/horoscopes).

'Initially, the role of our official internet partners was much higher than now,' says Natsuno. Today, the number of ISPs using i-mode portal sites or approved i-menu sites is not that different with the two services. The real changes pertain to the number of sites used, the volume of incoming and outgoing e-mail, and especially web pages accessed and ARPU. 'In 2003, e-mail accounted for some 14 per cent of the total i-mode traffic. Of the remaining 86 per cent, some 40 per cent came from our official internet providers and 46 per cent from the free internet providers. That's the evolution we've had – from official partners to free internet service providers.'

'The next stage will be the rise of what I call the "real commerce",' Natsuno believes. 'We already have e-commerce, but that's confined to the PC, which confines users to a place. The one difference between the PC and the wireless is the network. We can provide for your phone, wherever you go. Within the next five years, real commerce will prove very important. Entertainment, information, e-commerce – they're already part of Japanese people's life. They won't be eliminated. But there will be new content, real commerce content.'

By the autumn of 2004, the Japanese marketplace had become the mobile test laboratory of the world. However, the competitive rules were changing. In its first major move to revamp its ailing Japanese unit, Vodafone Group snared Shiro Tsuda, former senior executive vice president at DoCoMo (the top exec had widely been considered a candidate for the CEO but the post was awarded to another executive). It was a highly unusual move in Japan, and illustrated how dire the situation had become for Vodafone in the nation's cut-throat mobile-phone market – and how the corporate executive culture was changing. Vodafone KK, Japan's number three cellular carrier,

Table 3.2 NTT DoCoMo market research: subscriber behaviour

Younger Early-Adopters	According to subscriber breakdown, 51 per cent of i-mode users were men, 38 per cent women. With 3G (FOMA), the over-representation was even more significant (56 per cent v 34 per cent). Among the 2G users, the largest categories consisted of the 20–29 year olds (22 per cent) the 30–39 year olds (23 per cent) and 40–49 year olds (21 per cent). With the 3G, the early adopter categories are substantially younger, focusing on the 20–29 year olds (38 per cent) and 30–39 year olds (22 per cent).
Anytime, Anywhere	In February 1999, internet penetration in Japan was only under 15 per cent. i-mode offered instant internet access to subscribers from the minute they acquired a mobile phone. Unlike the PC, it was available anytime and anywhere, affordable and easy to use. The number of i-mode subscribers reached 1 million after six months, and 10 million, just a year later. The low initial internet penetration does not 'explain' i-mode's popularity. The mobile S-curve did not slow down with increasing internet penetration in Japan.
Continuous Improvement	Starting with its launch in February 1999, the S-curve of i-mode has been explosive. The continuity of the curve has been ensured with steady 'injections' of new innovation efforts, beginning with the colour LCDs, Java-based services (i-appli), corporate alliances, location-based services (i-area), dynamic content services (FOMA i-motion), camera phones (i-shot).
Mobile e-mail Volumes	By 2002, some 80 per cent of those with internet accessible mobile phones send and receive e-mail on a daily basis – which translates to more than 50 million Japanese using mobile phone e-mail every day. In 2004, each i-mode subscriber sent and received an average of 10 messages, or 750 Japanese characters worth of e-mail messages daily.
Peak Periods	The two time periods during the day when the DoCoMo i-mode centre is the busiest occur 12 pm and 10 pm. About half of the total volume (some 400 million messages per day) is concentrated between the periods 12pm–1pm and 9pm–11pm. The troughs occur during lunch hours and after prime time TV in late evening.
Complementary Communication	Friends are the top recipients of these messages, particularly those who are met on a regular basis. These exchanges do not substitute for phone calls or meetings, but complement them, especially when friends do not meet often. Mobile e-mails are also a considerate and less intrusive way to keep touch and convey one's thoughts quickly, yet without interfering with the other person's activities.
Expressive, Instrumental and Intimate	Most mobile e-mail messages are sent 'to tell others about something that just happened, or their thoughts of the moment'. In addition to serving as an expressive extension of chit-chat, mobile phone e-mail also fulfils instrumental needs because it is a convenient way to specify an appointment, confirm a location, and so on. It can also serve more intimate needs as a channel for touchy subjects that may be difficult to talk about on the phone or face-to-face. In Japan as well as elsewhere, cushioning the words by using emoticons and *hetamoji* (funny handwriting characters) has made it easier to get messages across in difficult situations.

Source: Based on NTT DoCoMo, and company reports (March 2002).

commented Tsuda, 'is certainly facing a lot of challenges right now' (quoted in Parker, 2004).

THE PROGENITORS

In 2004, operators were seeking new ways of differentiating themselves as they strove to gain a head start in the data game. Four years later, the mobile consumer applications market, which includes gaming, ring tones, video and music, was expected to amount to US $8 billion in Western Europe, where i-mode's progeny consisted of i-mode's alliance partners, Vodafone, and the FreeMove Alliance. The latter was formed in April 2003 by four major European mobile operators – Orange, Telefonica Moviles, Telecom Italia Mobile (TIM), and T-Mobile International – well established in the five principal European markets: France, Germany, Italy, Spain and the United Kingdom. With its 170 million managed subscribers in Europe compared with Vodafone's 89.2 million, the Alliance was calling itself 'the dominant European operator'. Worldwide, its subsidiaries and affiliates serve more than 230 million customers. With combined economies of scale and scope, they hoped to challenge Vodafone – the pioneer of European mobile services. Telecom alliances, however, have a notorious history.

How Vodafone redefined mobile services

The story of Vodafone Live! – an easy-to-use consumer service, bringing customers a world of colour, sound and pictures – originates from the inflated WAP hopes and the early failures with the Vivazzi service. At the group level, these disappointments led to a determined effort to alter the balance of bargaining power in the US $500 billion cellphone business, in relation to massive bulk orders. At the service level, it started with the bold effort to rethink the entire service operation.

The pilgrimage to Japan

As NTT DoCoMo's i-mode took off and achieved dramatic growth, Vodafone began to boost its presence in the Japanese marketplace by first snapping up AT&T's Japan Telecom stake and then launching a US $4.3 billion share sale and purchasing 4.9 per cent of J-Phone's regional operating units from BT. With this footprint, the UK-based company was executing a familiar strategy to force forward its vision through investments in new markets. The deal highlighted Vodafone's drive to play a role in the first 3G market. Vodafone chief executive Chris Gent said he wanted to take on the Japanese industry leader: 'The goal is to make J-Phone competitive and give DoCoMo a hard time' (quoted in CNN, 2001).

It was then that Thomas Geitner, Vodafone's chief technology officer, and his colleagues visited Japan. Geitner wanted to better understand the drivers of the i-mode success. 'As we walked in the shops, we didn't see technologies that were promoted. What we saw was a whole lot of very colourful phones. They were not selling technologies; they were selling phones with cameras.'[12]

Along with many others, Vodafone considered Japan a very technology-driven market. But what really intrigued Geitner was the fact that the market was already customizing. The transition from voice to data *preceded* the 3G launch. Vodafone's team had expected customization to go hand in hand with 3G. Yet, they saw people who were busy buying NTT DoCoMo's i-mode and J-Phone's J-Sky phones. 'We asked why the customers were buying these phones', says Geitner. 'After a while, we understood that it was really about the fun factor. "Look, we really need to forget about this technology stuff," I said. "Technology doesn't sell. Let's go back to basics." So we went back to the drawing board and examined what we were doing. "Let's design something that has a *wow* factor," I said. "Let's design something that's easy to use. And let's design something where the technology is embedded, but it's not something that you want to speak to the customer about."'

Then came the hardest part.

From vendors to development

Through the 1990s and the GSM revolution, the operators and vendors had struggled to satisfy the hypergrowth of the digital cellular markets. High volume compensated for the lack of differentiation. But as advanced markets were saturating, penetration was no longer the driving force; usage was. The mobile device, particularly usability and user interface, became increasingly important. In Japan, NTT DoCoMo dictated specifications to the vendors. In Europe, vendors dictated the specifications. At first, Vodafone approached lesser known and more flexible challengers that were not headquartered in Europe. But even these vendors were apprehensive. Would the Europeans be willing to change their form factor preferences?

'In September 2001, we went to see the representatives of Sharp, which had clamshell phones,' says Geitner. 'They told us that we won't ever be able to sell those phones in Europe because all marketers want to have just candy-bar phones. They told us clamshells were selling so well in Japan because the screen and the unit was bigger. Those reasons were all very convincing. "But isn't that precisely what we need?" we said. "If we want to push content, then we have to develop such phones!" So we decided to move ahead and convince operators. We asked them to let us know what the phone should be like.'

Partly by working with a growing number of Asian manufacturers willing to compromise on product branding, Vodafone was seeking progress towards an identifiable Vodafone 'look and feel'. In doing so, it was at crossroads with Nokia, which supplied about one in every two mobile phones sold in Europe. Even minor changes – Vodafone's budget for purchasing handsets amounted to an estimated $3.5 billion – had the potential to shake the entire industry. If customers could be persuaded to ask for a 'Vodafone handset' rather than, say, a Nokia or Motorola product, it would greatly enhance Vodafone's branding and pricing power.

Upon return to Europe, Geitner garnered a development team of some 20 people, and four to five companies that were specialized in critical competences: one in user interface design, another in usability representing the hi-fi industry, a third from J-Phone, and so forth. The team was assigned with two priorities:

> First, we wanted a very easy to use capability for consumers who use content. Design a telephone that's even easier to use than the one we saw in Japan, we asked. The second task we gave to the team was: Let's really create mobile content. What is mobile content? What do we need to do to present mobile content in an effective form to the customers? What does it mean to have local content? What should it look like to be useful to customers?

Geitner's team designed a prototype amidst a fierce debate between Vodafone and Vivendi on the future of the prior, ill-fated Vivazzi portal, which was quietly folded into the Vodafone Live! project:

> In December 2001, the J-Sky mobile internet service gave my colleagues a touch and a feel of the mobile picture, which at that time was something you would not easily see on a telephone. It had limited capabilities, it was a tri-mode phone, it didn't have a camera, but it enabled colour browsing. This phone really inspired both the developers and our marketers. 'Let's develop it!' we decided. We felt it needed to have an anchor service. With market research, we determined that it was not content that caught the customer's attention, but colour and pictures. So we added to the requirement the camera phone. The problem was that nobody had them yet.

Toward the launch

Pressures arose as CeBIT 2002, a major trade conference, was getting closer. 'We had to show something. We knew i-mode would launch and we wanted to intercept it by showing something to the press in Hanover. We showed them Vodafone Live!, which we would launch in October 2002. The name was already there.' Yet the road from CeBIT to October 2002 was tough. 'We needed to make a market for it, so it was a marketing story, but we also needed the technology,' recalls Geitner. 'We needed colour, pictures and ease of use. Content is not something that we can sell easily. Content is something people will use if they find it useful and easy to accept.'

Between March and October 2002, Vodafone designed what Geitner calls a 'demand-creating marketing story'. 'What does it require to make the customers hungry and to create the *wow* factor? That was the marketing story. What can we do with all the technology now available to best serve the customer's emotional and functional needs? The story was really about colour, pictures and ease of use. We put our case around those requirements.'

Geitner's team was less interested in putting the money in advertising the key features, such as browsing, than marketing:

It doesn't make sense to sell the phones for 50 euros. It makes more sense to create the desire and demand, and make it more expensive and put more money into communications. It doesn't make sense to sell a smaller number of telephones for the same amount of money and put up subsidies. For what?

In 2002, we launched with three telephones. Our key telephone was the Sharp GX10, which was really the best implementation of the camera capability and the ease of use concept, both on telephone and the navigation. Additionally, Vodafone had Panasonic and Nokia 7650 camera phones. Nokia was still struggling with the idea of Vodafone branding things and telling what the user interface should look like. The market took off:

We had never before sold telephones at 200 plus euros in any market! But it worked! People liked them! People liked the camera, they liked the idea that they could do something new with it. With content, they liked the fact that we had ring tones that were really like music; not like the ring tones we used to have. These things really began to make a difference in the pre-Christmas business of 2002. From then on, we expanded our range of services and our range of telephones. The first phones we bought around €400. Now the low-end phones are around €100–150, but those prices will come down eventually. These phones are now basically doing what the GE10 was doing when we launched it, in terms of technical features, such as camera resolution, screen size, the number of pixels. Today, we have a wider range of phones and services available. We have enhanced our content. We now know what kind of content categories work and sell well. We also know which kind of content doesn't sell well.

Vodafone Live!

Like i-mode in Japan and Nokia worldwide, Vodafone zoomed to young target demographics. The key target for Vodafone Live! comprises 18–25 year old urban adolescents, though the broader target extends to 34 year olds. Targeting seems to emulate the lessons of i-mode and FOMA. The majority of early adopters consist of younger age cohorts, which restrains potential average revenue per user. Unlike i-mode, the Live! service does not have a subscription fee. In spring 2002, i-mode debuted in Europe, as E-Plus in Germany and KPN in the Netherlands. In the autumn, service adaptations were implemented by Bouygues Telecom in France and BASE in Belgium. By the year end the operators had signed up 336,000 users; more than a third were in Germany. In Japan, the launch of i-mode had led to a subscriber explosion. Not so in Europe, where only 1.7 per cent of the operators' combined subscriber bases signed up. Vodafone followed in the footprints of the Euro i-mode. In October 2002, it introduced its flagship service simultaneously in eight countries (Germany, the UK, Italy, Spain, the Netherlands, Sweden, Ireland and Portugal). With a million target customers (1.5 per cent of Vodafone's total subscriber base in these country markets) reached five months later, just three markets (Germany, the UK and Italy) accounted for four of every five subscribers.

The Vodafone Live! interface is a colour, icon-based menu that is easy to use. In addition to news, sports and entertainment stories, customers can click one of half a dozen or so icons to access services, including picture messaging, polyphonic ringtones, games arcade, menu, mail and messenger (see "The Live! content package" over the page). The revenue-sharing model is about 40 (Vodafone) to 60 (content provider), though it can vary according to the attractiveness of the partner's content services. Bigger brands command greater shares (as with Vodafone's deal with Microsoft). With SMS, the revenue model is based on volume. Like NTT DoCoMo, Vodafone Live! provides billing for content providers, with its M-pay micropayment system. At the early stages, the services of Vodafone were fewer in number and weaker in quality than those of the European i-mode. In the marketing of these services, Vodafone, a better known brand in Europe, proved stronger initially, outselling i-mode substantially in those country markets where the two competed.

'Basically we have three big categories of services,' notes Geitner. 'One is messaging. The other is downloads: music, games, videostreams. The third is browsing. In Japan, browsing is slightly bigger than in Europe, for now. But we think there's also a time aspect to this. i-mode started earlier and Japan has a bigger population base for phone users. So we have to be careful with generalizations comparing Vodafone Live! and i-mode.'

By mid-2004, Vodafone had seen a slightly higher share of revenue from ringtones and games. 'The big surprise for us was the amount of game downloads,' acknowledges Geitner. 'Last year, the ringtone market worldwide was 10 per cent of the world music market and growing at the pace of 15 per cent, even though the industry was flat. Since every phone we sell has an easy download capability, this number will keep growing for a while. It has the capability to give the customer the polyphonic experience and the next generation real ringtones. Three years ago I had no idea that ringtones could take a 10 per cent share in the music market so fast.'

By 2004, the content package played a critical role in Vodafone's strategy, which was 'to delight its customers, delivering a superior customer experience and developing customer loyalty at all touchpoints, introducing end-to-end voice and data propositions to target customer segments, and achieving customer preference for the Vodafone brand'. At the same time, Geitner took charge of 'business integration within Vodafone to further leverage the scale of the global footprint'. The function was expected to improve speed to market for new products, while improving the company's strategic cost position (Vodafone, 2004: 10).

The Live! content package

The Live! package comprises several major elements:

- picture messaging, sharing moments with colour pictures and sound;
- polyphonic ringtones, with real polyphonic sound, letting people hear how the user feels;
- a games arcade with 3D graphics, full sound and vibrating handsets;
- the Vodafone Live! menu, with all the latest news, fun and info on the phone;
- Vodafone mail, never missing a message when the user is out and about;
- Vodafone messenger, the fun way to chat online.

The Vodafone Live! menu plays a critical role in content services. Instead of 'dull information', the package allows the user to 'experience fantastic full color pictures to go along with your news, sports and entertainment stories. Instead of reading about your news, sports and entertainment stories, see it and judge for yourself. Life's fun in color.'

- entertainment news: the latest showbiz news and gossip complete with pictures;
- football news and results, experiencing the thrill of scoring with the goal flash alerts, getting the latest updates on the user's team, plus the latest results;
- music news and charts: colour music news and charts, plus pictures of the hottest pop stars;
- WAP chat: making new friends, flirting and having fun, and letting fingers do the talking.

The Live! package is available to pre-paid and contract customers. Some services are charged each time content is consumed (such as events-based content like messaging). In other cases, customers pay a weekly or monthly fee, which entitles them to content access (such as *The Times* Online). In both cases, customers are also charged for the GPRS traffic used in the transaction.

Future prospects

By the summer of 2004, Vodafone Live! was available in 16 countries. Vodafone had leveraged the experience of its Japanese subsidiary in Europe and was intent on extending Live! across the entire global footprint. By focusing its handset development resources, the group aimed to offer a still wider range of handsets with enhanced functionality. The sourcing deals with Sharp and Panasonic led to two very attractive handsets (particularly the flagship device Sharp GX-10), while triggering a branding or cobranding debate with Nokia (now Nokia 3650 and Ericsson T610 are available as well). The first GSM-enabled megapixel camera phone launched in the European market, the Sharp GX30, had been introduced into 10 Vodafone markets. In marketing, Vodafone has promoted services rather than the technology, focusing on the 'fun' and 'exciting' experience:

> Vodafone Live! will bring your world alive. You're about to enter an exciting new age, it's all about colour, sound and pictures. Vodafone Live! will change the way you use your mobile.

The scale of the customer base together with the broader reach have attracted stronger content partners, including such established brands as Warner Bros. Online, UEFA Champions League Football, Sony Pictures, Sony Music Entertainment and Disney. In May 2004, the Group announced the phased introduction of 'Vodafone Live! with 3G' for consumers in Europe.

Verizon Wireless and the US catch-up

In the United States, the mobile operators have been catching up with technology innovation in Western Europe and Asia–Pacific. Verizon Wireless is the US leader in providing wireless data services. In June 2002, it launched Qualcomm's BREW-based content and application services nationwide, which made it the first carrier to offer US customers over-the-air downloads of games, ringtones, information and entertainment applications with BREW (see Box 3.2). It provides state-of-the-art wireless data services to 30 million customers via mobile phones. With the launch of the Get It Now service in September 2002, customers could personalize their mobile lifestyle. Fuelling the rapid growth of the data business have been partnerships with Microsoft, Qualcomm, Disney, Time Warner, RIM, and many others.

EXPLODING CONTENT MARKET

In the United States, the path to mobile content has evolved through phases that differ from those in Western Europe and Japan. 'The first milestone was the deployment of WAP 1.0 based services,' says Paul Palmieri, director of business development at Verizon Wireless and the architect of Get It Now. 'The US operators all met with some success, but not the success we'd expected. Another milestone was the success of the GSM equipment manufacturers. That taught the US CDMA carriers a valuable lesson about the importance of controlling the specification of the handset. The third one was the launch of SMS interoperability, which has the peer-to-peer impact that has been so great here. This also has had the ripple effect into really driving the operators through our trade association [Cellular Telecommunications & Internet Association, CTIA] to work together quickly towards common short codes. Finally, the launch of downloadable services across operators in the United States and their take-up far exceeds the Europe experience. In the rich application space, Europe is running behind.'

Box 3.2 GOING FOR GLOBAL MULTIMEDIA

'Global multimedia is the next big trend,' says Dr Paul E Jacobs, group president of Qualcomm Wireless & Internet Group, 'and wireless is going to drive devices and new services and bring new content providers into the industry. We address these issues from the technology side. We are developing technologies that are driving the cost per bit down. On the implementation side, we're building all the pieces into the chip and software.'

Cable paradigm

'People in the industry are looking at mobile multimedia in the wrong way,' says Jacobs. 'They're primarily looking at it as video on demand. The model of consumption is that the consumer gets in, looks at all the lists of video files, downloads some, and then plays them from another list of video files in a directory on their phone. It's clearly non-intuitive.

'The way most people consume multimedia and television is cable television. They search through channels and find the one that looks interesting and watch it. That's the paradigm we're trying to follow. The content providers are looking for a model in the wireless space that is similar to the one that they know in the cable TV industry. I think that's the right model. It's certainly been popular around the world.'

When television broadcasting began in the United States, broadcast technologists and marketers pioneered the new programme models. Today, systemic complexity and new technologies make things more difficult. 'Convergence requires both industries, so you have to find people who know each. That's what we're trying to do. We're trying to find the people who can understand the technology and the marketing side.'

Cannibalization and complements

'The wireless will offer multiple content distribution channels, and as always the best content wins. My kids are watching *American Idol*. They're participating in the interactivity, casting their votes in. These are small lessons that will be learnt and adopted. It's a process where people will feel out things. In the wireless industry, that's how we build new things.

'There's absolutely cannibalization going on, which happens any time there is a new channel. But that doesn't necessarily mean that one thing dies and another takes over. People may be watching television for a long time. They may all be paying for it. Today, almost 90 per cent of people pay for their television anyway because they buy it on a cable or a satellite system. The business model may change a little bit, but it won't go away.'

Source: interview with Dr Paul E Jacobs, group president, Wireless & Internet Group, Qualcomm Inc, 6 April 2004.

Like the founders of i-mode in Japan and Vodafone Live! in Europe, the US operators have begun to exert bargaining power in specifications, to protect their positioning in the industry value system.[13] 'I see industry players moving strongly to differentiate their services based on the service experience, not on the handsets. For us, it is very simply an evolution. Possibly the handset manufacturers may see it as a conflict.'

Contents and needs

The content providers argue that as long as they receive a minor percentage of revenues, the incentives remain absent. Are the players watching each other to take the first move? 'In the United States we are not at that stage,' says Palmieri. 'Small companies have been able to come in and invest in this marketplace. It's no more a chicken-and-egg situation, the market is now here and early movers and companies from Japan and Korea are the first real winners in this space. It remains to be seen what the role of the major entertainment will be in the United States, except for Disney which has already embraced mobile. The United States is leading in the mobile entertainment business, as evidenced by the explosion of the content market and entrepreneurial intensity.'

Palmieri believes that content categories in the United States are similar to others worldwide. 'But this has less to do with the content category than with the consumers' need state. There are primarily three need states that mobile content, no matter what the culture, is appealing to,' he says. 'One is keeping up to date and informed. Another is social interaction and fun, as well as information content and games. The third is expressing myself and instant messaging. In some cases, these need states are overlapping, and at the intersection you often see plain old SMS instant messaging. The content categories and the content itself can change from market to market. What is fundamentally the same is the consumer need and what they are fulfilling.'

Part 2

Mobile consumer services

4

Service innovation

While the last chapter told the story of the mobile service pioneers, this chapter focuses on their successful service categories. Despite differences between these branded services, there is much that is common to their portfolios, from 'texting' (the short message service, SMS) to rich voice, the mobile internet, messaging and personalized content.

SERVICE CATEGORIES

In the mobile business, each new innovation wave has been enabled by new technologies and new markets, which have given rise to new products and services. Prior to the late 1990s, voice reigned over data and service concepts were few, simple and bounded by national, or at most regional, markets. With multimedia cellular, data reigns over voice and service concepts will be many, complex and global.

From 'sexing' to 'texting' to new mobile services

Around the summer of 2000, porn emerged on wireless websites, even if analysts thought that the same audience on the fixed internet would never migrate to the tiny screen. 'The audience now ranks in the millions,' reported CNET (Charny, 2001). In March 2001, half of the most trafficked mobile websites, as monitored by Alloutwap.com, were still sex sites. The sites outranked the wireless web locations for Worldwide Wrestling Federation's mobile entry, two Nokia sites and Britney Spears. Despite impressive hype and anecdotal evidence, the early days of mobile sex proved enticing but treacherous business terrain.

Sex: the unexpected loser

The internet has had a dramatic effect on the porn industry, says Larry Flynt, the publisher of *Hustler* and other porn properties:

> In the 1980s, publishing was 80 percent of my business. Now it's about 20 per cent, and the rest is Internet or video. I don't think many people anticipated how the Internet was going to revolutionize the way we disseminate information. Now everybody does – but some did in time, and some didn't. That's one of the reasons *Penthouse* filed for bankruptcy. They were relying totally on publishing. We knew in the early 1990s that we needed to diversify and branched out into a lot of different areas.
>
> (Jardin, 2004)

In early 2002, total PC internet paid content in Europe amounted to €252 million. Adult content accounted for some 70 per cent of the total, whereas games, business news and other categories each accounted for just 10 per cent. At the same time, total mobile ancillary services amounted to 590 million euros. Ringtones and logos accounted for 95 per cent of the total, whereas alerts on news, sports and finance altogether made up just 5 per cent (Jupiter, 2002). Until recently, mobile handsets, with their small grey displays, have not been a particularly compelling medium on which to view images, pornographic or otherwise.

With much pornography available for free on the fixed internet, the demand for adult material was expected to be met largely by fixed internet services.[1] Nevertheless, the adage that 'sex sells' has been driving wireless adult entertainment initiatives. 'Technology still has many surprises for us down the road, particularly in the wireless area,' predicts Larry Flynt. 'It's going to be absolutely phenomenal. In the next two to five years, you'll see the computer and your home television set merging. You'll have one remote control, and they'll effectively be one device' (Jardin, 2004).

The role of porn movies and sexual chat was far more influential in the early days of home video and AOL's chat groups. As a medium, the PC provides a large form factor and greater sense of 'realism'. The user consumes porn in the privacy of home. With mobile porn, the form factor is small and provides a less impressive sense of 'realism', and the user consumes sex in public. When one is in a hurry, texting beats sexing.

SMS: the unexpected triumph

On Saturday 16 November 2002, more than 200,000 votes were cast via premium SMS in just one hour for the television show *Popstars – The Rivals*, according to O2 UK, the British mobile operator. Various models of SMS were already in use by television broadcasters across the globe. SMS had already been used as a channel for voting in Europe. 'TV producers are very interested in the use of premium SMS as an interactive channel,' said market researchers. 'We will start to see more and more quiz shows adopting an element of SMS interaction into the actual content of the show' (Hinchcliffe, 2002).

SMS – the ability to send and receive abbreviated text messages to and from mobile telephones – can handle messages made up of words, numbers or an alphanumeric combination. Originally designed as part of the GSM digital mobile standards, it is now available on a wide range of networks, including the nascent multimedia networks. Each short message can be up to 160 characters in length when Latin alphabets are employed and 70 characters when non-Latin alphabets such as Arabic and Chinese are used. Transmitted through the GSM network's signalling channel, SMS was initially incorporated for notifying mobile subscribers of waiting voicemail messages. The functionality was limited; the capacity was low. It was not thought of as something that would enable communication *between* subscribers.

With the transition to digital cellular, the first short message was sent in December 1992 from a PC to a mobile phone on the Vodafone GSM network in the UK. Two years later, Vodafone's Vodata became the first network operator in the UK to launch data, fax and SMS services over the digital network. It led to a 25 per cent increase in messaging traffic. Soon new initiatives enabled the exchange of messages between subscribers on different mobile networks. Meanwhile, the growth of SMS usage accelerated through the introduction of text messaging services for pre-paid phone users.

With limited initial appeal in the United States, 'texting' has proved very popular in Europe, Asia and Australia, particularly among young urbanites. In many markets, it is relatively cheap. In Singapore, for instance, hundreds of messages can be sent per month for free. As a result, the rapid and intimate mode of communication has thrived in grassroots initiatives. Among other things, it led to the resignation of the president in 2001, after a popular campaign based on SMS chain letters. By 2004, China's first novel delivered through SMS was being made into a film that will also be transmitted to cellphones and on the internet.[2]

In April 2002, the number of SMS messages sent globally exceeded the symbolic threshold of a billion messages per day. That was six times more than in 2000. The highly complementary service can be employed independently or with mass media. New SMS services offer automated 'alerts' sent on a regular basis giving news, weather, financial information, sporting event scores and other information. SMS is also increasingly used for 'real world' services. For example, some vending machines allow payment by sending an SMS; usually, the cost of the item bought is added to the user's phone bill. Market researchers expected the year 2004 to be the most successful year in terms of revenue for television-generated messaging, with global revenues reaching 9.4 billion euros that year from television alone.

SMS is one of the great mobile success stories, but it is an unintended success story. SMS proved successful *despite* its original mission.

NEW SERVICES

Until the mid-1990s, mobile services were driven by voice communications, and to some extent by text messaging. Today, multimedia cellular and wireless broadband enable vast new opportunities. The new services can be categorized into four broad groups of connectivity (Figure 4.1):

(a) Generic service categories

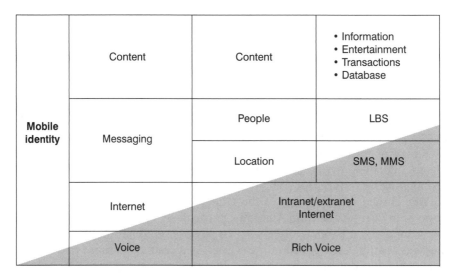

(b) Level of security/value of transaction

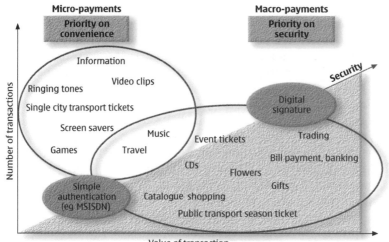

Source (b): Nokia Corp.

Figure 4.1 Service categories

- rich voice;
- the internet (mobile internet, mobile intranet/extranet);
- messaging (location-based services, people communications, such as SMS, MMS);
- content (including information, entertainment, transactions and databases).

Rich voice

In addition to voice communications, new mobile services provide always-on data communications. Mobility has led to shifts in communication patterns, but it is also transforming the culture of communication. According to the Swedish Ericsson, it is associated with 'the rise of the experience economy where consumers go from consuming out of needs to consumption out of wants and desires. There is also a shift in how consumers define value – from products to experiences' (Ericsson, 2004).

While voice will remain the critical service, high data rates allow additional functionalities. The rich voice service is real-time and two-way. In addition to traditional mobile voice features (operator services, directory assistance and roaming), it provides advanced voice capabilities (including voice over IP, voice-activated net access and web-initiated voice calls). Over time, it will include broadband-based mobile videophone and media communications. Between 2000 and 2010, more than 50 per cent of the voice traffic on fixed networks is expected to shift to mobile networks. At the same time, the voiceover IP market will go mainstream.

Videophone at day-care centre. Many women still find it hard to maintain a job and bring up children at the same time. In Hasaki Hikari day-care centre located in the town of Hasaki in Kashima Country, Ibaraki Prefecture, NTT DoCoMo allows parents and children to stay in touch via FOMA Videophone. Started at the request of a mother, the initiative supports peace of mind by allowing the parents to carry video of their children in the palm of their hand.

Push to Talk over Cellular. Push to Talk over Cellular (PoC) introduces a direct one-to-one and one-to-many voice communication service in the cellular network. It is not a substitute for any existing cellular services. It gives operators an opportunity to develop their voice service offering without having to change conventional voice services (Nokia, 2004b). It benefits a wide range of users, including:

- small businesses;
- leisure groups and communities;
- families, teenagers and social groups;
- corporate users;
- possibly demanding LMR/PMR users (even if it does not meet the stringent emergency public safety requirements).

The internet

In addition to enhanced voice services, the new data environment enables connectivity to content on the internet – mobile internet access for consumer markets, and, additionally, mobile intranet/extranet access for business markets.

Mobile internet

This service provides mobile access to fixed-line internet service providers with near-wireline transmission quality and functionality. It includes full web access to the internet as well as file transfer, e-mail, and streaming video/audio capability. In the long term, it will extend the user's desktop internet experience into the mobile environment, providing alternative access into existing content. As with i-mode, mobile access to existing e-mail accounts is anticipated to be a major initial driver for such a service. Targeting the current customer base of fixed internet subscribers, the service providers serve as mobile ISPs for consumer or business customers. Fixed internet users expect access to be provided at minimal or even zero cost.

Fall of Pioneers. By 2001, the first-movers included Sonera Zed, AOL Anywhere, Djuice.com, Vizzavi, Genie, and T-Motion. Launched by operators as well as traditional internet portals, these start-ups were competing to become the 'Yahoos' of the mobile market. Many were harvested with the telecom slowdown.

New Brands. Among the surviving brands, the bellwether services – i-mode, Vodafone Live!, Get It Now! and SK Telecom's branded services – represent the trendsetters.

Mobile intranet/extranet

These services offer secure mobile access to corporate local area networks (LANs), virtual private networks (VPNs), and the internet. Along with the consumer markets, the need for mobile internet services, particularly mobile intranet/extranet access, has been accelerating rapidly in the business market. With changing work patterns, employees expect access inside and outside their office. Mobile service providers are expected to profit from this opportunity by developing business enterprise services, building on mobile intranet/extranet access, including mobile access to desktop applications (e-mail, contact lists, spreadsheets, corporate management systems and so on), internet access and mobile access to the intranet and/or extranet portals.

Messaging

Building on always-on and IP-based data, SMS, multimedia messaging service (MMS), mobile presence, and mobile instant messaging have boosted mobile communities, from Asia to Europe and North America (see Box 4.1).

Box 4.1   MOBILE COMMUNITIES – ASIAN STYLE

'For now, the mobile space is very community-based. You can communicate with one person or another by using platforms, such as instant messaging, e-mail, dating or chat rooms and photos,' says the Singapore-based Randall Maxwell, who heads Yahoo! Asia's wireless services and used to oversee MTV Asia Online's operations. 'It is about sharing of experiences and identification with user groups.'

Mobile offerings

Yahoo! provides mobile versions of its PC offerings. 'We provide a search product. Second, we are an advertising medium. But we're also an enterprise division. For example we built an HTML portal for Hong Kong Shanghai Bank which allows consumers to apply for a credit card over the mobile phone.

'Our fourth offering is the mobile enterprise. In the United States, all major operators have approached us to create a Yahoo! brand and product that is specific to their mobile style. We create a layer of content that Verizon or T-Mobile users can access for their mail, instant messaging, photo products that can be customized.

'The business rules in South East Asia prohibit a large mobile operator, while limiting foreign ownership,' says Maxwell. In the absence of consolidation, economies of scale remain low.

Regional differences

'In South East Asia, phone landlines are often a luxury. It is much cheaper to build a wireless backbone than to install landlines into everybody's home. Many companies and state enterprises are regional. Yahoo! can provide them the ability to communicate on a regional basis with a centralized backbone.

'There may be 85–90 million mobile handsets in the marketplace, but less than 10 per cent have GPRS or WAP capabilities. We'd like to see the higher capability handsets reach about the 25 per cent penetration level. Then we can focus on direct access to Yahoo! services.

'In the United States the carriers will give you a handset if you subscribe to their services, whereas in Asia handset prices range from US $200–400. In South East Asian countries, 5 per cent of the population controls 95 per cent of the wealth. A massive section of the market uses second-hand phones.'

It's a communication device

As mobile devices acquire television-style capabilities, some observers anticipate disruptive changes. Maxwell believes the evolution will be more incremental by nature. 'There's great potential, at first in places like Japan and Korea. But you'll find something of a backlash as well. In the Philippines, I met someone who was using his handset to watch TV in real time, on a 2G format. "It was fun for the first three hours," he said, "and then it hurt my eyes." This was from someone in the business.

'Phones will return to being communication devices. Expectations have been inflated, despite the limiting screen size. Take multimedia messaging, or camera phones. As we've already seen in the United States, the initial take-up was strong but then it fell off. We've seen the same in Europe. It's a novelty phenomenon – until the phone returns to its purpose, which is communication.'

The content challenge

'The million dollar question is whether companies, such as Sony Pictures and Warner Bros, will format their content for delivering to mobile devices,' says Maxwell. 'The new applications are fabulous, but so is the cost to implement and produce them in a format that is deliverable to even 50 per cent of our subscribers. The cost of delivering that content en masse becomes a quantum leap for the revenue I can generate to serve that content.'

Source: the author's interview with Randall Maxwell, head of Wireless Services, Yahoo! Asia, 22 June 2004.

Short Message Service

Initiated in Europe in 1992, SMS was not designed, but discovered. Initially prescribed by an industry association, the text message service became available with digital networks. As the digital networks support SMS, it has grown into a universal mobile data service and is very popular among young people. By the same token, it has played a critical role in the multimedia migration path (Figure 4.2).

Multimedia messaging service

The MMS service concept originated from SMS, but – unlike its precursor – it allows for non-real-time transmission of various kinds of multimedia content, including electronic postcards, audio and video clips. In consumer markets, it enables instant messaging to closed user groups, which are defined by service

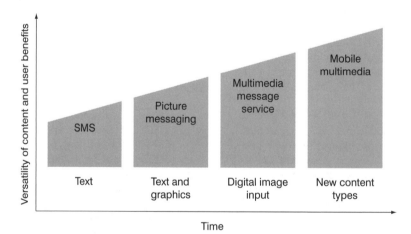

The global mobile communications industry is evolving from voice-driven communication to personal multimedia via text and imaging-driven intermediate stages.

Figure 4.2   Messaging migration: from SMS to multimedia

providers or specific communities of interest. In business markets, it offers MMS with always-on capabilities, personalization and user-to-user networking, while allowing for instant messaging. In this segment, the service typically targets closed business communities that may be defined by service providers or users themselves.

Mobile presence

With the transition from voice to data, the mobile phone is evolving into a highly personal device. The transition tends to favour those applications and services that support the user's natural communication patterns and individual needs, by contributing to lifestyle or productivity. Presence can serve as one of these supportive elements.[3] It is popular in youth segments because teens and adolescents use media to express themselves and build identity. In business markets, the uses of presence information can boost efficiency and productivity (Figure 4.3). Due to the extraordinary reach of the mobile device, presence is becoming a part of daily mobile communication.

Mobile instant messaging

Instant messaging (IM) allows users to send short and simple messages that are delivered immediately to online users. Empowering people rather than places, mobile IM extends the IM capability into the mobile domain. Coupling instant message delivery with presence information, it is an attractive messaging service. To boost growth and acceptance among the users, SMS has been employed to offer mobile IM services. The essential point is not the technology used, but the connectivity that allows the IM user over different access methods (GPRS, 3G and so on). New handsets provide larger, colour screens, which make it easier for users to carry on longer discussions on the screen.

Location-based services

Location-based services (LBS) are business and consumer services that enable users or machines to find other people or machines, and/or enable others to find users, just as they enable users to identify their own location. These services go hand in hand with the database function of the mobile devices. The value of mobile location services is boosted by drivers that underscore personal interest, topicality and the role of the location: the user wants the right service, at the right time, in the right location. The ability to pinpoint the location of an individual has vital, popular value in emergency services. Generic location-based services emulate basic mobility categories, including location, people connectivity and personal links (see eg, Nokia, 2002a):

- In consumer markets, LBS include typically enhanced personal navigation and route finding. For instance, the user listens to turn-by-turn directions to get to an unfamiliar address. In business markets, these comprise an array of tracking services, including fleet management, vehicle dispatch,

Blogging has gained tremendous momentum on the internet, enabling millions to share their lives and thoughts with others. Blogging is all about communication: we are interested in other people's lives, but at the same time we want to share our own experiences and thoughts with others.

Nokia Lifeblog is a PC and mobile phone software combination that effortlessly keeps a multimedia diary of the items the user may collect with his/her mobile phone. Lifeblog automatically organizes photos, videos, text messages and multimedia messages into a clear chronology the user can easily browse, search, edit and save.

Source: Nokia Corp.

Figure 4.3   New services and usage scenarios: lifeblogging

rental car tracking, and remote workforce management. Safety and emergency services include emergency dispatch, child/family tracking and auto theft tracking, as well as roadside assistance.[4]

- Community-driven people connectivity services include friend finder, location-based imaging and location sharing. Relying on enhanced personal communication (e-mail, MMS), the user for instance may receive pictures with attached location as an invitation to a birthday party.
- Personal content service groups comprise information and entertainment. The former comprise finding places of interest and information services. For instance, consumers may seek answers to simple questions, such as 'Where are the nearest restaurants?' The latter may include LBS versions of entertainment, as well as location-based gaming.

NTT DoCoMo has pioneered many of these services in mass markets. With i-mode, the 'i-area' service delivers users a broad range of location-specific i-mode content. Recognizing 500 different regions, the system pinpoints the location of the subscriber according to the nearest base station and provides him or her with a content menu specific to that area. Similarly, 'i-navi' service connects i-mode terminals with car navigation systems. In Japan, most operators have not charged extra for the location element. Location-based services have been employed to boost usage, which has translated to increased revenue.

Consumer location applications might generate over US $8 billion in global service revenues by 2008. The Asia–Pacific is expected to remain the dominant region for mobile LBS revenue growth, whereas Western Europe is expected to be overtaken by North America in 2006. Much of the momentum behind mobile LBS has dissipated in less than two years.[5] Three factors will play a critical role in the end-users' trust in mobile location services: privacy, security and ease of use. It is the customer and not the operator or service provider who must have control over the use of his/her location information.[6]

Personalized content

With the launch of i-mode in 1999, NTT DoCoMo developed four basic content service categories: information, entertainment, database and transactions.[7]

It is *personalization* that will make or break mobile portals. The mobile handset is a reflection and extension of the user's identity. Because of the smaller form factor and delivery issues, the mobile portal faces greater challenges than the fixed internet portal. The greatest challenge is personalization. Unless the services can be optimized for user needs, they will not thrive. Personalization has many aspects, ranging from the visual formatting of an individual's home page to user-selected alerts for news headlines, weather reports, stock quotes and personal calendar appointments. During the past few years, content providers, including the Wall Street Journal, have explored the challenge of mobile personalization.

Information services satisfy users' daily needs for factual news services. Entertainment services respond to their more personal and emotional needs. Transactions fulfil simple or topical retail needs, while databases facilitate information retrieval.

Information

Information includes sub-categories, which must be relevant and topical to the user, such as:

- news updates (national and local newspapers, business news, entertainment news, news from foreign media);
- weather;
- local information;
- sports events (horse races, car racing).

In the 1990s, the Wall Street Journal managed to develop a successful subscription model on the internet. In the 2000s, efforts at mobile publishing have proved less compelling (see Box 4.2).

Entertainment

Entertainment comprises sub-categories that must be intimately relevant to the user. Today, many content providers are seeking ways to extend their brands and platforms to the nascent mobile space:

- downloading (ringtones, characters);
- games (online / network);
- media (radio and television);
- trivia (club events, karaoke, fortune telling).

During 2003, the worldwide sales of mobile phone ringtones jumped 40 per cent to US $3.5 billion. First popularized by tech-savvy teens in the late 1990s, the standard ringtones with a few bars account for some 10 per cent of the US$32.2 billion global music market. Revenues for ringtones are divided between music labels, their artists and mobile phone operators. The average price of a ringtone is 60 cents.[8] The sales of ringtones are expected to remain brisk through 2008, when downloads are expected to top US$5.2 billion. Ringtones and games still lag well behind basic text messaging, which generated US $40 billion in 2003 for mobile phone companies. As phone users get into the habit of sending multimedia and picture messages, these figures should climb as well. The success of ringtones has been great news for the music industry, which has been struggling with piracy issues, substitute rivalry and declining revenues. To the operators, ringtones, along with other popular services, represent an important revenue generator. For the users, they have been a way to personalize the look and feel (and sound!) of the handset.

Box 4.2   WALL STREET IN THE PALM OF YOUR HAND

'Some 10 years ago mobility was limited to road warriors and people who could afford the expense of mobility,' says Jessica Perry, vice president of business development at Dow Jones Interactive Publishing. 'As mobility and flat-rate plans became more available in the late 1990s, the cost of technology went down. Only senior executives and technologists used to have devices such as Blackberry; now everybody has one. It is much more expected and necessary.

'The penetration of applications and devices has increased. There are some opportunities to [obtain] subscription revenue. The technology is becoming more sophisticated and the opportunity for graphics has increased the possibilities for ad revenue to go up. The business model is evolving.'

Personal journal

'The newspaper in your pocket is not that far off,' says Neil F Budde, the founding editor of the Wall Street Journal Interactive Journal. 'Today, I read the *New York Times* more often on my wireless palm than I do in print.'

When Newton – Apple's revolutionary portable and the mother of all mobile devices – made its first appearance via hand-helds, a software company encouraged the Journal to develop a news application. 'We tried to understand the nature of the device, its size and memory constraints, and the needs of the likely user,' recalls Budde, the creator of the only truly successful subscription model on the web. 'We created Personal Journal, a software application that could be set up to dial out to our computers and download a limited package of news tailored to the interests of the individual subscriber.'

Unfortunately, that generation of hand-held devices fell flat, and the Windows-like devices never reached stores. The Journal developers were stuck with a piece of software in search of a platform. To capitalize on the investment, the team decided to port the software to the Windows operating system. Personal Journal was released in 1994 with a monthly subscription price of US $9.95. It was designed for one device, and one kind of user. Released onto PCs, it had a limited news selection and functionality. Since it was launched as the internet was opening up vast amounts of information, it was dead on arrival. At best, Personal Journal had several thousand subscribers.

From hand-helds to palm-based services

The 'webified' Wall Street Journal allowed the publisher to explore the new medium, while developing a product that now served a half-million paying subscribers. 'Shortly thereafter, we started to develop a channel with AvantGo that allowed subscribers to download data to their devices,' says Perry. 'That was our first internet mobile device. It was launched in early 1997, but it never really had a business model.'

'Initially, it was more a channel for just introducing people to what the Wall Street Journal had,' says Budde. 'The strength of the Journal is not in breaking news. That's more of a commodity because you can get them from many places. The strength of the Journal is in a meaningful perspective, a long story with depth, and that does not land itself so well with the mobile devices.'

Despite scepticism and uncertainty, the publisher moved ahead to learn more about the medium. With the web version, Budde created the first HTML page in a Boston bar; since the Journal data was stored in XML, it could be easily reformatted into the AvantGo format.

Early in 2000, the Journal discovered that more people were downloading the WSJ.com channel on AvantGo each day than logging on to the Journal website. The Journal put a survey on the channel. Within a week, more than 1,000 responded via hand-held devices.

From electronic books to WAP

About a year after the mobile devices, the developers of early electronic book devices approached the Journal. These devices were designed for reading books, but early testers asked the developers to add news, particularly the Journal. Given the larger screen and intended use of e-books, the Journal decided to create a larger package of news, including full-length articles and feature stories. Because the audience was already paying for the content they download to their devices, it could offer a richer package as a subscription product.

As the palm went wireless, the Journal was faced with a different challenge. 'Bandwidth was limited and costly at first,' recalls Budde. 'How much should we provide? We decided to layer the content – first headlines, then summaries, with full articles available on demand.'

As WAP arrived, it faced similar problems to the early Palm VII, with slow access and an even more limited screen. The Journal kept the content limited to headlines and summaries. It also got engaged in various forays into audio content, which it thought might prove the ultimate portable format.

Size matters

With increasing bandwidth, declining costs and lighter devices, the key remaining factor is display. 'With the form factor, much depends on whether you are talking about the little tiny screen of a cell phone or something more, such as the palm screen,' argues Perry. 'With the cell phone screen, the form factor is limited to news alerts, maybe things that can't facilitate an immediate response. It is not for traditional advertising. These phones still feel like person-to-person devices; they're not mass media and mobile advertising doesn't really exist yet. If the bandwidth becomes less of an issue, form factor will be everything. Most people know that the Journal has the full piece, but they may not want to read it with the little screen.

'In the financial world, people are interested in alerts rather than information they must actively access,' notes Perry. 'They are more likely to purchase products associated with companies they are interested in. "Alert me when you hear something about company X." Mobile devices can provide them the news, via SMS and other mechanisms.'

Technologists focus on the interface, the publishers on the experience enabled by that interface. 'If we are to achieve the mobile electronic newspaper', says Budde, 'we must deliver a user experience that matches today's printed newspaper.'

Sources: the author's interviews with Neil F Budde, the Neil Budde Group; former founding editor and publisher of the Wall Street Journal Online, 12 March 2004; and with Jessica Perry, VP, business development, Dow Jones Interactive Publishing, 2 April 2004; Budde (2000).

With greater bandwidth, more capable phones and networks, consumers will download larger files, including video games, sports highlights and short video clips (see Box 4.3).

Box 4.3 MOBILE SPORTS AND GAMES

'I have seen the true 3G phones from Europe and Japan, and the soccer highlights on them, and they're fantastic', says John Smelzer of Fox Sports Interactive Media (FSIM). 'There is no substitute for television, but if the television set is not available the mobile device is a great substitute. Our biggest challenge will be the rights issue. Today, rights are primarily for television.'

ESPN versus Fox

Owned and managed by Fox Sports Networks (a subsidiary of Fox Entertainment Group, a division of News Corp.), FSIM develops new media initiatives. Along with ESPN and CBS Sports, Fox Sports is one of the top three brands in the United States that dominate cable, broadcast and internet wireless. The closest rival is ESPN, which Smelzer considers strong nationally, whereas Fox is heavy regionally.

'They have done a great job integrating their content products on multiple platforms,' he says. 'They have been a little slower getting into the wireless space, and we have heard that they are considering a MVNO, like Virgin Mobile. We don't think it's a good strategy. We try to create good quality products, get as broad distribution as possible and extend our brand and content of mobile devices.

Downloadables, games, voting and streaming

'In my division, we're extending the brand and platform to emerging markets. We produce Fox Sport.com, wireless, broadband internet, and are increasingly looking at new platforms, such as video on demand and interactive television. In our wireless base, we're focusing mainly on downloadables.

'Our flagship model is called Fox Sports mobile, basically all the content that you'd find on our website, but with a subscription fee of $4.99 which appears on the monthly phone bill. It's available for Sprint, Verizon and AT&T and we're going to roll it out to all carriers in the coming months.

'Currently, we focus on the arcade-style games and have partnered with Sorrent to produce all of our Fox Sports branded mobile video games. We have about nine titles now and downloadables on every major carrier in the US. Our other big mobile initiative is the virtual coach. That's primarily a marketing and promotional exercise, not so much a revenue exercise. We have successfully sold that feature to Sprint, as a sponsor for football and baseball, and Cingular, as a sponsor in our NASCAR auto racing broadcast. It's our high-profile mobile venture. But it's really a value-add that we give to the sponsor, not so much a stand-alone revenue generator.

'Our Fox Sports video is included on the Real One mobile pass, and we're also live with mobile television. That's actually streaming live television channels, which we provide with a condensed, slightly delayed package. You're not really watching a live television channel, but a very timely digest of television on mobile television.'

Apples and oranges

'It was around 2002 that we became aware of the mobile revenue potential,' says Smelzer. 'We operate worldwide and handle numerous properties. The carriers have their own bottom line to attend to. We were aware of what Sky was doing in Europe, but the market in the United States just wasn't ready for content that people would pay for on their mobile devices. Second, wagering is legal in the British sports world, but not in the US.'

Comparing Sky and FSIM is like comparing apples with oranges, argues Smelzer. 'In the United States, we have all kinds of SMS products, but for the most part the carriers do not cut us in. We do messaging and texting, but mostly for marketing purposes; it's not a revenue stream. Sky operates in a very different environment. They make money on every message sent.'

Source: the author's interview with John Smelzer, VP, business development, Fox Sports Interactive Media, 20 April 2004.

Transactions

In the post-war era, the United States became the first 'plastic nation'. In 2003, cash was used in 32 per cent of retail transactions, down from 39 per cent in 1999. Credit-card usage has remained stable, accounting for about 21 per cent of purchases during that time, but debit cards, which take money out of current accounts immediately after each purchase, have shot up to 31 per cent of purchases (Sapsford, 2004). The future, however, may well belong to the mobile.

The function of mobile e-commerce is to provide simple or highly topical transactional support, including banking, securities trading, credit card information, ticket reservations and shopping (books, games, music). By reducing the need to carry cash, credit or debit cards, the mobile device allows consumers to make purchases virtually anywhere, such as using vending machines without change or buying tickets while on the way to an event. In the adoption of mobile commerce services, key drivers include ease of use, cost efficiency and convenience, and the vital issue of security.[9]

Currently, digital content purchases dominate mobile commerce markets. Nearly all business today comes from selling operator logos and ringing tones, making the operator billing system the most commonly used and most practical payment method. There is a clear need for standardized solutions that merchants can implement and to make wireless processing attractive. In 2003 SK Telecom, for instance, established a national standard for mobile banking services, standardized mobile stock trading service and mobile banking payment service system (see Figure 4.4).

Database

Highly complementary to information, entertainment and transactions, databases facilitate users' information retrieval needs 'here and now', including

SK Telecom's 'Mobile Trading System' (MTS Service) lets customers access a wide range of stock information, and conduct mobile stock trading.

The mobile transaction payment service ('Moneta') employs a smart chip in a cellular phone that can be used online as well as offline. It allows the sending of credit card information for online transaction payments through the wireless internet.

SK Telecom also established the national standard for mobile banking, planning to introduce 'e-Bankbook' services and a variety of e-commerce services connected with the Monera card.

Source: SK Telecom.

Figure 4.4 Mobile trading, mobile banking, mobile transaction payments

telephone directory search, restaurant and city guides, recipes, dictionaries and delivery status inquiries. The database functionality goes hand in hand with location capability, with which the service provider can offer a sense of where the user is at any point in time relative to where he/she may want to go. LBSs include any mobile voice or data service enhanced with the added value of location information, maintained in a customer database by the mobile services provider. This may include local weather reports, news, hotel and restaurant information, traffic and travel reports, navigational services, telematics and mobile commerce.

CONTENT EVOLUTION

While observers often base their future estimates on potential revenue drivers, here the emphasis has been primarily on actual revenue drivers. As the mobile business has evolved through successive waves of innovation, it tends to be highly capital-intensive, which means rising entry barriers. Consequently, empirical business models may be more important than conceptual ones. Along with Vodafone Live! and Get It Now, even i-mode has changed and continues to be in flux. During the past five years, the usage has shifted substantially toward entertainment and free internet services rather than official i-mode service providers. Moreover, new content categories have surfaced (see Table 4.1).

The category of ringtones and standby screens underscores the trend toward customization (by service providers) and personalization (by users). Ringtones and standby screen images function as accessories for mobile phones, but they also reflect the user's sense of identity. The role of entertainment and entertainment-driven categories (games, horoscopes) has increased steadily. Information is a vital category, but not nearly as popular, as industry pioneers have concluded (see Box 4.4). Finally, transactions and database have been least important.

Table 4.1 Initial and evolving i-mode categories

Initial i-mode categories (1999)	Evolving i-mode categories (2003)
information	ringing tones/standby screens (37%)
entertainment	entertainment, games/horoscopes (39%)
database	information (12%)
transactions	transactions plus database (12%)

Box 4.4 NEW YORK TIMES: 'IT MUST BE 10× BETTER'

'It's going to take something really phenomenal to get people into the habit of reading a portable device in large numbers,' says Martin Nisenholtz, CEO of New York Times Digital. 'Certainly, it would have to be multimedia, interactive and have a deep level of application value. Among other things, if I'm to read such a portable, I would like to clip an article, file it and e-mail it to somebody. So far, the devices themselves are just not configured to do that.'

Martin Nisenholtz is a veteran of the interactive digital business, who began his career as a research scientist at New York University in 1979 and has work experience in advertising, interactive marketing and telecommunications. He has presided over the New York Times electronic media properties since 1995, and was named CEO of New York Times Digital in June 1999. Two years later, he cofounded the Online Publishers Association (OPA), while serving on the board of directors for the Interactive Advertising Bureau (IAB).

The New York Times, he says, has been interested in mobile retrieval from the beginning, 'for the simple reason that the newspaper is mobile information. The holy grail of electronic distribution is anywhere, anytime capability. You want to be able to get the Times online when you are in a train, plane or when you're sitting in your chair at the beach.'

The early experiences: AvantGo

'Part of the reason that these formats are held back sometimes is that they are not durable as they should be,' says Nisenholtz. 'AvantGo was among the earliest players in the mobile market to offer products. It was not a wireless product, but a card that was distributed to PDAs through the docking station. Nonetheless the experience was mobile. We actually found the AvantGo application to be very powerful. A lot of people liked reading us in that way.'

In contrast to the AvantGo, the cellphone proved something of a dud during these early years. 'We never had a good experience with the cellphone', acknowledges Nisenholtz. 'I think the cellphone is good for ringtones and games but it's got a form factor that is decidedly inferior for information retrieval, particularly for the kind of information that most newspapers provide.

'We have products for telephones, in fact last year we launched our first with AT&T and Verizon. These are marginal in terms of subscription take-up. We charge a modest amount of money for access and there is more advertising in there. Only about two thousand people have signed up. It has not been an exciting market for us and I did not expect it to be. We did it more as a learning experience to be on a platform rather than as an expectation that it was going to be a big business. On the other hand, as laptop machines, notebook machines and even PDAs become more powerful and incorporate better typography and graphical interfaces, those devices – as mobile devices – are becoming more exciting.'

It's the form factor

With regards to electronic publishing, would the New York Times require a hybrid between the wireless, the PC and the laptop? Would it mean a barrier?

'It would be a major barrier. The question can be answered differently for different kinds of media experiences. Clearly if it's a question about simply putting a movie over to a PC, we are already there. I see people watching movies on their Apple Notebooks all the time. But electronic publishing is quite different and you can't port a newspaper to a device. It is a broadsheet of information that has tremendous information density. It has a very large form factor.'

'The harder theme is to find an application that we haven't yet discovered. Last year Microsoft came to all publishers with their tablet system and they worked with the other manufacturers and created a version of Windows. They were most excited about taking magazines and simply putting the magazine over the tablet. Because a magazine is not a broadsheet, and the form factor on the tablet and the form factor on the magazine are almost identical, you can simply take the magazine and port it to the tablet. But I don't think that's enough. I have seen intriguing products and sites in Germany and the BBC's in England and elsewhere. But I don't see them as being much better than the sites in the United States.'

Andy Grove's 10x dictum

It is not easy to change consumer behaviour, Nisenholtz argues. With the dawn of the internet, many observers thought that newspapers were history. It did not happen. Nor is it likely to happen with mobility. Media are complementary. Truly transformational changes are predicated on disruptive innovation.

'Andy Grove's 10x rule suggests that the innovation has to be 10 times better for it to really catch on,' suggests Nisenholtz. 'Unlike a movie experience, you can't transport a movie theatre or a television set to the airport, so the only way to watch the movie is by watching on your laptop. That's why so many people are watching movies on their laptop on airplanes. Not only is it 10 times better, but it is the only game in town.'

'If I have to choose between buying a $2,200 machine or more likely paying a few hundred dollars for a machine that I have already bought and loading it up with a few magazines versus going to the newsstand and buying a magazine for $3.00, reading it and throwing it away, well… In the end I don't think it's 10 times better to do it electronically, and it won't catch on.

'When we're talking about instant messaging, that's a different story altogether. If my child is sitting in the back of the car and wants to communicate with her friends, but doesn't want me to hear her talking, the only game in town is to IM. That is a legitimate mobile application.

'The vast majority of consumers couldn't care less about technology. So, I go back to consumer behaviour and say, "What problem are we solving for the consumer, what magic are we making that hasn't been made before?" So far, I haven't seen anything come into focus.'

The limits of personalization

'Presumably personalization means that you only get the information that you are interested in and there are legitimate purposes for that,' says Nisenholtz. But he also suggests that while personalization has its privileges, it also has its limitation – and that is precisely where a newspaper can provide the kind of depth that the reader may find useful.

'The thing is that you may be interested in the stocks that you have in your portfolio but you may also be interested in the stocks that you might want to buy. On the other hand, if you are a person looking for a media experience, you are not going to be delighted if the only thing new in the world is the stock that you are interested in. The whole purpose of a news organization like the New York Times – in effect, most newspapers and magazines worldwide – is to go out and look at the whole world and say, "We think that these things are really interesting and we want to make sure that you know about them."'

Source: the author's interview with Martin A Nisenholtz, CEO, New York Times Digital, 14 April 2004.

There are qualifications, however. Different market segments pose different requirements to content services. For instance, business markets underscore the role of information and database, while different verticals may require quite different service capabilities. Second, mobile services are dynamic. Just as the current categories have replaced the initial categories, the ongoing shift toward dynamic content (mobile media) is likely not to underscore the role not only of entertainment but of information as well (mobile CNN, MTV, and so forth). Enabled by increasing bandwidth, spectrum and device capabilities, the potential of service innovation in LBS (local database) and mobile e-commerce (transactions) is expected to escalate in the next few years.

MOBILE PORTALS

As far as the user is concerned, the mobile portal may be just a leveraged extension of the (fixed) internet portal. While the two exhibit many commonalities, they also have fundamental differences, which pose additional challenges. First of all, with mobile portals, content must be optimized for the smaller devices. Second, the content must be delivered to the mobile user.

The mobile portal has been defined as 'an entry point to a wealth of information and value added services' (UMTS Forum, 2002). A 3G mobile portal is a mobile portal accessed via any of the 3G family of systems. Based on the internet/intranet, it has a browser user interface, which can be personalized and which delivers content, according to device characteristics and user needs. The transition from voice to data communications, however, was not predicated on 3G adoption. The early mobile portals – i-mode in Japan, and the first WAP portals in Western Europe – did not have 3G capabilities. Over time, most mobile portals will have 3G capabilities.

Early mobile portals

With the advent of i-mode and WAP (using cHTML and WML as page description languages), many industry players – mobile operators, internet service providers and phone retailers – invested considerable sums in tailoring their own portal offerings. The content and services provided by these early mobile portals fell into half a dozen main categories:

- communications and community, such as e-mail, calendar and chat;
- information, such as news, weather and directories;
- lifestyle, such as listings of events, restaurants, movies and games;
- travel, such as hotel listings, direction assistance and timetables;
- transaction, such as banking, stock trading, purchasing and auctions;
- other, which includes information about personalization, LBS, device type and advertising, and also about the openness of the mobile portal, billing and target group.

After the false start of WAP in Europe, NTT DoCoMo's i-mode pioneered mobile services in 1999. Two years later, it rolled out the 3G network FOMA. In Europe, Vodafone Live! was introduced in 2002, and a year later, Vodafone Live! with 3G. In the United States, Verizon Wireless was the data service pioneer, and first 3G networks were introduced around 2004. As the pioneers, challengers and new entrants began to extend their properties across borders, globalization drove content services as well.

From bellwether providers to category specialists

While there are many *potential* trajectories of development, *actual* paths remain few. The example of bellwether providers draws from actual empirical success. These provide actual paths for success, which have been widely emulated in the industry. Category specialists offer conceptual potential for success and thus potential trajectories of development.

Bellwether providers. It is the successful pioneer offerings – including NTT DoCoMo's i-mode in Japan, Vodafone's Vodafone Live! in Europe, SK Telecom in Korea, Verizon Wireless – that define the evolution of mobile portals. As the bellwether service providers, these are widely followed and imitated by industry rivals and cooperators.

Category specialists. Mobile services can be categorized into four broad groups of connectivity: rich voice, the internet, messaging and content. As the marketplace evolves and matures, these categories also provide a frame of reference for growing differentiation. Each can serve as a nodal point for specialization, for instance:

- Rich voice portals: a mobile portal that focuses on advanced voice capabilities, including voice-over IP, voice-activated net access, web-initiated voice calls and – over time – broadband-based mobile videophone and media communications.
- Mobile internet portals: a mobile portal that offers mobile access to content services with near-wireline transmission quality and functionality. Typical services include browsing, downloads, gaming and mobile transactions.

- Mobile intranet/extranet portals: a mobile portal that provides secure mobile access to corporate LANs, VPNs and the internet. Typical services include corporate e-mail, calendar, training and customer relationship management tools. These are critical in corporate markets and enterprise solutions.
- Messaging portals: a mobile portal that offers non-real-time, multimedia message access allowing third-party content. Examples of typical services include multimedia 'postcards', video clips and movie trailers.
- Content portals: a mobile portal that provides device-independent access to personalized content anywhere, any time. Typical services include streaming music, short film/video clips and m-commerce applications.

Naturally, different classifications – or classification where sub-categories serve as main categories – would lead to slightly different results. One of these sub-categories is location-based services.

- LBS portals: a mobile portal that enables users to find other people, vehicles, resources, services or machines. It also enables others to find users, as well as enabling users to identify their own location via terminal or vehicle identification. Typical services include emergency services, asset tracking, navigation and localized shopping information.[10]

In the past, network operators were in the business of voice. Today, they are increasingly in the business of data. The introduction of content-based services allows mobile operators to expand their services. Because of their position in the mobile value chain, the operators stand closest to the users. The key assets of the mobile operator in this business model are the micropayment billing infrastructure, a large end-user base, an established mobile brand, the users' location information, established dealer channels and the mobile network infrastructure itself.

In order to make optimal use of their mobile portal, they may develop partnerships with content providers, other ISPs, application service providers and financial institutions to expand their expertise into service provision, such as value-added information, games and e-commerce – as NTT DoCoMo first did in Japan. Companies can sponsor airtime or content services for their user relationship management programmes. Mobile portals can act as managed gateways for targeted wireless advertising.

Mobile virtual network operators (MVNOs)

As mobile markets expand, they will specialize and globalize. This gives rise to a growing separation between those who own and operate mobile networks and those who sell mobile services. The mobile operator provides the network to MVNOs to maximize returns on network investment, thereby increasing its share of revenue from bearing traffic. An MVNO is an operator that buys capacity from network providers and markets services under its own brand name. While an MVNO does not need its own network, it must have supporting infrastructure, including marketing and sales, advertising, distribution, channel relations, customer relations, billing and fraud control. Since those that already have many of these elements in place are most likely to succeed and pay less entry costs, the MVNOs tend to be large marketing organizations, or great brands, or both (Shosteck, 2003).

By 2004, MVNOs were ubiquitous in Europe and Japan, and beginning to emerge in the United States. MVNOs typically add value such as brand appeal, distribution channels, and other affinities to the resale of mobile services. Unlike simple resellers, who often have little or no brand recognition, MVNOs are typically well known, well positioned companies, with a good deal of marketing clout. For example, Virgin Atlantic Airlines is an MVNO in the UK that uses its market recognition to position itself for selling directly to its airline customers and others. Tesco, a UK supermarket chain, may match most of the criteria – and in the United States, Disney has great potential to do so as well.

As fixed and mobile networks were slowly converging, network operators were also looking at service convergence to stay on top of the game. These challenges meant new revenue opportunities to agile vendors, which sought to leverage their global presence, wide business networks and familiarity with the dynamic marketplace. Take, for instance, Ericsson Mobility World (EMW), initially formed to encourage the rapid creation and market deployment of mobile Internet applications and services. By late 2004, it was pushing a "plug-and-go" solution for operators to launch new services on the fly. "There has been a lot of demand from operators to provide a ready to go, end-to-end solution, including billing and content for services such as movies, music, and enterprise packages,"[11] says EMW vice-president Kurt Sillen. The plan allowed an operator to achieve faster time-to-market for different services, created an opportunity for content developers to globalize their solutions, and offered a provision to EMW for matchmaking.

New opportunities required new imagination.

5

Content services

Today, compelling content is the key driver in the mobile space. Because of display requirements (screen size and resolution, and local memory), mobile content differs from other media, making it essential to design the content to suit the mobile device and the method of distribution. Starting with NTT DoCoMo's pioneering, content services have evolved rapidly, from multimedia messaging services to mobile phone television. The breakthrough came with the explosive rise of ringtones and mobile music.

NTT DOCOMO'S PIONEERING

Increasing technological capabilities enable emerging content services, which Minoru Etoh, the chief of NTT DoCoMo R&D in the United States, calls the 'mobile multimedia frontier'. The ultimate goal of mobile multimedia technology development is to make any type of multimedia content and services available anywhere and anytime (Figure 5.1) (Etoh, 2003). While e-mail is expected to remain one of the killer applications in Japan, users today download and store a variety of dynamic applications. Movie trailers, news highlights and music files are among the many types of increasingly rich content to be offered.

The rise of dynamic content

In addition to shortening development cycles, several developments have served to prepare the industry firms and users for dynamic video content, including colour displays and ringing tones, Java-enabled terminals, higher speed, digital camera capabilities and mobile e-commerce.

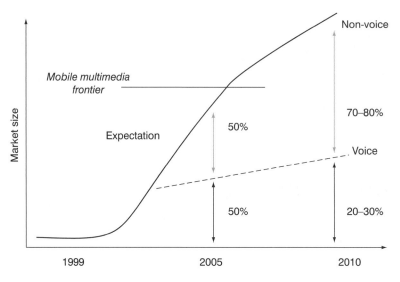

Source: NTT DoCoMo Inc.

Figure 5.1   The mobile multimedia frontier

Shortening development cycles

With the transition from voice to data, the pace of mobile phone evolution has accelerated substantially. The shortened development cycles of handsets in Japan illustrate the trend. During the first year of the i-mode service, there were just four i-mode-capable models. When the number of i-mode subscribers began to grow, resources started converging on the i-mode models. By October 2000, some 21 i-models had been launched. With such a variety of models on sale, each manufacturer must come up with distinctive features of its own in order for its models to sell.

Colour display and ringtones

In December 1999, colour displays became available with the launch of the 502i series of terminals. These displays made content more attractive and engaging, while the ability to download ringing melodies allowed subscribers to add a personal touch to their mobile phones. From the vendor standpoint, colour displays and ringtones allow leading suppliers to better extend branded properties and trademarks into the mobile space.

After weariness with the hype and execution, colour re-ignited the interest of content providers in the mobile space. When the Java-enabled handsets reached the market and saw the rapid transition from the simple black-and-white models to colour-screen handsets, more complex games and more compelling content arrived in the marketplace.

Java-enabled terminals

LG Electronics was the first company to introduce a Java technology-enabled handset in August 2000. Paying close attention to developments in South Korea, the Japanese market followed suit and quickly became the leading wireless market worldwide in terms of Java-enabled device penetration. In January 2001, NTT DoCoMo introduced the 503i series terminals capable of running Java applications (i-appli). The launch provided a substantial boost to mobile services because Java allowed subscribers to download applications such as games, which can then be stored on the phone and played without having to reconnect. It also facilitated the reception of automatic information updates, while enhancing data security. The massive adoption of Java technology has created mass-market business opportunities for operators, application developers, content owners, applications service providers and aggregators.[1]

Digital camera capabilities

NTT DoCoMo developed the mobile phone further with the release of the 251i series terminal. With digital camera capabilities, this phone supports the service (i-shot) that allows subscribers to take digital pictures and attaches them to e-mail messages. Images can be sent to both mobile phones and PCs, and the service automatically converts the image into the optimal format for the receiver. In early 2003, the penetration of camera phone handsets in Japan topped 5 million subscribers, only eight months after DoCoMo's picture mail service was introduced. By 2004, the 505i series terminals came with a high-resolution screen, a built-in digital camera and infrared communications capability.

Mobile e-commerce

The new generation of products and services has also meant the rise of mobile e-commerce and increasing transactional security.[2] In September 2001, Coca-Cola (Japan), NTT DoCoMo and Itochu Corp. jointly launched the Cmode service. The new prepaid membership-based consumer service linked i-mode mobile phones with Cmode information terminal vending machines from Coca-Cola, with built-in computer, display, speaker and printer. Coca-Cola's vending machine network comprised about a million machines across Japan, near pedestrian traffic.

Boosting i-mode

FOMA

In October 2001, NTT DoCoMo expanded the diversity of i-mode with the introduction of FOMA, the world's first fully commercialized 3G service (W-CDMA). In July 2004, the number of FOMA subscribers surpassed the 5 million mark. The FOMA terminals support advanced visual communication services like videophone i-motion, including NTT DoCoMo's video clip service, and i-motion mail, which enables users to e-mail video clips taken either with the built-in camera on FOMA terminals or download from i-mode sites (Figure 5.2). The role of entertainment content has steadily increased in the i-mode content portfolio. According to Takeshi Natsuno, 'i-mode handsets are ready for the entertainment and interactive content. The 3G phones, for instance, are capable of providing PlayStation-class games. The quality of the display is already at the level of the PC. The same goes for the flash, Java and 2 mega-pixels inside the handset. We're already there. People in Japan are already enjoying high quality of content.'[3]

Payment and authentication

Today, NTT DoCoMo's services are focusing on how to connect with real-world needs. As a first step, the 504i handsets were introduced in May 2002. These phones were all equipped with infrared wireless communication interfaces. Subscribers could now, for example, register as members of a video rental shop on the i-mode site, obtain IDs, and take their mobile phone to the shop, and use it as a membership card by exchanging information via infrared at the counter.

Mobile wallet: toward transactional capabilities

In July 2004, NTT DoCoMo introduced the i-mode FeliCa Service for mobile wallet applications and began marketing its first i-mode smart-card handset, the mova P506iC. With the contactless IC card and through collaboration with Sony, the new service and smart-card handsets may be used for a variety of

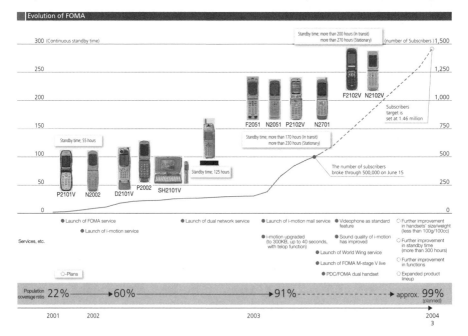

Figure 5.2 NTT DoCoMo advanced service innovation from 1999 to 2010: evolution of FOMA

unprecedented functions that were previously possible only with IC-equipped cards, including train travel, debit card (electronic money) and credit card-based withdrawals and transactions, and personal identification (Figure 5.3) (NTT DoCoMo, 2004b).

Converting cameras to scanners, and screens to bar codes

The camera-equipped 505i series was built with the capability to read one- and two-dimensional bar codes. Mobile phones could now read such bar codes printed on paper, or display bar codes for use as concert tickets or discount coupons for restaurants, with compatible scanners. With this capability, subscribers can eventually store on their mobile phones things that used to be in their wallets, such as money, receipts, bills and coupons.

Cmode: branding purchase stations

In September 2001, Coca-Cola (Japan), NTT DoCoMo and Itochu Corp. jointly launched the Cmode service. In the past, a number of companies had experimented with cashless purchases of drinks using prepaid cards or IC cards. The Coca-Cola Japan/NTT DoCoMo approach was different. It was not just about buying; it was about branding the purchase situations, and thereby leveraging the brand images of i-mode and Coca-Cola as fun and exciting.

Mobile wallet service

In July 2004, NTT DoCoMo launched the i-mode FeliCa service for mobile wallet applications and marketed the company's first i-mode smart-card handset, the mova P506iC. The FeliCa chip enables users in Japan to buy train tickets, debit card (electronic money) and credit card-based withdrawals and transactions, and personal identification.

Source: NTT DoCoMo Inc.

Figure 5.3   From digital cameras to scanners to mobile wallets

With the motto, 'Put everything you carry around into your mobile,' i-mode sought to break out of the internet world and connect with various services in the real world (NTT DoCoMo, 2004c). 'In addition to the entertainment and interactive capabilities, we shall have an IC card in the wallet,' says Natsuno. 'You can use it to access the gateways. You can use your phone as your wallet. If you are into certain kind of entertainment, this wallet will allow the provider to take better care of the supply. Ultimately, it will contribute to revenue flows, vis-à-vis real commerce. Our main focus is now to turn the handset into the wallet. Your credit cards, loyalty cards, money, keys, all that stuff in your purse or wallet, can go into the phone.'

The mobile wallet concept was not something new. Trials had been common for several years. The notion was developed by mobile operators to boost non-voice revenues, from Vodafone's M-Pay, which allows the customers to charge low-cost items, to alternative offerings from Sonera, AT&T Wireless, Cingular, Hutchison 3G, Telenor, T-Mobile and SK Telecom. But as market research indicated, the critical lesson had been that vendor-driven or bank-driven 'solutions' focused on the value for the operators and banks while ignoring value for customers. The key was to gain an understanding of the customers' need for simple solutions that added value to their lives (Shosteck, 2002a).

EVOLUTION OF MOBILE CONTENT

With the new mobile services, mobile browsing remains one of the most important phone applications and the basic way to discover downloadable content and infotainment. The rich browsing experience may be driven by pull or push. In the case of pull, the user consumes the product by clicking links and form buttons to request the next page. In the case of push, the server initiates the action to deliver content to the terminal. Ringtones were the first downloadable media objects. Screen savers, polyphonic ringtones and Java MIDlets followed on footprints. Authors' collection societies collected US $71 million in royalties from ringtone sales in 2002, up 58 per cent from the previous year. The royalties figure, typically 10 to 15 per cent of the total sales from ringtones, indicates that the overall market was over US $700 million annually, possibly as high as US $1 billion.[4]

Dynamic mobile content

Multimedia messaging services (MMS)

As the pioneer operators demonstrated, video messaging can be launched with pre-3G technologies, even if these new services thrive and can be optimized with a more advanced infrastructure. If each wave of mobile innovation can be illustrated with an S-curve (analog for 1G, digital for 2G, multimedia for 3G, and so on), the evolution of each reflects a 'mini' S-curve of its own (MMS still pictures and animations, video messaging, video download and streaming, and so forth). And just as the waves of innovation can be illustrated through their development phases (introduction, growth and maturity), these mini-waves may be illustrated as similar sub-phases (see Figure 5.4).

MMS still pictures and animations

The evolution of mobile media services took off with MMS still pictures and animated presentations, which were launched in the pioneer markets in the second half of 2002. In the pioneer markets, these were followed by video MMS. This translated to an important shift in the sensory experience, as SMS was augmented by MMS. 'In the Mobile Information Society, the user can take a digital picture, annotate it with text and send it to a friend or a colleague,' said Nokia's senior executive Matti Alahuhta in 1999. 'This is also why we say that the content within personal mobile communication is expanding from ears to eyes' (Nokia, 1999).

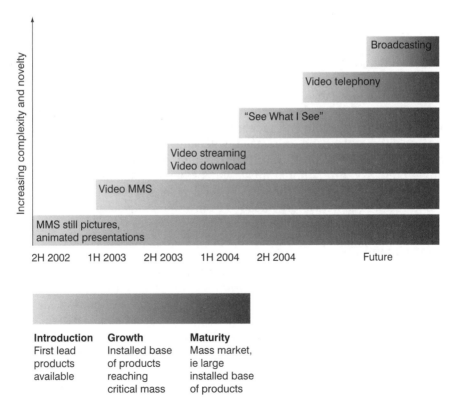

Figure 5.4 Evolutionary phases of mobile video services

Video messaging or video MMS

With video messaging, users send or receive a multimedia message, which contains a video clip, to a mobile device from another device or an application. The clip may be opened and played back for viewing, or saved.[5] Video messaging was the first video service experience by mobile users. With FOMA, NTT DoCoMo made available i-motion, a video-clip distribution service which allows users to enjoy dynamic video content, including sports highlights, press conferences, movie previews, promotional videos and music videos. According to the early experiences by Korean and Japanese pioneers and market research in the lead markets, mobile imaging and messaging boosted revenue, while colour display phones increased the value of the end-user experience, which meant a rise in average revenue per user.[6]

Video download

Mobile users may view video content in several ways, typically via downloading or streaming. Each has different merits. Video download allows the user to select, save or play back video content, whereas streaming provides the user access to large video files which may be real time. Due to the nature of the models, the issues of DRM are essential in video downloading, but not in video streaming.

Video download refers to the delivery of video clips to a mobile device, typically through discovery, such as browsing, and downloading by the user. It is reminiscent of pay cable, where the viewer obtains programming for private use. As part of FOMA, the i-motion service allows subscribers to download content combining audio and video data. The service delivers three kinds of content: video with sound, still images with sound, and sound-only files. It has resulted in a proliferation of compatible content, offering subscribers access to movie previews, promotional music videos, news and more. Similarly, the i-motion mail service lets subscribers send videos recorded by the mobile phone's built-in camera or downloaded from a website by attaching them to an e-mail.

Video streaming

In the past, users had to download the entire clip or file before they could view multimedia content on the internet. More recently, streaming has matured and gained high user acceptance (Nokia, 2002b). Today, it includes one or more media, which are streamed or transported over a network (see Box 5.1). Meanwhile, value chains are becoming increasingly complex, as different business models from the PC, content and mobile worlds are converging. For operator services, streaming is one of the key areas that differentiates true multimedia cellular (3G) from digital cellular (2G) or enhanced digital services (2.5G).

Box 5.1 MOBILE STREAMING

'We provide a universal platform for the delivery of any digital media from any point of origin across virtually any network to any person on any internet-enabled device anywhere in the world,' says Rob Glaser, the legendary founder and CEO of RealNetworks, a pioneer internet media firm. The internet was built to handle text-based information, not audio and video and other rich media. Glaser foresaw the need for specific solutions that could handle the creation, delivery and consumption of media via the internet. That led to the RealPlayer and RealAudio in 1995. Now RealNetworks and its offerings are mobilizing.

Just a matter of time

'Our focus has been on digital media ever since we started in 1994', says Rob Glaser, who first worked on the PC, since he spent his early working years at Microsoft. 'But we had a high level of openness to whatever the environment would be that would give people the access to media anywhere and anytime they wanted it. If that's your philosophy, then at some point you say to yourself, "Look, just having access in the home or office only gets a small piece of people's lives." The power of the mobile phone is that it's the first pervasive network and travels with the user anywhere he or she goes. It was clear that eventually we'd want to work with the mobile industry. It was only a matter of time. The time was right around 1998–9.'

Mobilizing RealNetworks

'Our first major initiative to deliver mobile media services was with Nokia,' recalls Glaser. 'We started at the service foundation level because when you get involved in a market early, you have to start with the enabling foundation. We brought to the table a very specific technical expertise and experience on how to bootstrap and develop these markets.'

Ahead of its rivals, Glaser made important deals with mobile vendors and carriers to deliver content using wireless networks. By spring 2004, RealNetworks had part-nered with some 26 mobile operators, including UK wireless giant Vodafone, O2, Telecom Italia, Telefonica and Wind. In the United States, it established partnerships with vendors Sprint PCS and AT&T Wireless. It also had deals to build its digital media technology directly into mobile handsets manufactured by Ericsson and Motorola.

From Communicator to Vodafone Live!

'The first project we worked on was software for Nokia's communicator,' recalls Glaser, 'not because we thought that those were high-buying products but because Nokia made a commitment to produce Series 60 architecture. It would be the delivery mechanism for mobile media, which Nokia would drive into its mainstream product line over the next few years.

'After putting together a product line over regular GPRS network, we set it on a path to be a broad based consumer service. That led us to work with operators such as Vodafone and its Vodafone Live!, Sprint and other carriers in the United States. It led to the creation of our first generation of mobile services.'

'Vodafone Live! is at the very high end in terms of ambition and competency relative to most of the carriers,' says Glaser. 'It is in many ways a global brand. Vodafone Live! is an integral part of what they want the brand to mean to consumers.

In Spring 2005, as multimedia services took off, Nokia and Real Networks extended cooperation 'to bring audio and video to the mobile masses worldwide'.

Source: the author's interview with Rob Glaser, CEO and Chairman of RealNetworks, Inc, 19 June 2004.

Multimedia streaming enables new and attractive service concepts, including:

- news and information services: streaming hotline, sports, news and so on (audio, still images, video);
- entertainment: streaming before downloading games, pre-listen to music, preview movies before buying tickets, internet radio;
- web cam: or preview digital content, pre-listen to digital music, image manipulation software;
- communication and messaging: viewing video content after a message is received, 'See What I See', talk and share video content by streaming (Session Initiation Protocol, SIP), SIP voicemail control;
- new market channel: since only a small amount of content is shown at any time, streaming offers a relatively secure means of content distribution, and as content is not actually stored on the terminal, content copyright issues are already supported.

Streaming and MMS have an evolutionary trajectory. The first MMS messages consisted of 'slide show presentations' containing still images, text and audio, but eventually video clips will be part of the multimedia message content – as demonstrated by the FOMA V-Live service (October 2002).

SK Telecom's mobile movie channel

In December 2003, June, SK Telecom's mobile multimedia service, positioned itself as a new movie channel one year after its launch. This service offers digital fragment omnibus movies (called 'Yigong'), which consist of 20 movies that are each about five to eight minutes long. As the first offerings hit the market and the revenues began to accelerate, even the larger players moved quickly into the mobile space. The scale and scope of value activities increased dramatically in just a year or two (see Figure 5.5).

'See What I See' (SWIS)

SWIS refers to real time person-to-person communication, where one person is sharing what he or she can see with another person. A kind of a mobile variation of the ICQ, familiar to the internet users, it is based on a concurrent voice call, coupled with the video session to share content. Like the easy-to-use online instant messaging program and similar to America Online's popular

In the past SK Telecom used to introduce only previews, cuts of regular movies, and films made exclusively for mobile phones. In December 2003, its mobile multimedia service (June) positioned itself as a new movie channel. The service offered digital movies (called 'Yigong'), produced by 20 famous Korean movie directors. Each was about 5–8 minutes long and designed to be run in the movie theatres.

Sources: SK Telecom, Nokia, NTT DoCoMo.

Figure 5.5   From mobile video to mobile television

Buddy List and Instant Messenger programs, it is used as a conferencing tool by individuals on the internet, to chat, e-mail, perform file transfers, play computer games and so on.

Video telephony

Basically, video telephony is the mobile version of internet telephony. Through video telephony, the mobile user can make or receive a video call, which allows the user to see and talk to the other person. By 2009, mobile video services are expected to generate US $5.4 billion in annual revenues (about 15 per cent of total wireless data revenues) in the United States (In-Stat/MDR, 2004c).

FOMA videophone service

NTT DoCoMo's FOMA videophone service allows subscribers to speak to each other face to face. It is coupled with multi-access, which allows subscribers to communicate by voice while using packet transmissions. In a business setting, the service allows salespeople to talk to customers, while accessing a corporate database. For consumers, the service enables a chat with friends, while reviewing restaurants on i-mode. The terminals enable subscribers to take still images and send them as e-mail attachments while talking on a phone.

Mobile phone television

From the late 1930s, broadcasting has enabled information and entertainment, but on analog technology. In the 1970s the digital revolution was restricted to production facilities, whereas consumer markets were driven by VCRs, home video and remote controls. It was only in the 1990s that television broadcasting was swept by digital broadcast technologies.[7] At the same time, consumer electronics manufacturers became committed to new mass customizing media, such as personal video recorder (PVR), including TiVo and replayTV, which have steadily expanded their reach.

By 2004, several leading mobile vendors, including NEC, Nokia, Samsung and Toshiba, were introducing phones with built-in tuners that can receive broadcasts. In contrast to some high-end phones that already enabled users to download and play back streaming video via mobile internet, the new television phones pick up signals directly over the air.

Mobile broadcast and internet

Broadcasting refers to mobile users tuning into content that is being 'aired'. It is the mobile version of traditional broadcasting, which until recently was restricted to fixed places. Through mobile phone television, the user may watch news, entertainment, explore directories, conduct transactions and enjoy location-based services when, where and how ever he or she chooses. Some observers and industry practitioners consider 'mobile TV' a disruptive force (see Box 5.2). Enabling high-bandwidth channels and high transmission speeds, digital broadcasting can provide a wide variety of content, including television services, to mobile users. It is enabled by a combination of digital broadcast and internet protocol (IP datacast over DVB-H).[8]

A likely spearhead service of mobile broadcast is mobile phone television, a way to receive television-like content to mobile phones delivered over a mobile broadcast network. Mobile broadcast will enable cost-efficient mobile mass delivery of any multimedia content. This is believed to be likely to strongly increase the consumption of media content using mobile devices.[9]

The drivers – the development of digital content, capabilities to broadcast and bill for the content, and the growth of the user volume – boost the 'mobilization' of traditional television, enabling new, compelling services to the consumer. Unlike digital television, mobile handheld enjoys savings in power consumption. Moreover, conventional television delivers three to five programmes for a large screen, whereas IP datacast makes it possible to send

Box 5.2   DISRUPTION THROUGH MOBILE BROADCASTING

'It will be disruptive,' says Paul Palmieri, director of business development at Verizon Wireless. As US networks and handsets enable television-style capabilities, he expects shifts in the content market. 'We are talking about high bandwidth for very reasonable types of rate transmission. This will be ideal for mobile phones. In the United States, consumption seems to be more a la carte and fragmented than worldwide. Here you have hundreds of different cable channels and 27 different kinds of salad in a bag at the grocery store. The US market and persona is very "I want what I want when I want it!" and I believe that this opens up a great opportunity for a broadcast paradigm in America.'

Importance of original programming

'Users will be open to different types of programming and scheduling with the phones that handle media,' says Palmieri. 'With mobile broadcasting, I'd think that subscribers would have tolerance for having a window to watch a one minute clip of say one hour. From the start, content must be made specifically for this medium. It has to be relevant to the need states and the users' general state of mind when they're mobile.' Industry evolution will shift as the content players join the mobile value chain, Palmieri suggests.

Brand advertising and big marketers

'With market growth, there will come a point where the dollars spent on advertising will be more substantial than the revenue share on the new medium. As that transition takes place, there will be a period of confusion on everybody's part. How do I work with this other company in a way that is different from the one I work with today? Wireless ad spending in the United States is at an all-time high. A delicate balance will need to be struck between the programming value that can be brought to the media companies and the advertising value. But 85 per cent of advertising dollars are still brand advertising dollars. The direct marketing promises of the internet is even greater with the mobile.'

Source: the author's interview with Paul Palmieri, director of business development, Verizon Wireless, 14 June 2004.

50–80 programmes over a single network. However, mobile handheld sets have small screens, the power supply is limited and the reception mode is mobile.

Still, the opportunity was too attractive to ignore. By February 2005, Verizon's 'V Cast' – following in the footprints of content providers in Japan and Korea – offered one-minute mobile episodes of '24 Conspiracy', Fox's spin-off of the popular TV show, along with 300 video clips. For $10 a month, the subscriber got 20 channels of mobile TV. And this was only the beginning.

What makes mobile phone television intriguing to content producers is the fact that it enables an interactive return channel, because of SMS. While the broadcast content is delivered via the broadcast channel, potential responses (such as transactions, voting or requesting additional online information) take place via an interactive channel over the cellular network. In this way, these two infrastructures complement each other, boosting a wide variety of new opportunities and business models (see Figure 5.6).

It's the best of two worlds. Digital broadcasting is highly cost-efficient in delivering media content to large audiences, while the mobile business provides billing mechanisms for the new broadcast services.*

In October 2003, Nokia announced its first media category device, the Nokia 7700.

In May 2004, NTT DoCoMo revealed its 'OnQ' model, a concept mobile phone capable of showing terrestrial digital TV broadcasts. Metadata allows relevant data to appear on the left hand side of the display.

*During 2002 and 2004, pioneering efforts included a Finnish trial of the IP Datacast network, the Japanese-Korean mobile television satellite, as well as pilot mobile television broadcasts in Berlin. In June 2004, achieving a first for the Asia–Pacific region, Nokia, MediaCorp Technologies, M1 and the Media Development Authority of Singapore jointly showcased a live end-to-end mobile phone television broadcast over a DVB-H network at the Nokia Connection event in Singapore.

Sources: Nokia Corp., NTT DoCoMo Inc.

Figure 5.6 From mobile video to mobile phone television

MOBILE MUSIC: RINGTONES EVERYWHERE

She blinded me with science
She blinded me with science
And hit me with technology

('She blinded me with science' in *The Gold Age of Wireless*
by Thomas Dolby Robertson, 1982)

In 1982, Thomas Dolby Robertson, now president of Retro Ringtones, climbed the pop charts with his album *The Golden Age of Wireless*, scoring a major hit with his new wave classic 'She blinded me with science'. Two decades later, he was spearheading a music content firm, Beatnik. 'Given that a small hand-held device will always have a limitation on screen size, there's only so much you can do with graphics,' Robertson said. 'Sound is one way to make it a lot better' (Ankeny, 2002). Images of hard living and brash poses belong to the music business, but sex, drugs and rock'n'roll are no longer enough. Today, the definition of cool for some acts includes mobile phone ringtones. In August 2004, Warner Bros Records began showing commercials on MTV and MTV2 for a set of voice-greeting ringtones recorded by members of the punk band Green Day. It was the first time a record label had paid to run its own ads for ringtones in the US market. The lords of the ringtones have arrived.

The world's first downloadable ringtone – hangover, Finnish style

'It was a Thursday morning in March of 1998,' says Vesa-Matti Paananen, a mobcom veteran and the founder of Add2Phone. 'March in Finland is terrible, very dark and windy and rainy. I woke up in the morning with a terrible hangover. My phone rang, and it was the standard Nokia ring. De–de–de–de. I thought, my God, I want to change that thing. Then I thought, I'm sure I'm not the only one on the planet who wants to change it. Then it turned out that the Nokia guys actually had the technology to do it. And so we started planning. What sort of service would this be? Who would be the composers? I approached Radiolinja (a leading Finnish telco) to ask if they wanted the service. It took me six months to convince them. The payback time was under two months. And then of course, the rest is history. Today, 30 per cent of all SMS messages in Europe are requests for down-loadable ringtones. Back in 1998, no one could have imagined anything like that' (Shalit, 2002).

Operators, vendors, and content providers followed these developments – and not just in Finland.

'Not another Napster!'

Around 2001, record companies realized that they were losing much revenue through ringtones being distributed without licences over the web. With music sales falling worldwide and CD piracy on the rise, the times were bleak for the industry. Global music sales were down on 2001, hit by CD piracy and online music sharing. The record labels blamed the plunge of sales on the explosion of online file-sharing services. An estimated 900 million music files were available for download every day without a single penny ending up in the pockets of artists or the record companies. As many CDs were copied as were sold (IFPI, 2004).

'Downloading ringtones is very popular and the music industry could be losing millions of pounds because of the huge number of sites that don't appear to pay royalties on the ringtones they sell,' said Ben Coppin, chief operating officer of Envisional, which monitors the internet for abuse of its clients' material. Some 1,400 sites based mainly in the UK and the United States were offering ringtones, but most did not pay royalties. 'The music industry doesn't want another Napster-type situation to develop and is starting to crack down on such sites' (McLindon, 2001).

Ringtones were already a substantial business in Europe and Asia, with more than US $300 million worth being sold in Japan in 2001 alone. As the market began to emerge in the United States, record companies were concerned. At the end of the 1990s, the controversial Napster had sparked an intense debate in the United States on copyright protection. It lost a copyright infringement court battle against the major record labels in 2001, and went offline to develop a subscription service.[10] By then, only one lawsuit had been taken against a ringtone seller. Record company EMI sued US wireless advertising firm YourMobile for copyright infringement.[11] But things were changing rapidly. The breakthrough Nokia–EMI deal provided a new deal framework for music and mobile industry leaders (see Box 5.3).

The breakthrough for online music

World sales of recorded music fell by 11 per cent (whether measured by units or value) during the first half of 2003. The industry was haunted by piracy. In North America, Europe (particularly Germany) and Japan, the numbers of unauthorized downloads of tracks and copied CDs reached, and in some cases exceeded, the levels of legitimate track and CD album sales.

However, 2003 was also the breakthrough for online music services, as major and independent record companies licensed hundreds of thousands of tracks for legitimate download in Europe. The total market for music downloads in the United States during the latter half of the year stood at 19.2 million, as measured by Nielsen SoundScan. Downloads outsold physical singles by three to one over the period. Initially, the success of Apple's iTunes Music Store drove the take-off of legitimate online services in the United States. The industry had grown very competitive, as services sought to secure new marketing routes via partnership deals with:

Box 5.3 MOBILE MUSIC: THE NOKIA–EMI DEAL

'This deal marks a further development in our new media activities and is the first global initiative of its kind,' said Jonathan Channon, senior vice president of Film, TV and Media at EMI Music Publishing. In August 2000, mobile ringtones moved to a new pitch of personalization after a trendsetting deal between music publisher EMI and Nokia.[12] It allowed the manufacturer's handsets to ring out with users' favourite tunes from a range of artists, including Robbie Williams, the Spice Girls, Matchbox 20, Sting, Puff Daddy, Aerosmith, Lenny Kravitz, Enrique Iglesias, Janet Jackson, TLC and Phil Collins.

Even as they signed the exclusive six-month agreement to launch the product, both Nokia and EMI were negotiating with other parties to extend the reach. Motorola and Ericsson followed the footprints.

The ringtone opportunity

Initially, the fee for downloading a favourite song was well under £1, recalls Channon. Downloading a song to a mobile became available in the autumn of 2000 through Club Nokia on the internet, or by sending a text message to a phone number to obtain the song. By 2003, both companies expected 'tens of millions of downloads'. Since users were also anticipated to change their songs frequently, both expected substantial revenue as well.

The two companies were not the first movers in the emerging ringtone market. A few companies were already offering similar services, including Worldpop.com with its selection of 10 songs favoured by Ibiza fans. But despite the popularity of Moloko's 'Sing it back', Nokia and EMI had the kind of reach that the first movers lacked.

The business potential had emerged around 1998. 'That's when I started using the handset,' says Channon. 'Sometime later it occurred to me that the handset was a business opportunity.'

Changing deal structures

'After I'd had the mobile for some three to six months, I realized there were embedded ringtones on the phone,' Channon says. 'As a music publisher, I began to ask questions about demand and copyright clearances. At EMI, we started talks with Nokia's people in London because they were the market leader. After a few months, we were approached by a number of other handset manufacturers. The deal with Nokia was always going to be a non-exclusive deal.

'The defining moment came when we went down to Nokia. We sat in a room where they had a chart on the wall showing the revenue flow, operators and other industry players. Our proposal was based on the traditional media publishing model. But as we took a look at the chart and the way it was structured, we realized that it was not going to work. We were entering untouched territory.

'Subsequently, business activities have been streamlined among vendors, publishers, record companies, operators, talent and other stakeholders. Now we have standard ringtone deals, and many record companies, especially independents, recognize that the mobile platform is a major distributor of their products. After the Napster experience, we like the mobile more than the internet because the billing system and the infrastructure are more secure for licensing rights.

'Several of Nokia's executives participated in these discussions. They were pretty savvy about intellectual properties. It was a learning curve for Nokia and for us in terms of how the mobile business worked, the relationships between operators, distributors and handset manufacturers, and so on. It was complex because it was a whole new business model. The business has really kicked in during the last three years or so. In the UK, the ringtone market has superseded the singles market.'

From publishers to record companies

'Initially, the business engaged only one party of rights owners, the music publishers, because actual recordings were not used with the ringtone. There were no artists involved. This early business model was driven by the publisher. Today, ringback tones, or true tones, involve the record company. The battleground is now open.'

'When you bring the master recording and the artist into the value chain, it heightens the number of potential marketing operations,' Channon believes. 'If the music industry does not work closely along the mobile business, the industry will complicate the cost of rights and the value chain. Moreover, the rights owners have a real opportunity in bundling the music rights with other rights because now the mobile phone has the camera capability and can play short clips from music images.'

Globalizing innovation

'Usually America is at the forefront of music initiatives, but with ringtones that has not been the case,' acknowledges Channon. 'When we talked with Nokia, nothing was going on with mobile or ringtones in the United States. Traditionally international business repertoire has been Anglo-American but there has been a significant increase of successful local repertoires since the late 1990s. It is noticeable particularly in South East Asia, where this repertoire is driving new mobile businesses.

'When EMI did the deal with Nokia, Nokia was very keen on having access to EMI's offices locally to ensure that the local Nokia would be able to speak with local EMI people and the local repertoire.' The ringtone market was born global.

Source: the author's interview with Jonathan Channon, senior vice president, EMI Music Publishing, 2 April 2004.

- broadband suppliers: iTunes and AOL, Rhapsody and Comcast;
- hardware manufacturers: Musicmatch and Dell, Napster and Samsung;
- other established brands: iTunes and Pepsi, RealPlayer Music Store and RollingStone.com;
- academic institutions: Napster and Penn State University (IFPI, 2004).

In January 2004, Apple decided to license the technology of its digital music player (iPod) to Hewlett-Packard, which bundled the iTunes Music Store software into its PCs, but was also working on its own digital music player. A thriving online music market took shape in Europe, with almost 30 legitimate services. As these developments in the online space were mirrored outside the United States and Europe, the digital breakthrough provided a powerful boost to the nascent mobile music market – mobile networks and devices were expected to become a critical distribution platform for music in the near future.

Changing market

In 2003, ringtone sales were around US $1–2 billion worldwide and the industry began to get excited about the mobile, says Keith Jopling, director of market research at the IFPI. 'The mobile market is great for raising some new revenue through fairly discreet deals and it can package content quite nicely and market it through a mobile as artist promotion.'[13]

'Unlike with iTunes, Napster and Rhapsody, there's critical mass that's attracting industry players. Mobile users are quite happy to get notice of particular artists that have a release coming up and to download a ringtone or a voice-activated content involving those artists. It is still more about video clips and tones; we have yet to see people using their phones as personal music players. That's something people are still doing with their iPod, or their MP3 player, or their personal portable CD player.'

In late September 2003, ringtones were outpacing traditional forms of music revenues (see Box 5.4). The top-selling single in the United States, rapper Lil' Kim's 'Magic stick,' moved 7,000 retail units, whereas Moviso sold *17,000* 'Magic stick' ringtones over the same period. With its 70 per cent of the ringtone market, the company had become the biggest mobile media publisher in North America, boasting the industry's largest catalogue of entertainment content, copyright licences to more than 100,000 songs and an extensive list of partnerships with wireless carriers, device manufacturers and media organizations. Shawn Conahan, president of Moviso, envisioned a music library that stretched into infinity, its limitless holdings encompassing songs old and new, legendary and obscure, from Bach and the Beatles to Britney and beyond.

**Box 5.4 LICENSING THE RINGTONE REVOLUTION
IN THE UNITED STATES**

'Mobile entertainment, including ringtones and streamed and downloaded music accessed through cell phones and portable computing devices, promises to be one of the big growth areas in the digital music space,' said Richard Conlon, vice president, marketing and business development of BMI, in the spring of 2003. 'If the US markets perform like the markets in Western Europe and Japan, we may be able to generate significant revenues. We've been proactively working with these companies for the past three years to help develop business solutions to cover our songwriters' rights.'

The role of BMI

Founded in 1940, BMI is a US performing rights organization that represents more than 300,000 songwriters, composers and music publishers from around the world in all genres of music. Through its music performance and reciprocal agreements, it grants businesses and media access to its repertoire of approximately 4.5 million musical works.

Under Conlon's direction, BMI's digital licensing group has negotiated agreements for a wide variety of leading digital media properties including Yahoo!, MSN, MP3.com, AOL and pressplay. In addition, the team has negotiated royalty agreements with leading mobile entertainment providers for ringtones and other entertainment and information services delivered to cellphones.

'After the mid-1990s, we started watching what was going on in Japan,' says Conlon. 'We signed our earliest deal for mobile in late 2000. We've been monitoring this marketplace for half a decade now, and the year 2004 was the first in the United States when we saw significant business.'

Scrambling for royalties

During the past few years, BMI has been scrambling to ensure its artists can reap the fruits of the ringtone revolution as these grow increasingly popular in the United States. In March 2002, BMI embraced the burgeoning ringtone/mobile entertainment marketplace in the United States by establishing new licensing agreements for the performing rights of the musical compositions that the group represents. Two months later, it signed a licensing agreement with Colorado-based Cellus USA, a leading international provider of SMS content applications for wireless telephones, including ringtones, downloadable logos and picture messages.

BMI's traditional business, licensing musical public performance copyrights for radio, television, cable and commercial establishments, has expanded since the mid-1990s to encompass a growing roster of client industries ranging from internet sites to digital music subscription services and portable wireless services.

BMI's agreements grant mobile entertainment firms the rights to publicly perform the approximately 4.5 million musical works in the BMI repertoire over both internet and wireless cellphone delivery systems including WAP and SMS. Both systems enable users to download or stream e-mails, specialized web pages, music and other content directly to their mobile phone. Once payment and performance data are received, fees collected from the public performances on the site will be distributed as royalties to the songwriters, composers and music publishers of the works BMI represents.

'The new media market is still very small, about one per cent of the total revenue, but the growth has been rapid,' says Conlon. 'And it will contribute to changes in the music business.'

From Asia to Europe to the United States

'Ever since people began to think about the internet as a music archive and MP3.com, many sites have become totally devoted to breaking into music and launching new talent,' says Conlon. 'They provide an opportunity for emerging artists to get exposure and for existing artists to repackage and resell their work in a new way.

'At some point, mobile music will be a real source of revenue, but now it's primarily promotional. However, the medium has a very different cost structure, so it's possible to make money at much lower volume. We follow mobile reports from Europe to Japan and Korea to get a feel on how consumers are using the medium. We have watched with great interest how record labels in Japan are using mobile ringtones to pre-promote releases and the rollout of broadband services in South Korea. We can learn from those experiences before they hit the United States, even if we don't know yet whether they're resulting in a retail or subscription market or new business models.'

Anticipate commodity pricing

'With the mobile, one can develop a one-to-one relationship and highly segment the marketplaces,' says Conlon. 'For instance, you can place an ad to promote a Jessica Simpson release with girls from 12 to 16. That provides tremendous opportunities to truly micro-market and target products.'

As far as Conlon is concerned, the mobile is also another validation that certain signals industry observers have seen for a long time are getting stronger. 'Consumers do not want to buy an album that has 12 songs, to listen to that one song they really care about. The music industry is now faced with new packaging and pricing questions, which also translate to tremendous opportunities.

'The price range for ringtones will probably be set with the download pressure. When you'll see smart phones, which enable more sophisticated solutions, they will boost changes as you can make and store your own ringtones, or start dubbing CDs into your cellphone, and so on. In such a dynamic environment, the industry needs to be experimenting and anticipate commodity pricing.'

Make it compelling

'What the internet has taught in the business is that you got to have a market before you can realize revenue, just as you must have a product that people are willing to pay for,' says Conlon. 'It has to be compelling so that it can't be rapidly commodified down to a value of zero. After the dotcom bust, everyone has talked about focusing on the business fundamentals. But it's as important to have something attractive to sell.

'As the mobile applications are growing out, we need to focus on a much more quantitative role in marketing these services. We must see a much more measured approach. It's not enough to just say, "Oh, this is cool, people will buy it." We need much more quantifiable data to take this business seriously and to build a business that will provide consumers what they really want.'

Source: The author's interview with Richard Conlon, vice president, marketing and business development, BMI, 10 March 2004.

Ringtones are the new single, thought industry observers, 'and if airtime helps promote an album or a single, then ringing phones represent the new airplay. We're seeing a fundamental paradigm shift that is no less important than the shift from radio to the Internet' (Ankeny 2003).

The ringtone shift was transformational – it went hand in hand with extraordinary complexity and novelty, from technology to rights issues (Figure 5.7).

'A few years ago, everybody from California to the rest of the universe was on a drug trip,' quips Christa Haussler, BMG Entertainment's vice president of new technology. 'There were great ideas, but no business models. The idea was basically that "if you can give a lot of your content for free, I can make you millions!" Well, now the dumb money is gone and it's time for a reality check. Skepticism is healthy because it forces us to focus on core competences rather than pipe dreams. The digital music will come. The real question is when.'[14]

As operators were launching high-speed networks and vendors accounted for rising handset penetration, new mobile services were developed and initiated, including music downloads. Mobile operators, record companies and music-related companies (such as MTV) formed a number of partnerships that led to a wave of new services. In the UK, O2 launched its service allowing mobile users to download music and transfer files to a Siemens player device. In the United States, Warner Music was the third major record company to make material available for Sprint Music Tones, a ringtone service. The agreement followed the Sony Music deal in July 2003 and a Universal deal in January 2004. Meanwhile, AT&T Wireless was set to launch its mMode service in 2004 using the handset as a channel for clips and full tracks downloadable to the PC.

At this early stage, the mobile music business was driven by promotional partnerships between mobile operators and music companies. These alliances allowed mobile subscribers to stream and sample new music while offering personalized artist-related material via the handset. Even Nokia stopped

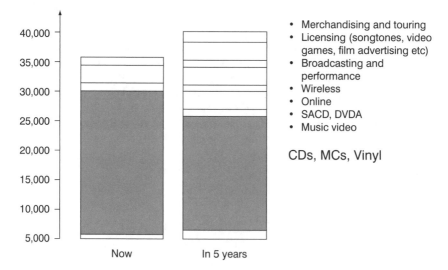

Source: Industry reports.

Figure 5.7   The changing context of music

selling ringtones, games and Java-based games in a move that reflected the changing balance of power in the mobile industry. The ringtones and mobile entertainment market emerged first in Japan and South Korea. In the aftermath, business spread throughout Asia and to Western Europe, and more recently to the United States.

In May 2004, Vodafone and Sony Music Entertainment (SMEI) announced the world's largest single mobile operator/music company content distribution agreement. The deal called for music content from hundreds of Sony Music artists to be provided to Vodafone around the world. Presumably a 'billion dollar industry' in Japan and Europe, ringtones ranged in price from 99 cents for monophonic tones to about US $2.50 for higher-quality polyphonic versions. US consumers purchased 4.8 million ringtones in 2002, translating to US $16.6 million in revenue. The mobile arm of KDDI, Japan's second largest telecom group, was about to launch the world's first service offering full song downloads directly on to mobile phones.[15] In 2005, US consumers were expected to download 30 million ringers, accounting for US $404 million in sales.

Changing consumption

As the industry moves from static content to dynamic content, so must ringtones change as well. Low-fidelity, electronic monophonic ringtones decline with richer media capabilities and polyphonic ringtones, which incorporate a series of tones by real voices and real instruments. And as the musical experience is rapidly growing deeper, mobile carriers can move beyond ringtones into additional music applications like streaming audio clips, animated content, album cover screen savers and artist information. These changes reflect technology evolution, but that is only part of the transformation.

As ringtones have taken off, music continues to be a critical part of people's daily lives. The labels seek to discover and invest in a new and existing artist roster, just as they try to create the right environment for artists to achieve their creative potential, while exposing the results of the process to the widest possible audience. However, the industry is witnessing the shift of its revenue sources as the new context of music consumption undermines old drivers of industry profitability (Figure 5.8). For decades, music fans had purchased whatever material record companies deemed worthy of releasing on compact disc, vinyl and other physical formats, which meant vast amounts of recorded material never reached consumers, unless it was bootlegged. With the online space and ringtones, the industry has entered a different era (compare Smith and Wingfield, 2004).

Instead of the full-frontal assault record labels have mounted against online file-swapping services, the music industry is embracing the possibilities of mobile music. Unlike CDs or digital music files, consumers can download premium mobile content regardless of time and place, with the resulting cost discreetly tacked onto the subscriber's monthly phone bill. In an industry

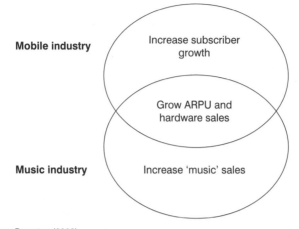

Mobile industry

Increase subscriber growth

Grow ARPU and hardware sales

Music industry

Increase 'music' sales

Source: Adapted from Downton (2003)

Figure 5.8   Complementary objectives

where some players would like to see alternative outlets to MTV, mobile devices offer to developing artists and potential hits a new channel. With carriers monitoring mobile activities, a library of rich media files can be created for download and distribution over mobile devices, without a Napster déjà vu whereby users exchange free, unlicensed and pirated content. Likewise, applications developers and handset manufacturers can add checks and balances to their products to restrict premium content to playback only on the device that received the original download. The opportunity triggered extensive industry cooperation – even between Microsoft and Nokia.

The online space is enabled by PCs that people use, whereas mobility empowers people who use PCs. Digital downloads confine users to locations; ringtones are available to users anywhere and anytime. Ringtones herald not only the transformation of music content, but the very context in which music is consumed. Along with the online music space, it is part of the changing context of music consumption (Downton, 2003). In the new competitive environment, the industry must rethink marketing and distribution by applying integrated marketing models and maximizing all income sources – a shift from one-way shopping to a multi-level entertainment experience, which better matches the new environmental conditions (see Box 5.5).

Ringtones' most appreciative audience is among the young 18-to-24-year-old demographic. But with their mass appeal of individuality, they herald any downloadables that enable users to personalize their phones to their own specific tastes. The ringtone is far more than the generic virtual downloadable; it reflects the customer's class, lifestyle and sensibility. It is not the song that the customers buy, but a manifestation of their personality that – for now – just happens to be the ringtone.

Box 5.5 INTEGRATING MOBILE MUSIC

'We first seriously addressed the wireless space around 2003,' acknowledges Pete Downton, marketing, planning and new media director at Warner Music International. 'We're now working on the new emerging channels in business development, specifically focusing on online wireless and all the new digital channels. In the past, new media issues had been dealt with by a specific department; now we try to bring those new and emerging channels into our frontline business.'

Through its 47 affiliates and numerous licensees, Warner Music has a presence in 70 countries, with a roster of more than 1,000 artists covering all major nationalities and music genres. Headquartered in New York City, its international activities are driven by the London operation. 'We're trying to put our system in the digital space at the heart of what we do in the business.'

Integrating new channels

'Since early 2003, the wireless space has accelerated due to the ringtone business in Europe. We need to understand which primary consumers buy ringtones, how and why they are buying them, and at what point we should put the record on the radio. In the past, one of our key problems was that we separated the new media business development from our traditional business. We weren't moving quickly enough to get the products to the street. The challenge has been to overcome that separation.

'In the past, 90 per cent of a record label's employees were working toward exploiting music believing they could carry both CDs and alternatives, including music DVDs and VHS,' says Downton. 'You only got to hear about a product once it reached its release date. It was quite a passive activity. People were disconnected from the deal making.

'Most of our marketing takes place at the very early stage of the release of our records. We'd put a record to radio usually about six weeks in advance of the release of actual single, and so that could be up to 10 weeks in front of the release of the physical album. Now we're capturing the digital product and creating it by download and trying to use the radio as the point at which we begin to make those products available to market. That is when we spend the vast majority of marketing dollar and that is when we have the artist in the marketplace doing promotion and that is the most effective time to have new digital products available.

'Things change from market to market. But the consensus is that we have to ensure that when we are spending most of our marketing dollars, we have as much products in the marketplace commercially available as possible.'

Changing context of music consumption

'Basically there is a link between digital networks and file sharing ability to get music to the consumers quickly and fairly easily online. That has had an impact on our ability to commercially exploit single products. The genres of music and the pop records that are targeted to demographics that tend to be more computer literate and probably have more access to things like broadband. Combine that with the television, X Box and digital television, and the access to and perception of music is often seen as being free at the point of consumption. At the same time, music sales are falling, due to the free music from the internet and the fact that consumers are being bombarded with a host of different places that consume that music.

'The context in which people consume music has changed greatly and we have not been terribly successful at adapting to the needs of the consumers. Since 2003, we've tried to focus on how that context in which people consume music has changed. With certain bands, we're not just proving ringtones, but trying to take into account the changing context. We've provided editorial information for driving links to the act, we've signed an international distribution deal with T-Mobile. We managed to offer the Kevin Lyttle track. We were able to offer his second single even before we took the product to radio. We gave two weeks of exclusive ringtones more than what the radio stations got.

'With ringtones, we need to concentrate the business on making the right music available at the right time. We are starting to see success both in terms of sales and ringtones in the UK.'

From ownership to access of music

'On the demand side, we've seen the beginning of the larger transformation. These business models are based on the ownership of music. We are going through a transitional period when people are moving from owning music, probably a more subscription rental-based model. The old school of thought favours dealing with traditional music retailers and focuses on selling the physical product. Looking at what's available online and the PC listening experience, it's difficult to see how consumers could have the same kind of music experience they used to have with CDs.

'We're witnessing the beginning of the convergence, the linkage of PC to mobile phone, media centre, television. Owning a piece of music isn't any longer as important as it used to be to the consumer, assuming they have access to a track that they can listen to at any given time.

'Consumers, who used to own a physical piece that they could listen to, have now access to music almost instantaneously on mobile phones. That's what happens when you have an effective opportunity to associate with an artist and a piece of music that means something in terms of your identity. When I was at school, I'd buy a particular album because I wanted to be associated with a particular piece of music and activity. Ringtones fulfil a very similar function.

'The degree to which consumers are able to fully consume music is really being hit with mobile technology. If we have the ability to sell music and if consumers will buy ringtones, I am sure that it will be a very prevalent market.'

Source: the author's interview with Pete Downton, marketing, planning and new media director, Warner Music International, 5 April 2004.

6

Mobile media and entertainment

'The whole world is watching!' chanted the demonstrators in Chicago's streets in 1968, as television cameras beamed images of police cracking heads into homes everywhere. Today such images can reach ears and eyes anytime and anywhere. Meanwhile, the sales of mobile handsets are already in hundreds of millions of annual units worldwide, and an escalating proportion of these unit sales include camera phones. In the near future, mobile content will transform media and entertainment consumption worldwide.

THE EMERGING VALUE CHAIN

Rights, licensing and convergence

Most business models are variations of the generic value chain underlying all businesses. They are typically associated with upstream activities (design, manufacturing, purchasing), downstream activities (distribution, marketing, advertising, sales), or both. With mobile innovation, each new platform (analog, digital, multimedia, broadband) has given rise to new products, processes and services. Until the early 1990s in the most advanced markets, the focus was on upstream activities, especially technology development. As business shifts from aggressive penetration to usage promotion, innovation is migrating from upstream to downstream activities.

Advanced mobile content reflects a variety of forms, from television to music and publishing. These forms go with familiar revenue and business models that set initial expectations and will be extended into the mobile space.

Paying for media is not a new experience; watching mobile media and entertainment is. In the most advanced markets, initial services in mobile video, entertainment and messaging share certain common patterns. With pricing, for instance, all seek to model charges according to generally accepted parameters (data, content length, content item, message, video air time (see Table 6.1). With increasing customer base, the market is expected to stabilize around prices that ensure profitability. As illustrated by the costly struggle over digital rights in the music business, the technological potential of a business does not necessarily demonstrate its commercial viability.

Digital rights management

Following NTT DoCoMo and other Asian players, the European vendors have launched Java-enabled phones for the mass market boosting the development of mobile content. The business of downloading has accelerated with the availability of content, such as Java applications and ringtones, and phones with increasing multimedia capabilities. The evolution of digital rights management (DRM) reflects the mobile industry's efforts to avoid the kind of rights issues that have plagued the music business (Figure 6.1).

Table 6.1 Media and entertainment services: payment, revenue sources, time-use

	Payment	Revenue sources	Time use
Broadcast TV (analog)	Free	Advertising	Scheduled
Cable TV (analog)	Subscription (t)	Advertising plus subscriptions	Scheduled
Cable TV (digital)	Subscription (t, v)	Advertising plus subscriptions	Scheduled (v)
TV on demand	Fee	Customers	User
Satellite TV (digital)	Subscription (t, v)	Advertising plus subscriptions	Scheduled (v)
Movie theater	Pay per content	Customers	Scheduled
VCR	Fee	Customers	User
Newspaper, magazines, books	Fee	Customers	User
Video games	Fee	Customers	User
Internet file sharing	Free (but issues of legality and quality)	Users	User
Mobile media and	Subscription (t, v)	Subscriptions	User

Since the 1950s, traditional media and entertainment services (broadcast TV, movie theaters, newspapers, magazines and books) have been augmented with new channels. During this evolution, advertising- and customer-based revenue models have been coupled with subscription-based revenue models, which provide increasingly complex and novel alternatives. Concurrently, the bargaining power over time use has shifted from producers to users. As a result, the emerging mobile media and entertainment is likely to embrace existing business practices, particularly those in cable.

t tiered

v variable

* This is the emerging category and comprises several models, including video (multiple models), video messaging (per message, MMS model), video telephony (per airtime), video entertainment (first unlimited, later per content/usage), and so on.

(a) The evolution of DRM

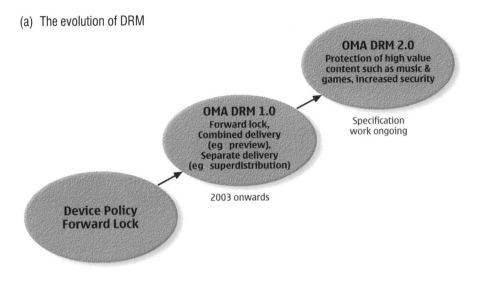

(b) Three DRM methods (Oma DRM 1.0)

Currently, the standard provides three DRM methods: forward-lock, combined delivery and separate delivery

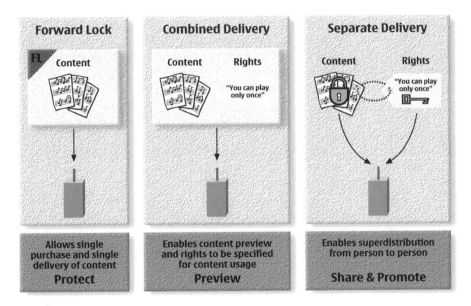

Source: Nokia Corp.

Figure 6.1   Digital rights management (DRM)

Between 2001 and 2004, entertainment companies embraced mobile devices as a means to market their artists and as another avenue to sell their goods. DRM had become an increasingly important technology for content providers, which were coping with daunting piracy challenges. Initially, a wave of competing and incompatible DRM products hit the market from Microsoft, Apple Computer, Sony, IBM, RealNetworks and others, creating interoperability problems for consumers. Today industry players are ready to found new and more open licensing entities.[1]

Leading vendors and operators expect DRM to protect the rights of all players in the industry value chain, while offering them an extension to the current model of distributing and selling content. To operators, higher usage of content download services means higher data traffic and revenue per user.

Licensing

As content owners expect to be paid for the use of their content, they have increased their activities in the mobile space through licensing: that is, leasing the rights to a legally protected (trade marked or copyrighted) entity.

Merchandising began more than a century ago, but licensing really took off in the 1930s, with comic strips, comic books, film celebrities and radio stars especially popular, from Felix the Cat and Batman to Shirley Temple and Roy Rogers. The 1950s marked the debut of lucrative television properties. The start of the licensing business, as it is known today, originates from the licensing programme surrounding the movie *Star Wars* (1977). The US $2.5 billion effort demonstrated the upside of licensing. The 1990s witnessed the maturation of the business, including the first-ever annual declines in total sales of licensed merchandising in the early part of the decade. The first decade of the 2000s has seen a continued increase in corporate licensing, with a particular focus on brand extension. Despite the fluctuations of the music business, music licensing has witnessed growth (Raugust, 2004).

Licensing is not a strategy in and of itself, but like advertising and promotion, a tactic that should be aligned and support the company's strategic objectives. Content providers view licensing royalties as an important part of the total potential profit picture for a franchise, along with fees from television stations, syndication, home video and global sales. With new mobile services and dynamic content, Hollywood studios – the world's largest media and entertainment conglomerates – began to invest in mobile innovation at first through licensing (see Box 6.1).

Convergence

Converge is complicated. In mobile entertainment, content originates from entertainment, but the value chain is dominated by the mobile industry. In entertainment, core competences tend to be marketing-driven. In the mobile business, core competences have historically been engineering-oriented. At the

Box 6.1 MOBILE MEDIA LICENSING

'Licensing can involve everything, from licensing television shows for broadcast to licensing for instructional purposes,' says Jeremy Laws, executive director of media licensing at Universal's consumer products group. 'Mobile licensing is a new form for Universal. It's a consistently growing business.'

Eager to avoid the digital rights problems of the music industry, Hollywood studios adopted a more proactive posture toward the mobile internet around 2001–2. In media licensing, Laws has watched the transformation closely. 'Our primary activity is to license content for reuse in broadcast products, for instance when there's a documentary about sharks and they'd like to use some clips from *Jaws*. We may license intellectual property content, including character elements and story ideas for reuse in various forms of advertising, such as television ads featuring the Frankenstein character. We also license intellectual property for reuse in location-based entertainment and in new corporate media, including internet applications and mobile telephones.'

Simple applications, unsophisticated players

With Bill Herzberg, vice president of Universal's interactive licensing, Law noticed a real opportunity for Universal's intellectual property in the wireless space around 2003 and 2004, due to Java. 'We work with portfolios of some 4,000 properties that are primarily motion pictures but also television programmes from the Universal library, which goes back to the 1920s,' says Laws. 'Despite the ever-growing content portfolio, television remains Universal's powerhouse.'

Initially, the studio's experience in the wireless space comprised licensing simple content-based applications and working with parties that were relatively unsophisticated about the licensing business. 'Still, people were generating revenue from these non-compelling products. At first, the operators got Universal Pictures into licensing black-and-white logos. Similarly, they were needed when, say, a teenager in Italy was interested in downloading the *Jaws* logo, which allowed the studio to make 5 cents.'

Java games and colour handsets

Along with so many others, the studios were caught up in the exuberance of the wireless community in a very early stage. They thought they could make money from very simple applications. 'Then people realized that doing simple applications is not enough,' says Laws. 'Maybe the content needs to be just a little more sophisticated to be compelling to the consumer. At the same time, we had become disillusioned at Universal. Many were asking questions whether the wireless would be attractive for revenue or focus, especially as we watched the development and publishing communities go down.

'Our interest became reignited when the Java-enabled handsets reached the market. That's when we began to see the development of simple Java games, which were compelling. Now developers could create more applications based on our intellectual property. The simple black-and-white handset was replaced with the colour screen handset. In the United States, the change has been really dramatic. It has affected the development of downloadable games. Sprint and Verizon Wireless have created compelling premium content services. For instance, the Get It Now service could be compared with America Online in the early days of the internet.

'Colour and Java reignited our licensing interest,' says Laws. But as the studio follows developments in Europe and Japan, it is also paying increasing attention to cultural differences. 'Universal content plays well in Japan, particularly applications targeting younger segments, including Wood Pecker and animations. Snoopy applications may not play very well in the United States or in the United Kingdom, but they work in Japan where adult women download such applications.'

Mobilizing temple properties

Starting with simple applications – black-and-white handset, logos and wallpapers – mobile media licensing has grown more complex with novel technologies, including colour handsets, logos and wallpapers, and Java games. And because of their intellectual properties, the studios were even more interested in the next stage, mobile streaming video – and even more dynamic content. As a television powerhouse, Universal and certain other studios were particularly well positioned for mobile television.

'In trade fairs, we've already seen a lot more interest in library properties that have proven equity, as the developers are tapping into the nostalgia factor via television shows, such as *Miami Vice* and *Knight Rider,*' notes Laws. 'Historically, the interest has been in the big releases or the 'temple properties'. With games, that means titles such as The Fast and Furious (PS2), and the Dracula game. Certain games are also doing fine in Japan, including the Wood Pecker game. But the business is still looking for a blow-out success story.

'Across the Hollywood community, there is a general interest in the interactive space video games. But it has not yet translated to the mobile space. Mobile content is still a relatively new phenomenon in the US market, so perhaps it's not in the radar screens yet. As the content grows more sophisticated and closer to the platform-based space, we will see more interest from the creative community. Still, it's difficult to imagine a person watching an entire film on a mobile device. It's more realistic to assume that some users might watch episodic television.

'As the mobile network becomes more robust and the devices grow more sophisticated, our goal is to protect and monetize our content, while we seek to establish relationships with industry players who are legitimate licensees and distributors of our content.'

Source: the author's interview with Jeremy Laws, executive director of media licensing, Consumer Products Group, Universal, 15 April 2004.

retail end, the revenue model of mobile carriers depends on rate plans, whereas the entertainment business model is driven by subscriber fees and advertising revenue.[2] Historically, the mobile value chain has been driven by two strategic groups: mobile operators and equipment manufacturers. More recent entrants comprise IT enablers, consumer electronics conglomerates, and content providers, including Hollywood studios.

Equipment manufacturers

These are companies involved in the design, manufacture and marketing of mobile devices and their operating systems. Players include Nokia, Motorola, Ericsson, Siemens, Samsung, Microsoft and Texas Instruments.

IT enablers

These are companies involved in mobile chips and application software, including Intel, Microsoft and Texas Instruments. They also comprise vendors specializing in mobile entertainment, particularly software platforms (streaming audio and video, ringtones), and authoring tools.

Operators

These are carriers responsible for the billing and maintaining a relationship of trust with subscribers. They include wireless network operators like Vodafone, Telefonica, NTT DoCoMo, AT&T Wireless and Sprint PCS, and gateway service providers like mBlox and Mobileway. Over time, these players may also focus on:

- Providing customer interface and content selections. Mobile portals include wireless network operators, such as Vodafone and Telefonica, and independent portals such as Yahoo! Mobile.
- WASPs (wireless application service providers) develop, implement or operate mobile entertainment platforms. They include Cash-U, OpenMobile, UCP Morgen and corporate divisions like Qualcomm's internet Services division.
- Others may focus on display, marketing, billing, collection and customer care, including MVNOs (mobile virtual network operators) such as Virgin Mobile, resellers and divisions of mobile delivery companies, and broadcasters (such as SkyTV) that distribute mobile content.

Content providers

This group of companies – large brand owners, such as Disney, Vivendi Universal and Sega – create original content or provide recognizable brands, characters or themes for mobile entertainment applications. They may also be application developers and designers. In mobile entertainment, they are often the content owners and/or the ASPs. They work closely with publishers/aggregators.[3]

Subscribers

These are the users of the service, who enjoy (and pay for) it. The subscriber is also the target audience of campaigns in a free-to-air model.

Currently, industry participants take on several roles. Over time, competitive pressure will force players to focus on their core competences. The key part belongs to large operators which control access to the end-user and thereby have relative power over revenue-sharing agreements. Despite their dominance, operators need to coordinate the value system, just as vendors have been forced to accept co-branding by operators. It is in this changing environment that content providers must develop their unique positioning. Such efforts can be illustrated by three types of content providers: cable news (CNN), mobile games (N-Gage and others), and family entertainment (Walt Disney).

PIONEERING EFFORTS

The rise of CNN Mobile

More than three decades ago, Walter Cronkite's reports from Vietnam forced the Nixon administration to formulate new policies. In the early 1990s, Peter Arnett's satellite reports from Baghdad compelled the allied forces, the Iraqis and international organizations to tackle the policy challenge of CNN's real-time satellite images. But imagine the future confrontations – from suicide attacks in the Middle East to 'dirty bombs' in global cities – where mobile phone cameras can record anything, any time and anywhere to worldwide audiences and in real time. Mobile media is about to enable these sounds, voices and images (Steinbock 2003b). Ted Turner's cable news empire has been preparing for the new world of mobile media and entertainment since the 1990s.[4]

Mobilizing cable news

'In the early 1990s, the media wasn't much involved with analog cellular,' says Mitch Lazar, vice president of wireless and emerging technology for Turner Broadcasting System International, Inc (TBS). 'Things didn't change too much even when GSM was introduced and it began to evolve into the global standard for mobile communication.'[5]

Founded by broadcasting pioneer Ted Turner, the Atlanta-based TBS is the primary television subsidiary of media and internet giant Time Warner. It is home to an array of cable television networks, including multiple CNN news properties and a number of websites affiliated with its many channels. It also owns the TBS superstation, the Cartoon Network, Turner Classic Movies, Turner Network Television, a majority stake of the WB Television Network, as well as the New Line Cinema film groups and professional baseball's Atlanta Braves. The extensive TBS and CNN wireless properties have evolved with the explosion of the internet, the hypergrowth of the digital cellular, and the popularity of SMS (see Table 6.2).

As the GSM triumphed in Europe and Asia, the United States moved slowly toward digitalization and many content providers – including CNN, ESPN, AccuWeather, C-SPAN and Yahoo! – signed their first mobile contracts with PageNet, once the largest paging company in the United States. When it overextended and fell apart, mobile vendors and operators entered the messaging business and began to develop content distribution businesses. 'Without the web, SMS and the mobile markets, there was no way to disseminate the emerging content services,' says Lazar. 'Around 1997, case studies of PageNet attracted attention in trade conferences, and got the interest of Nokia.'

Birth of CNN Mobile

CNN and Nokia began to develop a service for WAP and SMS. As Lazar began to cooperate with Nokia, CNN's first mobile service was commercialized in

Table 6.2 CNN mobile services: timeline

TIMELINE	WIRELESS BUSINESS (v 1.0)
1996 CNN launches pager service in the United States with PageNet. Service distributed in eight categories, updated every half hour to alpha numeric pager subscribers.	**CNN Mobile:** • Distributed in more than 30 countries on 50+ operators. • Available to more than 300 million mobile subscribers. • Launched in 1999. • Product features SMS alerts, browsable content, Java ticker, video.
1997 CNN presents pager case study at 3GSM World Congress in Cannes.	*CNN Mobile delivers the following services:*
1998 CNN strikes deal with Nokia to roll out CNN news services in SMS and WAP on Nokia's first WAP device, the 7110.	• **SMS News Service:** CNN's SMS service is available worldwide through mobile network operator partners and direct to consumers via CNN.com/mobile. The service delivers over 25 categories of content, updated 24-hours a day.
1999 CNN announces Nokia deal at 3GSM World Congress, along with nine charter operator distribution partners from Europe, Middle East and Asia.	• **Browsable news:** CNN's browsable news services provide longer news reports delivered to mobile devices in colour and featuring photographs, graphics and maps.
2000 CNN operator distribution grows to more than 30 operators worldwide, including an i-mode service in Japan with DoCoMo.	• **CNNlive:** Launched in 2003, CNNlive is a Java news service which features the top 10 stories from the CNN.com international news website, available on numerous devices in both MIDP and Doja.
2001 CNN launches Avantgo service for PDAs. Operator distribution grows to more than 50 operators worldwide.	• **Video service:** CNN's live 24-hour international news channel is available on selected European and Asian operators in live video streaming format.
2002 CNN launches direct to consumer SMS breaking news alerts. CNN rolls out service on new Vodafone Live! portal in the UK.	*Deal structures:* • Licensing of content for flat fees with or without revenue share. • Revenue share with or without minimum guarantees. • Content for incremental ad buy. Sometimes combined with licence fee for content creation.
2003 CNN launches CNNlive, a multimedia Java news ticker service developed in partnership with Mediabricks, a Sweden-based Java developer. The service debuts on KPN Netherlands, with distribution deals subsequently announced with other European mobile operators. CNN teams up with Nokia for the launch of the Nokia 6600 mobile phone, embedding the CNNlive service on the phone's MMC. CNN upgrades its WAP service to XHTML, adding colour and photographs.	• Per subscriber fees against minimum number of subscribers. • Deals with developers to create content services based on share of revenue generated. *Distributors:* • Primary: mobile phone operators. • Secondary partners: mobile phone manufacturers. • Tertiary: web portals specializing in mobile download as well as mobile phone manufacturers.
2004 Commercial streaming services of CNN International. Global alliance with Vodafone for CNN & Cartoon Network.	• Others: retailers, newspaper and magazine publishers.

February 1999, with the launch of CNN Mobile. Directing the development of the project, Lazar travelled worldwide to partner with nine charter GSM operators in Europe and the Asia–Pacific. SMS began to find a comfort zone in subscriber behaviour, but the WAP service did not meet the expectations. 'The emergence of the content business took place in very adverse circumstances, and it required significant changes in the philosophy of the mobile operators and content providers,' says Lazar. 'Despite difficulties, media companies got into the act, with the end of the technology downturn. Today, many are focusing their mobile efforts, but they remain reserved and conservative. The real business of mobile communication is still 95 per cent in voice rather than data.'

By 2004, CNN Mobile was accessible to more than 300 million mobile phone subscribers around the globe.[6] CNN's internet service, CNN.com, produces and constantly updates content for CNN Mobile, drawing on CNN's nearly 40 bureaus and worldwide news-gathering resources. The goal is to keep the subscriber up to date on breaking news, world and regional news, entertainment, health, nature, weather, sports, and of course business headlines and market numbers from around the world. Mobile devices enable consumers to experience the news services faster, but they are also transforming the way news organizations gather and disseminate information.

'The content providers are eager to get more involved in the mobile space,' says Lazar, 'but they've realized that in order to become more user-friendly the business needs time for devices, charging systems and new services. There is also a real generation gap between young kids who know how to use these devices and the 30–40-year-olds who find it difficult to navigate a mobile phone. We must look at new opportunities and define the revenue potential, even while extracting money from the old analog businesses. The Generation X and Y and their successors will use the media differently, and they will be more familiar with interactive content. That creates a big business opportunity – and that's where the focus should be.'

Getting advertisers aboard

'I got the SMS alert in New Orleans, via my mobile phone,' recalls Lazar. 'According to CNN news, the United States had declared war in Iraq and President Bush would address the nation at 9 pm Eastern Time. That same week in March 2003, CNN made available a channel that can give the users and subscribers 24-hour access on a regular basis so that when they hear a news story they can dial into CNN and watch it live. That's when I really felt the power of the mobile.'

The reach of CNN is compelling. In 2004, more than a billion people worldwide watched CNN each day on 2.5 billion screens across the globe, while Cartoon Network, for instance, is enjoyed by more than 73 million homes worldwide in 17 languages. CNN's revenues come from channel distribution and the ads its sells in airtime between programmes. A similar model, says Lazar, could lead to more solid business models between media companies and wireless operators, but that requires a different approach on the part of the operators.

Despite the rising power of the mobile in news production and entertainment consumption, even in mobile media (see Box 6.2), the great US marketers have not yet got aboard. 'Any successful media model is based on advertising, but operators are reluctant to include advertising in their offerings,' says Lazar. 'Yet they must create a business based on media. Otherwise, advertisers will not jump on the bandwagon, even if they'd want to. McDonald's, Procter & Gamble and other big advertisers want to do a lot in the mobile space, but they cannot evaluate the return on their business without appropriate measures for reach and frequency. Operators need to devise a system for measuring audiences and audience behaviour.'

Box 6.2   MAY THE BEST CONTENT WIN!

'Just like with enhanced television we add SMS to our applications,' says Bruce Gersh. 'My hope is that the interactive capabilities of cell phones will be another added layer to the interactivity of the internet.'

In May 2004, ABC promoted Bruce Gersh to senior vice president of business development at the network and Touchstone Television. He was responsible for online properties, which could take ABC into broadband, video-on-demand and e-commerce initiatives.

'As evidenced by the voting success of *American Idol* in the United States, people have an interest to use these applications to interact with television shows. The challenge is whether people will pay incrementally to interact. That's the million dollar question.'

The Precedent of Big Brother

'Today, everybody looks to *Big Brother* as an ultimate example of a programme that has been able to create interactivity and a large revenue stream,' says Gersh. But US broadcasters are newcomers in the mobile space. Around 2002, Brian Fons became the head of ABC daytime. Coming from Europe, he had seen the success of mobility and asked Gersh to put together some ideas for mobile marketing revenue programmes for ABC daytime. The Walt Disney Co. had been generating revenue for many years, as a result of their mobile deals in Europe and Asia.

As they develop their scheduling and programming, the broadcasters look at mobility from the standpoint of advertising and direct revenue. 'On our network and other networks, there are non-premium programmes; occasions where a sponsor pays an advertising fee to be an exclusive carrier for a specific programme,' says Gersh. 'Then there is the carrier premium programme that we've done as well. The non-premium is always driven by our creative group because there is only one carrier involved or an exclusive advertiser. In the premium world, we look at the content, but what we're really trying to figure out is whether there is a business and who we are targeting.

'We are identifying some other elements like ABC daytime and the scripted drama space as one opportunity of taking a loyal audience to create interactive development that gives them added value.'

Interactivity and loyalty

'*Man in America* was the first crowd carrier premium SMS campaign in the States,' says Gersh. 'We narrowed down thousands of contestants to 25 and over the next five weeks allowed our audience to vote on who they thought was the sexiest man in America. That person ended up on our television show. We then launched a programme called *Sub-Confidential*. It's Soap Club where for US $2.99 per show you will be able to get SMS from different soap characters.

'We have been able to embrace our audience and we have figured out a business model within soaps. As you move into other scripted products, whether it's comedy or other prime time dramas, it's more challenging because you have to have the audience that is really passionate about the show, like you do for soaps.

'Certain genres are going to make sense for premium products. Take, for instance, breaking news if people are willing to pay for it. Categories with added fan base will be successful. The same applies to certain games. *Who Wants to be a Millionaire?* is doing very well in the wireless sector. However, if you try to introduce interactivity into a comedy programme and charge people 25 to 50 cents to vote on a certain question, I'm not sure the US audience is going to pay for it. Content will drive this business so we will always put a premium on that.'

Mobile broadcasting – challenge and opportunity

NTT DoCoMo's rise in Japan is predicated on industry conditions that do not prevail in the United States and in several other important country markets, Gersh thinks. 'In Asia, people use cell phones for everything, whereas in the United States they don't. However, DoCoMo's content packages are amazing. In the US, AT&T and some of the other companies are trying to mimic it but it takes time to get there.'

Even as designers struggle to expand the form factor of the mobile device, broadcasters regard the enterprise as heroic but futile. 'I probably would never watch television on my phone. The larger the screen, the better. Unfortunately, we do not control the technology side of business, so all we can do is keep producing great content. We are focused on taking the contents we own and developing great applications, including ring tones and graphics. We believe that mobile provides a marketing tool. The question is how can we reach all of those people? I haven't seen a truly valuable solution yet.

'We have very restrictive privacy policies to avoid mobile spamming. You need permission-based marketing. With television, you can put up an ad as long as it is OK for broadcasting standards. With mobile, you need permission from individuals to send them information, which limits your base. The good news is that since these users want the information, the odds are that they'll respond better. Also, you'll have the opportunity to target market these individuals. But your base is going to be much smaller.'

To broadcasters, television-style mobile capabilities provide a terrific challenge and opportunity. 'Those capabilities will provide great opportunities, but we're in the business of television so we need to make sure that we don't disrupt our business with new technologies like broadband and video on demand. We want to ensure that our core business is always being supported.'

Source: the author's interview with Bruce Gersh, VP, business development, ABC Entertainment, 19 May 2004.

'We do not believe that a business model where operators take a large portion of our subscription revenue is going to be viable in the long term,' says Lazar. 'Part of the success of i-mode in Japan can be attributed to the fact that DoCoMo took less than 10 per cent of revenues generated in return for handling the billing. It encouraged content providers to experiment, invest and market, allowing all to prosper and create a new business. Likewise, our brands can help operators attract more subscribers, generate more average revenue per unit and drive more traffic, creating a successful data business, provided we are reasonably compensated for such a contribution.'

Revolution in your handset

Mobile is more advanced in Asia than in Europe, while the United States has been behind the cutting-edge developments, says Lazar. 'But America is a nationwide market. Operators, such as Spring, AT&T and Verizon Wireless, have a tremendous number of subscribers and can offer services in a national marketplace. That's something you can't easily do in Europe and Asia. If I developed a CNN service with an operator in the United Kingdom, it would not apply to the rest of Europe. In the United States, you'll have an audience of some 150 million people. Once they get the premium SMS concept, it'll be a phenomenal business, especially when it's integrated with television broadcasting.

'The new devices will be interactive and integrated. You can use the mobile phone as a remote control to change your television channel. Your electronic programs can be downloaded into your phone, depending on your selection. You can programme your VCR or your TiVo box by sending an SMS from your phone. As it provides a way for people to interact with programming, this interaction and integration assists media to cross over and complement each other.

'For any content provider, form factor is an important point', acknowledges Lazar. 'Increasing technological capabilities will translate to a more compact device with nice screen, like the larger Blackberry with colour screen. It's a perfect window for seeing television. The new phones will be radically different, very thin with a nice screen for interacting in a fulfilling way. They will revolutionize video on the handset.'

Mobile games: from Snake to Hollywood

Rise of video games

The story of modern video games – companies like Nintendo and the game units of Philips, Matsushita (Panasonic), Sony and Sega – precedes the cellular era. When the first cartridges and programmable consoles were released, Bell Labs was still working on cumbersome car phones. As Nolan Bushnell launched Atari and 'Pong' in 1972, Martin Cooper was completing Motorola's first cellphone. As the video games took off, developers were already working on the first hand-held programmable machines.[7]

With PacMan, the most popular arcade game of all time, the business was booming. Nintendo was launched in the United States, and the revenues of US arcades peaked at US $5 million. A bust followed in 1982, when Atari announced that its sales did not meet predictions. Revenues took off again after the mid-decade, when Nintendo began to test market the Nintendo Entertainment System (NES) in the United States. While Sega followed the footprints of Super Mario Brothers, Nintendo's market power was overwhelming.

In the 1990s, the cutting edge games were in Japan, where Sony's PlayStation emerged as the superior machine against the Sega Saturn. It became the most popular gaming system in the world, with an installed base of more than 3.2 million units in the United States alone. In November 2002, Microsoft released the successful X-Box Live online gaming service, which allowed users to play games with people all around the world.

Electronic games were attracting big-dollar deals with sports leagues, Hollywood and advertisers, and more gamers were facing off in professional venues. The pay-offs have been particularly rich in Korea, where computer games began to thrive with the nationwide broadband around 1999–2000. Instead of expensive consoles or hand-held games, which were not widely available at the time, teens used the internet. By 2004, three Korean cable television channels were broadcasting matches 24 hours a day. Live matches took place weekly in Seoul, attracting as many customers as movies, while young gamers were lured by prospects of fame and six-figure incomes (Fong, 2004).

Nintendo's Game Boy and hand-helds

Throughout the 1970s and 1980s, several companies – including Coleco and Milton Bradley – made lightweight table-top or hand-held video game devices. But since they would play a single game, they cannot be regarded as consoles. It was Nintendo that popularized the hand-held console concept with the release of the Game Boy (1989). The concept was predicated on a light-weight portable electronic device for playing video games. It differed from video game consoles because the controls, screen and speakers are all part of a single unit.[8]

Even with a tiny monochrome screen, the hand-held Game Boy began to build a historical sales record. As NTT DoCoMo's i-mode exploded and 3G was introduced in Japan, in June 2001 Nintendo introduced the Game Boy Advance, a 32-bit colour hand-held system, which could be combined with a cellular phone for internet access. It was the only game in town. With a 98 per cent market share, Nintendo now owned the hand-held game world.[9] As the stakes grew in the gaming business, minor players began to establish a foothold in niches. US Sega exited from hardware to become a software developer.

In early 2003, the Game Boy Advance was upgraded to the Game Boy Advance SP (as in 'Special Project'). The industry buzz, however, was around the new offerings by Nintendo and Sony. Like before, Nintendo was creating something new by its focus on the gameplay experience. In late 2004, the Nintendo DS, with its two 3-inch LCD screens, would be able to play Game Boy Advance games and support Wi-Fi for wireless multiplayer. It would compete with Sony PSP, another highly expected hand-held game console.

Mobile games

In 1997, Nokia's new phones allocated a tiny slice of memory to a game. Like early video games on other platforms (Pong, Space Invaders), Snake was a simple but addictive diversion. It was the reach that made all the difference. Until Nintendo's hand-helds, video games used to be played at home. Snake came with the cell phone. In short order, Nokia added other games like Space Impact and Bantumi to its phones, expanding the content available to customers. The opportunity to establish a foothold between the Game Boy and cellphones was too attractive to ignore. In video games, unit volumes were in millions; in mobile phones, they amounted to hundreds of millions.

The creation of Snake coincided with the introduction of the WAP service. Since many of the early content pioneers were game developers, the WAP debacle constrained the growth of mobile games in Europe. In Japan, however, the success of i-mode and the 503i series terminals running Java applications boosted a new generation of game developers. NTT DoCoMo began to create expanded services via i-mode partnerships. Two game services stood out. VF.NET connected users to arcade games, whereas PlayStation, which already had more than 14 million subscribers, enabled i-mode connectivity for games. It was a win–win situation. Cellphones entered homes, videogames entered phones. As DoCoMo's Takeshi Natsuno put it: 'The tie-up enabled us to make home into another space for i-mode.'[10]

Soon mobile games were thriving in Japan. Despite small player fees, sales of the amusements were adding up fast, creating multiple revenue streams. Cellphone game sales totalled ¥31 billion (US $287 million) in 2003, excluding carriers' download fees. At NTT DoCoMo, small-screen games were bringing in more than ¥1.3 billion per month to its content providers. It was deploying popular game brands to bait young, hip users, Japan's early adopters.[11]

With appetites for the digital diversions spreading fast, worldwide cell-phone game sales were expected to reach about US $4 billion by 2007, compared with US $584 million in 2003. It was a highly profitable value proposition because incumbents could reuse their vast libraries of old console games at relatively low cost on the new platform.[12]

Mobile game value chain

Projections of substantial industry growth have given rise to a wide variety of scenarios.[13] As content providers and game companies have entered the mobile business, the nascent value chain has specialized and globalized. The roles of mobile game publishers and developers have been augmented by independent niche developers and publishers. At the same time, the growing market potential has attracted PC and console video game publishers, while providing new opportunities to Japanese video game companies and Korean developers:

- publishers: JAMDAT, Gameloft, Airborne and Mforma;
- developers: Centerscore, Blue Heat, iomo, Nuvo Studios, Monkeystone and Handy Games;
- independent developers/publishers: Blue Lava, Sorrent, Morpheme (Argonaut);
- PC and console video game publishers: Sega Mobile, THQ Wireless; Activision, Microsoft Studios, Atari;
- Japanese video game companies: Bandai, Namco, Taito, Dwango;
- Korean developers: Com2uS, Game VIL.

Mobile game sales remain far behind console games and mobile voice revenues. Still, the market is expected to grow to US $7 billion by 2008, while the number of worldwide mobile game users may rise from less than 200 million in 2002 to almost 700 million in 2005.[14] Even in the United States, many mobile games services (including Sprint, Verizon, AT&T) were rolled out in 2002.

Positioning N-Gage

In the early 2000s, gamers were increasingly carrying a cellphone and a Game Boy. Nokia spotted an opportunity. Why not marry the most popular cellphone with the most popular hand-held game system into a singular unit? After a set of tools was developed for game developers and top-name publishers were signed up, the original N-Gage was launched worldwide in London in February 2003 (see Figure 6.2).[15] Despite great pre-launch attention by gamers, the N-Gage's expected sales of 1–2 million in the first two years did not materialize. That was not exceptional. Microsoft has predicted that it would not make a profit on the X-Box for at least three years after the console's debut. A comparable benchmark for N-Gage would be late 2005 or early 2006. With most console marketing strategies, the console is sold near cost and profit is made on software licensing fees. It is the 'razor and blade' business model (Pachter and Woo, 2004).

But critics had other issues as well. N-Gage was criticized for high costs and a poor selection of games, compared with Nintendo Game Boy Advance. As a cellphone, it was carried by only one or two mobile phone providers and suffered from design issues. The N-Gage QD, the more sleek and stylish new version, appealed to casual gamers rather than power users. As the underdog in the gaming business, Nokia sought to build N-Gage for a position of strength – before the arrival of Nintendo DS and Sony PSP (see Box 6.3).

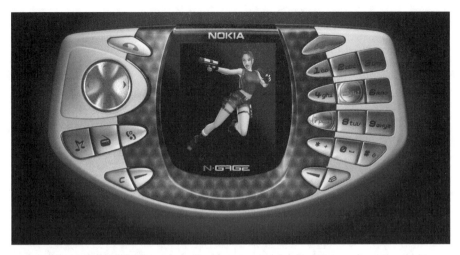

In design similar to Nintendo's Game Boy Advance, N-Gage's screen was in the middle of the device with game controls and a numbers pad on both sides

A unique platform that provides opportunities for game developers and publishers, network operators and service providers

Source: Nokia Corp.

Nokia N-Gage business model

— Nokia N-Gage game deck device

— Sales and distribution of branded games

— Nokia as game publisher

— N-Gage as a platform for game publishers

— Mobile operators – airtime & services

— Service providers – N-gage online services

Figure 6.2   N-Gage

By summer 2004, Nintendo's Game Boy consoles continued to dominate the market for hand-held or portable games. It garnered 98 per cent of hardware and almost 100 per cent of software sales a year before. Since the introduction of the Game Boy in 1988, several companies have attempted to launch and support hand-held consoles with little or no success. The original GBA debuted in Japan with eight software titles; by mid-2004, there were over 1,100 titles available. Over the previous year, more than 140 software titles had been introduced for the GBA, including Mario Bros 3: Mario 4, Donkey Kong Country, Mario and Luigi Saga, Finding Nemo and Yu-Gi-Oh Sacred Card.

Box 6.3 DEVELOPING UNIQUE POSITIONING

'It's not that difficult to create great game devices,' says Ilkka Raiskinen. 'You just need a big screen, a big battery, and a big processor, and then you got to know how to put it in a mobile device. But developing the business model and making money, that's a different story.'

Ilkka Raiskinen has been working in mobile services since the early 1990s. At Nokia Mobile Phones, he oversees the entertainment and media business unit. He is focused on games, music and media mobile – including the Nokia N-Gage game deck.

Expectations and realities

'The critical feedback came from hardcore gamers. They compare the N-Gage experience with the game experience on the consoles. From that perspective, they're certainly right. But to us N-Gage is about mobile online gaming. It's not the device, but content and games that count.

'Certainly, we made mistakes, and we need to improve our ability to execute. In order to have a good solid business, we need to address in a better way the hardcore gamer and the games magazines. The game business is all about the details. You must get everything right in a very detailed way.

'We began to develop QD before the global launch of the N-Gage,' says Raiskinen. 'We've had a tight schedule and we intend to continue adding new N-Gage decks. We have been criticized on various features of N-Gage, but we believe that it appeals to young people and perhaps casual gamers.'

Boosting critical capabilities

'It takes a while to build a brand, and N-Gage is going to be a brand in Nokia, with a variety of devices that can play N-Gage games,' says Raiskinen. 'We're beginning to see this with the N-Gage and the N-Gage QD. We're developing a range of new games that can offer a richer experience for the user. Original titles, original ideas, much more multiplayer games, different genres, a lot more work on the community side, on the back-end side, so that you can chat and communicate while you play, things like that. That's the goal, to improve all these strategically critical areas – the device, the portfolio, and the back-end, enabling N-Gage Arena.'

Developing unique positioning

Nokia seeks to define a unique identity for its N-Gage, or 'the unique N-Gage flavour', as Raiskinen puts it. As a result, the vendor is focusing on exclusive software and services offerings, which capitalize on the mobile abilities of the platform. By the same token, it has been developing the N-Gage Arena service, adding new functionality, focusing on the development of multiplayer mobile gaming titles. Take, for instance, such multiplayer titles as Sega's Pocket Kingdoms and Nokia's own Pathway to Glory.

'One might also measure mind share, penetration, creation of new markets, and usage areas like N-Gage Arena. The idea is to give the N-Gage three Christmas sales periods, so realistically we'll assess it in the first quarter of 2006.'

Source: the author's interview with Ilkka Raiskinen, SVP, entertainment and media, Nokia Corp, 13 June 2003 and 5 November 2004.

Nokia introduced its hybrid cellphone/video game device in late 2003, with only a handful of titles initially. While the QD cellphone demonstrated substantial improvement over design flaws, battery life remained a drawback. The real issue, however, was the business model. N-Gage was in a razor and blade business, without adequate supply of blades (read: software titles). There was also the lingering question on the usage patterns. Historically, portable gaming has been a form of individual, visual entertainment, whereas mobile communications is based on 'connecting people' via audio. Consequently, if the N-Gage obstacles have been empirical, Nokia's persistent investments could generate positive results over time, as the optimists thought. If, however, these issues were conceptual, the market launches of the Nintendo DS and Sony PSP had the potential of reducing N-Gage sales to a bare minimum, as the pessimists thought.

Mobile entertainment: Hello Mickey!

Since 1999 and 2000, Hollywood has gone mobile. Hollywood studios are taking the initiative and distributing movies, trailers, ringtones, logos and other movie-related content on mobile devices.

The Story of Disney Mobile

Around 2000 and 2001, all major Hollywood studios were creating separate mobile divisions or boosting the mobile focus of marketing divisions, or both. The launches were triggered by the maturing mobile media, dynamic content (colour-screen phones, Java for games) and DRM. US operators alone are expected to generate US $1.1 billion by 2005 from movies, movie trailers, ringtones, graphics and games. That compares with US $214 million today (see Boxes 6.4 and 6.5). Different strategic groups are extending to and embracing the mobile space, including Hollywood studios – and among them, Disney has played the lead.

First Japan, then the world

'The Disney brand is very strong in Japan; we have a very significant presence there', says Larry Shapiro, executive vice president of business development and operations for the Walt Disney Internet Group (WDIG). Shapiro has steadily consolidated and expanded Disney's new media properties. 'In August 2000, we signed a deal and launched with NTT DoCoMo. It has been a great partnership for us. We expanded to other carriers in Japan. We built an organization of 30–40 people and some 3.8 million monthly subscribers; that's about US $50 million a year. Thereafter, we have expanded our distribution relationships and have contacts in 25 countries with 37 carriers. This has been increasing on a monthly basis or so.'[16]

Disney modelled its US experiments after these initial tests in Japan, even if it has also provided wireless content from ABC, Disney, and ESPN in the United States for several years. Mobility has also meant a historical reversal at

Disney. In the past, technology innovation – from Disney's cartoons to video games – emerged first in the United States, which had the lead markets where these products and services were diffused into mass markets. Today, technology innovation can occur in multiple locations worldwide.

In mobility, the most advanced IT developments continue to take place in the United States, but mobile technology, product and service innovation occurs now in Japan, Korea and the Nordic countries, whereas the large-scale growth markets are in China and India. Disney is using Japan and Korea as a test laboratory for content introduction in the United States.

Studios must follow the customers (see Box 6.4).

Box 6.4   WHERE ARE YOUR CUSTOMERS?

'During the next five years, the mobile will become a more pervasive and ubiquitous part of lifestyle,' predicts Rio D Caraeff. 'It will have a profound integrated effect on television, print, retail, film and radio. All traditional forms of media will be fused eventually with aspects of mobility. From the standpoint of the device and the network, the actual experience will be quite rich, but it tailored on the core aspects of communication, information and entertainment.'

As vice president of wireless services for Sony Pictures Digital Networks, Caraeff is responsible for developing and distributing new mobile-specific entertainment applications, games and services featuring Sony Pictures Entertainment properties for current and emerging wireless technologies and platforms. Sony has entered mobile entertainment on a similar timeframe to Disney. 'We see the mobile becoming a greater and integrated part of lifestyle and we see a significant volume and uptake of these services.'

Focusing on content and user experience

'Our objective as a mobile entertainment publishing company is to deliver branded entertainment to the consumer, irrespective of whether based upon Sony Pictures property or a third-party property that we license,' says Caraeff. Created in Los Angeles in January 2002, Sony Pictures Mobile has three major objectives. It is focusing on managing the merchandising and revenue-generating opportunities inherent in the mobile marketplace. It seeks to leverage the wireless via marketing and promotional opportunities with the Sony film and television businesses on a global basis. And it is focused on building value for Sony Pictures through managing its own distribution and production of mobile products and services, with Sony Ericsson in the wireless handset business.

'The definitions change, but our perspective is focused on the handsets and terminals, they are the platform for us,' says Caraeff. 'As the publisher of mobile entertainment services, we are not very focused on the hardware. We are more focused on the content and the overall experience to the end user. If the content and experience are attractive, they will diffuse into different markets and countries, just as they will scale with different infrastructure and devices.'

Entry drivers

Like several other studios, Sony entered the business amidst the worldwide technology stagnation and 3G slump. This decision resulted from mobile maturation and the confluence of other determinants. 'First of all, colour screen is a major demand driver for branded media entertainment, whether it's an image, game, video clip or screensaver. The other major driver is the high-speed network, which enables a more sophisticated user experience and is friendlier toward content publishers and providers. The establishment of the billing system has been critical in provisioning to allow content providers to be paid for the delivery and consumption of their product. Finally, whether combined with Java or Brew, the middleware application environment inside the handset makes possible applications that enable a rich user experience on the terminal'.

Leveraging across platforms

'In the case of a major film, console video game release or television show, you can launch a successful mobile entertainment programme that generates revenue and creates new marketing opportunities with the network operators or handset manufacturers that can promote the movie, television show or console game,' says Caraeff.

In the United States, Spider Man II mobile entertainment was launched in May 2004, a month before the film promotion. It served as a personal 'teaser' or 'trailer' for the temple property. 'With Spider Man II mobile games and mobile entertainment programmes, efforts will be revenue-generating and premium in nature. They are being exclusively distributed in some countries by certain operators. In exchange for that exclusive opportunity, they are marketing our games and mobile entertainment products heavily, including the movie release date and the film itself.'

'We have also linked our mobile game to Spider Man. We can promote this game for PlayStation 2, while the Activision marketing of the Spider Man II game promotes the availability of the mobile game. There are thus all kind of linkages between the films, games and other existing platforms. The major attribute of mobile entertainment publishing and distribution today is that they are already inherently revenue-generating. They solidify the existing relationship with the consumer, while offering an integrated billing opportunity. They can also drive promotion and awareness.'

Source: the author's interview with Rio D Caraeff, vice president of wireless services, Sony Pictures Digital Networks, 15 April 2004.

Personalization, utility and entertainment

With mobility, Disney pays attention to three categories: personalization, utility and entertainment. It is 'focused on pull-driven content, because we think the push-driven will tip over into spam. With personalization,' says Shapiro, 'we explore the things you do to your device to make it reflect your personality, how you use screen savers, ringtones and attachments to make them personal. Equipment is used in the internet as well, but not to the same degree, and not through universally customizing your experience. We do extremely well on the basic kind of content, the screensavers and ringtones. In personalization, we're looking for evergreen content that lives forever.

'The next category is utility. In other words, what are things that a user would want to benefit from the mobility and what is a good use of a mobile device, what are the things you need on a daily or hourly basis that are useful to your daily life, for instance, weather updates, stock prices, and so forth? ESPN provides a whole variety that fits this category. In Japan, we also have a host of things of the Disney brand, calendars and so on. In comparison to the fixed internet, the access is a lot timelier with mobile devices.

'The third category is entertainment, from games to eventually some form of video. It can be a similar experience with a mobile device and an internet device, but the extent of mobility poses challenges of its own to entertainment. It is a short 10-minute experience. For now, we don't feel it is necessary to make a 24-hour channel or anything like that.'

With greater bandwidth and more capable mobile devices, personalized media is about to become reality, as evidenced by developments in Japan and South Korea.

Disney's mobile expansion

In March 2001, images of Disney's popular cast of characters and songs from its classic movies became available on AT&T wireless phones. It was the first time Disney-branded ringtones and graphics were available to US wireless subscribers. Disney ringtone and graphic content launched in Japan in August 2000 and has since garnered more than 2 million subscriptions. It was available throughout Asia and in Europe. In November 2001, Sprint PCS became the first US carrier to offer the games, which were based on Disney movies *Monsters, Inc* and *Atlantis: The Lost Empire*.

Others followed suit and entered into similar revenue-sharing deals. The small screen enabled primitive games, which Shapiro dubbed as being part of the 'pre-Pong era,' but he also saw them as part of Disney's future forays into the US and European wireless markets. Besides coping with the technological gap, Disney will face competition from downloadable games played on personal digital assistants (PDAs), which make for a better experience. The studio wanted to create a wireless entertainment service that carriers in Europe and the United States would sell on a subscription basis.

By late 2002, Mickey Mouse, the Lion King and other Walt Disney Co characters lit up wireless phones buzzing with tunes from Disney films under deals announced with two European wireless companies, the French Bouygues Telecom and the Italian Telecom Italia Mobile Sp. Anchored by a 3.1 million subscriber base in Japan, its biggest market for mobile entertainment, Disney now had deals to supply games, news and ringtones to wireless providers in 21 countries, with contracts in six more countries not yet announced.

By spring 2003, Disney believed that the entertainment industry had barely begun to scratch the surface of the potential market for wireless entertainment services. 'We're at the tip of the iceberg of what can be the true third screen: the PC, the television and the wireless device,' Shapiro says. 'Current content emphasis is on ringtones, graphics and games, with many in the wireless industry predicting that games will prove to be the 'killer app' that engages the mass market of consumers. WDIG has had considerable success with these categories during its three years of operation, he said, but 'this is the year for us to move to more sophisticated, more engaging and more entertaining content'.[17]

By October 2003, following signs of 'astronomical' growth in its wireless data offerings in the United States, Walt Disney Co planned to add a new internet promotional site, as well as new wireless content based on Disney's Pixar movies, including *Finding Nemo* and *Toy Story*. Shapiro said such growth is notable because Disney counted no wireless revenues in the US market in 2002. Thereafter, Disney greatly expanded its wireless offerings in the United States, including new deals with Verizon Wireless for its Brew application download service. That year, the studio saw significant growth in its wireless data business. Two months later, WDIG launched its first comprehensive consumer internet site devoted to its wireless content offerings.[18] 'We saw significant growth in both consumer awareness and usage of our mobile content, primarily driven by carriers' marketing efforts,' said Shapiro. 'The US market had matured to a point that allowed us to begin marketing directly to our customers.'

Starting in spring 2004, WDIG began selling a 3D wireless game, which worked on both Brew and Java application systems. '3D technologies are a major step forward for mobile entertainment. With them, consumers can begin to experience games and game play that they've come to expect from consoles and PCs,' says Shapiro. 'We've been very aggressive in leveraging new technologies to expand our consumers' experiences. We feel we've got a franchise that can really benefit from this technology and showcase its capabilities.'

Discontents of carrier power

In the mobile business, vertical integration simply does not exist. As their channel power is more limited, content providers have lower incentives to invest and innovate. 'In most countries the carrier is the gatekeeper, a benevolent gatekeeper trying to increase data revenues and looking to content providers and looking for clear navigation. Your experience is controlled by your carrier.

'Additionally, the carriers had a lot of consolidation and capital investment through the late 1980s to 1990s. With head-to-head competition, they are really battling each other with such intensity that you don't really have in other markets. They are very focused on customer additions, that is, new customers per month or quarter as they are measured on Wall Street. Consequently, their attention is on garnering new customers, as opposed to driving revenue or new services.

'On the internet it is much easier to have a broader and deeper experience,' says Shapiro. 'That is harder with the wireless because you are working with the constraints of memory enhancements and latency in the network, but most importantly because of the carrier control of what your screen looks like.'

It is the content that makes or breaks new services. Content, however, requires appropriate incentives. Only quality sells (see Box 6.5).

Box 6.5   QUALITY SELLS

'Mobile entertainment is different,' says Doug Dyer. 'Mobile entertainment is all about five minutes a time, five times a day. The form is short and one has to get right to the point.'

In the autumn of 2003, Warner Bros Online officially launched its wireless initiative with the appointment of Dyer to the post of vice president of wireless, Warner Bros Online, with a mandate to expand the group's wireless business beyond licensing into developing, producing, publishing and marketing its own content to mobile operators and handset manufacturers.

The announcement came on the heels of a cross promotion between US wireless carrier Sprint and the upcoming theatrical release of *Looney Tunes: Back in Action*. The deal marked WB Online's first significant foray into wireless content production, creating everything from original screensavers to custom games.

The games man

'It's still too early for mobile content to make waves,' says Dyer. 'With repurposing, the most popular game on mobile will be Tetris. For now, people are buying games that they are comfortable and familiar with. People are only buying things they can understand.'

Before Warner, Dyer created a career in the games business, starting with Microsoft's product portfolios, which led to business development for Infogames (Atari). He also founded and ran THQ Wireless, a division of THQ dedicated to publishing and distributing wireless games, launching interactive mobile games and services for such popular brands as The Simpsons, WWE Wrestling and Major League Baseball. 'At THQ Wireless, the first three years were slow, as the mobile was only beginning to take off. But now it's growing to a real business. But mobile entertainment is different. It's about content, putting it into a small device and understanding how people will use that device.

'User patterns will definitely change over time, if the medium can be made more compelling,' Dyer believes. 'Teens used to spend money on PlayStation and gaming; now they also go for mobile games. The publishers and the equipment manufacturers are trying to understand how people are going to use these devices. It may be five minutes five times a day, or watching 30-minute mobile game shows on television, as in Korea.

'Ultimately we'll find new and different types of programming for the mobile media, maybe short-format film or short-format commercial entertainment that can grab attention and hold it for 30 seconds, or even three to four minutes. The handset manufacturers are no longer paying attention to just usability with the phones, but with the menu, the user interface and the user experience as a whole. And as the screen technology is getting better, we'll see more made-for-mobile content and specific production budgets for mobile entertainment.'

Think mobile, think global

'We're at the test phase, this is the period of market making,' says Dyer. 'For mobile video to be truly successful, the big studios must become involved. In Warner Bros, everybody has jumped on the bandwagon, including theatrical movies, home video and television, animation and DC Comics – and the same goes for CNN, Turner, Cartoon Network, AOL and HBO. Each has its own properties, but all are very excited about the mobile potential.

'*The Lord of the Rings* has already seen a margin of success on Verizon. In addition to DC Comics, cartoon properties like *Scooby Doo* and others lend themselves well to the mobile platform. The interaction of mobile with television is already a reality with the success of texting in Europe and *Big Brother*, and MTV *Video Clash*. From *American Idol* and *Harry Potter* to *Looney Tunes* and animation pieces, the opportunities are many and growing with video streaming.'

As Warner Bros Online seeks to move beyond licensing to take an active role in producing and marketing content, leveraging existing content and current libraries will no longer suffice. 'Some simply repurpose content, but that is not going to translate too well into the small screen,' says Dyer. 'If they want to be truly successful and if they want the market to grow, they will have to develop made-for-mobile entertainment. They have a good brand, and the mobile is a media now.'

Video games are Dyer's precedent for mobile content. 'Cutting corners won't do it, quality sells. That's what Electronic Arts did with games. They won't even do a video unless it sells over one or two million units.' In addition to scale and quality, he underscores the need to think global. 'Most US companies don't think beyond the United States, whereas Warner Bros has a global view.'

Terms of revenue sharing

As content producers are moving beyond licensing, operators' revenue-sharing deals can encourage or discourage industry expansion. Operators would like to see themselves as mobile Wal-Marts, or even wholesale retailers, but revenue sharing requires the smooth functioning of the full value chain.

'Publishers like the DoCoMo model because it is successful and has resulted in benefits to the operator and content producers alike,' says Dyer. 'It operates in the very crowded Japanese market, where consumers are already paying some 200–300 yen per month. They expect upgrades and new features, which can be very expensive for the publisher. Due to price sensitivity, the value of the mobile content is going down. Over time, people are not going to be paying US $2–3 for a ringtone. That will force publishers and developers to come up with new and interesting content that people are willing to pay a higher price for. Publishers, developers and operators are in this business together. That requires business models which provide incentives to each.

'Mobile entertainment will not make things more difficult for existing brands,' says Dyer. 'It is going to support them. Mobile is not going to be a threat. It has already been integrated into so many properties. It is everywhere.'

Source: the author's interview with Doug Dyer, VP, wireless group, Warner Bros Online, 8 March 2004.

7

'Device formerly known as cellphone'

Like the artist formerly known as Prince, the cellphone is really the 'device formerly known as the cellphone,' as Motorola's marketing chief Geoffrey Frost says with tongue in cheek. Mobile devices are Janus-faced. They come with a physical form, but serve as emotional expressions. During the past two to three decades, the design has evolved from Motorola's large and heavy 'brick' to Nokia's segment categories. With maturation, the models have been swept by style, mass customization and imitation, price competition and commodification. Today, the industry deploys a variety of segmentation principles (technology, lifestyle, functionality, experience), while preparing for smart and wearable phones.

FROM BRICK TO SELF-EXPRESSION

A dual role

Like Nike's footwear, mobile devices are favoured by youthful demographics. Both products draw from innovation in technology and fashion. Both have a physical form, but that is only part of what they are. 'When I moved from Nike to Motorola, the sports industry was becoming very saturated,' recalls Frost, who sees many parallels between mobile devices and sneakers. 'The next big thing was going to be personal technology. The cultural position of the running shoe had begun to be consumed by Nokia and the cellphone, as the almost 10-year icon of self-expression.'[1]

With maturation, the marketer must understand and develop the physical form, and the more intimate role of this seemingly innocuous gadget to its user. In their first role, mobile devices are tangible and objective. In their second role, they are intangible and subjective. Both matter.

The form factor

The most obvious visible characteristic of the handset is its physical form. By 2005, the most popular mobile phones have been around for years, including blocks (candy-bar) phones, flip phones and folders (clamshell phones). Historically, the candy-bar phones have been typical of Europe's GSM markets, whereas flip phones have been popular in the United States and the Asia–Pacific. More recently, clamshells have gained popularity in China and other markets.

Block phones (candy bar)

Aside from the buttons and possibly antenna, the block phone has no moving parts. To prevent keys from being pressed accidentally while the phone is in a pocket, these phones typically employ a keyguard feature, requiring a special key combination to 'unlock' the keys. Longer, thinner block phones are often referred to as candy bars. This form provided Nokia the base for its segmentation.

Flip phones

Seemingly identical with the block type, these phones also have a thin piece of plastic that flips open. When closed, it covers the keys to prevent accidental keypresses. Most flips 'flip' down, below the keypad. Some phones flip up, with either separate arms or a clear plastic window allowing the display to be seen when the flip is closed. In this class, Asian producers (Samsung, LG, Kyocera, Panasonic) have had a substantial presence, along with US firms (Motorola, AT&T).

Folder phones (clamshell)

This type consists of two halves, connected by a hinge. The phone folds closed when not in use. Usually, the top half contains the speaker and the display or battery, while the bottom half contains the remaining components. Most folder-type phones feature active flip. The model has been popular since the 1980s.[2] In 2004, Nokia reportedly paid a price for missing the trend toward stylish clamshell handsets, while Samsung Electronics reported soaring profits – not least due to Chung Kook Hyun, Samsung design boss.

Self-expression

Unlike the traditional simple handset, the new and complex gadget can be called a personal trusted device. It is used and carried by one person most of the time. It is an application platform for transaction-related services, including banking, payment and loyalty schemes. It has security functionality for transaction-related services, including secure sessions, authentication and authorization. As a personal trusted device, the mobile device has become a life management tool for business, work and leisure:

> This focal lifestyle accessory will also be a tool for storing and exchanging personal information and experiences. It will deliver practical and rational benefits, but equally importantly, the sharing of experiences and emotions.

> (Nokia, 2001b)

Since the 1990s, the cellphone has been morphing into something more emotional and intimate, a reflection of one's identity. Like Madonna's 'Express yourself,' it has become a matter of self-expression. 'Phone makers are busy designing handsets for nearly every sort of person,' commented the *Wall Street Journal* in 1999. 'There are products for tech-types who want to surf the Internet, colorful, snappable plastic covers for fashion-conscious teens, and easy-to-use toy-like models for the 12-year-old set' (Kaiser, 1999). These trends were new in the United States, but old in Scandinavia, where Nokia introduced them around 1994 – at a time when the mobile industry moved from the mass marketing model to segmentation.

DESIGN EVOLUTION

The most successful industry products fulfil both physical form and self-expression requirements. This duality is demonstrated by the evolution of mobile design, from Motorola's 'brick' to Nokia's segmentation and mass customization (see Figure 7.1).

The brick

In the pre-cellular era, the first portables came with the Walkie-Talkies and Handie-Talkies in the 1940s. The development of the civilian markets started after the Second World War, first with emergency and industrial services, then with car phones. In 1973, Dr Martin Cooper and his colleagues at Motorola developed the first truly portable phone model (see Chapter 2). The brick was heavy, black and rudimentary technologically, but it defined the 'look and feel' of mobile phones until the late 1980s.

During this analog phase, the customer base comprised dispatch employees, corporate professionals, and high-end consumers. Dominated by the selling concept, the marketing mix was driven by sellers through the 1980s. The products were characterized by high prices, low volume and penetration, and minimal differentiation. As long as business markets were more important than consumer markets, function reigned over style – as evidenced by pioneer designs in Nordic countries and Japan.

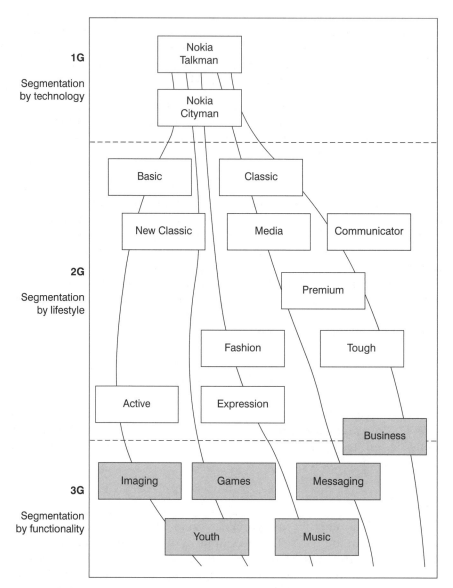

Figure 7.1 Nokia's design categories: evolutionary branching

Nokia: the successors of Mobira Talkman

Launched in 1984, the Nokia Mobira Talkman, for instance, was the first transportable phone. Heavy by today's standards, it was still 5 kilos lighter than its predecessor, the Mobira Senator of 1982, which had weighed 9.8 kilos. In 1987, Nokia cut the size of its phones dramatically, introducing its first handheld model. The Mobira Cityman weighed only 800 grams with its battery. By the end of the 1990s, the handsets had become very light, while single product categories had been replaced with extensive product families (Steinbock 2001: ch 10).

NTT DoCoMo: the successors of the 'shoulder phone'

Ever since 1999, i-mode subscribers – as well as FOMA subscribers after 2001 – have relied on prior technologies for achieving size and weight reduction of the handsets, including stacking for high-density mounting of electronic components, space-saving circuit boards, and high-quality communication with internal antenna. In Japan, the first truly portable mobile telephone was launched in 1985. The NTT DoCoMo Shoulder Phone (Type 100) weighed about 3 kilos. By 1998, the mobile phone grew progressively more compact and light, weighing less than 100 grams. Despite the size and weight reduction measures, higher functions escalated (NTT DoCoMo 2004d).

From mass marketing to segmentation

With the digital transition, the industry witnessed a massive shift, which resembled another in the automobile industry some six to seven decades before. In the mass marketing era of the automobile business, Henry Ford devised a strategy that called for total concentration on a single, 'universal' car aimed at everyone, settling on the Model T as its sole market entry in 1908. This was the profit-through-volume stage of the automobile industry. In the 1920s, the automobile market had grown large enough and the problems posed by the used car had proved vexing enough that there was an opportunity for a new strategy of segmentation. At General Motors, Alfred P Sloan, Jr seized the window of opportunity by introducing the legendary price pyramid with the 'car for every purse and purpose'. That led to the profit-through-value stage. Ford established the mass market; Sloan segmented it.[3]

In the early 1990s, Motorola was the Ford and Nokia the General Motors of the mobile industry. Like GM in the 1920s, Nokia segmented the markets to capitalize on its strengths and to exploit Motorola's weaknesses. The customer base exploded from business to consumer markets. Driven by the marketing concept, the marketing mix shifted toward the customer. Declining prices made possible high volumes. Penetration accelerated dramatically in the most developed markets, while differentiation took off. New mobile device models proliferated. Continuous product introductions and the new design language coincided with Nokia's move from geographic segmentation to customer segments and value-based segmentation. These shifts went hand in hand with the move from narrow business markets to broad consumer markets. The breakthrough design was the classic 2100 of 1994.

Some marketers define design in narrow aesthetic terms, but it should be considered more broadly as an integrative force, encompassing the totality of features that affects how a product looks and functions in terms of customer requirements (Kotler, 1984: 16–21). This is vital in maturing mobile markets. In the past, function reigned over style. Now style reigns over function. Since tech features no longer differentiate mobile vendors, consumers purchase phones that suit their individual lifestyles. Nokia's CEO Jorma Ollila hired designers from Europe and California to give Nokia phones their distinctive look and feel. Segmentation came to be considered a prerequisite for success. By late 1998, Nokia was pumping out new models every 35 days. Like Procter & Gamble fills up the supermarket shelves, Nokia proliferated segments to dominate categories (Steinbock, 2001: ch 10).

Maturation

Segmenting growth markets

'In the beginning, there was only one category, the brand product,' recalls Frank Nuovo, Nokia's chief designer. 'When you only have one or two products, or even three of four products in your portfolio, you're not thinking in terms of how to extend the offering. You're just trying to get your products out there.' But even in those early days, Nuovo argued that one could appeal to certain segments with the same product, just by changing the colour.

> Take, for example, a lighter, more colourful, friendly phone; or a more fashionable phone; or black, silver, a darker, serious colour that may be more apparent for a business target. The standard was the black plastic. But even then we asked ourselves, 'How can we demonstrate the expanding mass-market interest in the product?'
>
> We gave the business professionals the form they wanted; the black classic, or the 'serious black suit', as we used to call it. People don't want just black suits, but all kind of colours. When you're using bright colours, pretty colours, patterns and textures, you're broadening the product appeal and making it friendlier and easier for people to accept.[4]

During the early 1990s, the challenge was much about colour. There was no discussion about changing the whole form yet. As digital phones hit the marketplace, the industry was swept by dramatic expansion. The pipeline escalated, prices declined, the volume of users soared, and the operators lowered prices. No longer did the phone belong to the business user, but to the general consumer. 'What was once a dream became a reality,' recalls Nuovo. 'As you opened up beyond a single target [the business users], the whole game changed. You used to appeal to a profession. Now you're appealing to an individual. And when you appeal to an individual, you can begin to target the style value, even as you're providing essential performance value.'

Meanwhile, the base of competition was shifting. It used to be about performance capabilities; now it was about the needs of the consumer. 'That's when we began to target a creation of a product that was easier to use, had fewer keys, with overall style that was more friendly, less professional and serious,' says Nuovo. 'It had to be something that your grandmother could use without much instruction.'

Style categories

A number of style categories were identified at Nokia. 'The categorization began with the expansion of the appeal of a standard product through the means of colour and materials,' recalls Nuovo. 'The idea was to expand beyond the basic business unit, to create more interest in something that was not just a business tool, but had the potential to expand into the general consumer marketplace.'

Gradually, new categories evolved. They were predicated on differences between business users and general consumers, but also between stylistic categories, which appeal to a wider range. Changeable covers did a lot to cover a tremendous breadth of different user types. Nokia began to break into more sophisticated and more mature product categories, including Premium. 'We gave it all the same functionality as a business phone,' says Nuovo. 'But it was more about the style. It was efficient, it performed, but it also had to match what matters to the target customer and the premium style category. It's about the look, the feel, the appearance, good solid functionality, and obviously user-friendliness, but it was not about hyper-performance, and it was quite successful.'

The style categories were about functionality as well. After Premium, Nokia broke into the blue-collar, tough rugged phone, which was all about durability, even as it began to develop the active sports category, which was water-resistant and had an inbuilt compass. The categories were running parallel, expanded quickly and multiplied (Figure 7.2). 'The idea was that with changeable covers, we can combine the very high-end premium approach and make it more fashion-oriented. It's a much more exotic foreign language that appealed to a more refined sense of style. It had to be much more colourful, more expressive, not just the classic silver chrome metal case. With our 8200 series, the fashion category was born. Meanwhile, I began to drive the luxury category. It was first introduced in 1995, reintroduced at the turn of 1998 and launched in 2002 via the subsidiary Vertu.'

All of this expansion – multiplication of product categories and subsequent segmentation – reflects the maturation of the marketplace. The style categories differ from functional categories, but are predicated on matching functionality.

Mass customization

By the late 1990s, the mobile marketing mix was driven by the customer concept. Mass customization became the new slogan, endless variety the new dogma. Growing flexibility went hand in hand with increasing scale

Colour displays

Nokia 8310 coloured covers, fan shot

From fashion to luxury

Nokia 3210 coloured covers, fan shot

Nokia 8860

Vertu

It was the introduction of Nokia's 8860 – the 'first fashion phone' – that made Nokia's chief designer Frank Nuovo a fashionable subject of *Vogue*, in which he was praised as 'the designer who made wireless technology a fashion statement'.

Figure 7.2 From colour to fashion to luxury to imaging

Huge market opportunity

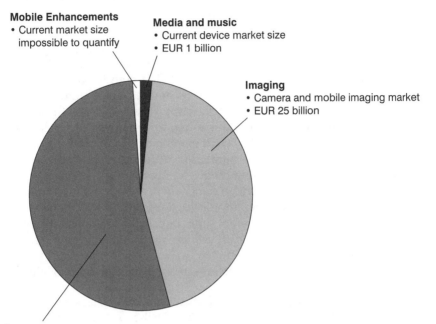

Mobile Enhancements
• Current market size
  impossible to quantify

Media and music
• Current device market size
• EUR 1 billion

Imaging
• Camera and mobile imaging market
• EUR 25 billion

Games
• Current games industry (device and software)
• EUR 30 billion

Mobile imaging value proposition

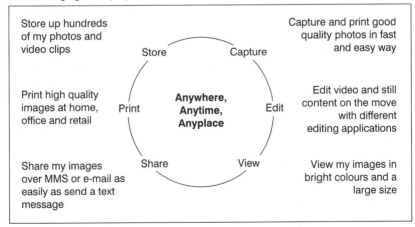

Store up hundreds
of my photos and
video clips

Capture and print good
quality photos in fast
and easy way

Store   Capture

Print high quality
images at home,
office and retail

Print   **Anywhere,
           Anytime,
           Anyplace**   Edit

Edit video and still
content on the move
with different
editing applications

Share my images
over MMS or e-mail as
easily as send a text
message

Share   View

View my images in
bright colours and a
large size

Figure 7.2   continued

and scope. As entry barriers grew higher and escalating R&D costs were leveraged across markets worldwide, original demand gave way to replacements, which led to increasing price pressures. Segmentation by technology prepared the way to segmentation by lifestyle, which led to segmentation by functionality.

The focus on functionality originated from the Communicator category in 1996 (Steinbock 2001). At Nokia, it was the first combined mobile phone, personal digital assistant and mobile internet device. Yet the significance of the category went beyond existing product groups. 'That was really the beginning of thinking in terms of what does this thing do, what else can it do?' recalls Nuovo. As N-Gage became Nokia's first gaming device, 'we were looking at a new functionality and style in a number of different ways. Today, we have camera phones, which have found themselves both uniquely and more traditionally styled; that is, a phone with a camera in it, as opposed to a camera with a phone in it. You can take either approach. We also have MP3 players, which happen to be phones. These different types of categories are getting into new functions with new capabilities, such as high-speed data and movies that are changing the features of the product.'

Initially, the designs were trying to breach out from pure functionality:

> The size factor of the devices was so huge that there was great concentration on getting the product physically more acceptable to mobile use. Working with hefty technology was the challenge. The notion of easy-to-use was one of the first influences. The second influence was targeting the design and the style to complement the ease of use. People want to carry an object which complements their own needs and functionality. In those early days, design was just about voice and SMS. There were no additional functionalities. That fashion sense of technology worked and continues to work very well.
>
> Now the functionality has resurfaced and we must make sure that the designs appeal to people who want these new functionalities. Others have made the phone a gaming device, but we will appeal to those who see themselves as gaming types. A multimedia device having a large screen should take on a new look, it should not just look like another phone. Today, people are not only sophisticated on the functionality they want. They are also sophisticated on the options they want, such as the form factor and the style.

Segmentation by technology, lifestyle, functionality, or even experience are not mutually exclusive. They are accumulative and complementary. When the form factor changed with lifestyle segmentation, technological segmentation was not excluded. As a complement, lifestyle segmentation has to live with technology, not against it. Maturity is natural evolution, which allows one to explore the same form and how one can make that form more interesting. 'Maturity is a natural thing,' contends Nuovo. 'It's no different than the watch market with its high-end simplicity. If you have a US $30,000 Philippe watch, you have to wind it every morning before use, even if you could walk down the street and buy a US $5 Timex with a battery. You can get more functionality at a lower cost, but you're paying for a whole different principle.'

In the early 1990s, Nokia's segmentation and design were original. But as the pioneer set the tacit standards for the 'look and feel' of the segmented mobile phone, it also attracted increasing numbers of imitators worldwide. 'You try to protect these properties,' says Nuovo. 'We have many design patents. Some have been brutally stepped on by the competition. Much of what we have established in terms of ease of use and simplicity has become a global standard.'

Price pressures and commodification

In the pre-cellular era, the mobile phone had been confined to emergency services. Its function was safety. In the 1980s, the cellphone – more precisely the car phone – penetrated the business markets, but remained a household luxury. In the 1990s, it turned from a consumer tool to a household commodity. Meanwhile, its significance shifted from safety to basic needs, instrumental uses and expressive functions (Figure 7.3a). With the transition from voice to data, value has migrated from hardware to software. Increasingly, great applications boost great services. Conversely, the pace of evolution demonstrates relentless price pressure via commodification. With greater performance and capabilities, today's high range is more often than not tomorrow's mid-range – and the day after tomorrow, a low-end utility (Figure 7.3b).

VARIATIONS OF SEGMENTATION

At the broadest level, segmentation refers to the process of subdividing a market into distinct subsets of customers that behave in the same way or have similar needs. Each subset may be chosen as a target market to be reached with a distinct marketing strategy. The effort is initiated by selecting a basis for segmentation. Usually this is a product-specific factor that reflects differences in customers' requirements or responsiveness to marketing variables, including sought benefits, usage, preference, loyalty or purchase behaviour. In turn, the basis for segmentation leads to choices of segment descriptors (demographics, geography, psychographics, customer size and industry), based on their ability to identify segments. To have strategic value in marketing, these descriptors should be measurable, accessible, sufficiently different, and durable.[5]

Layers of segmentation

While industry producers have carved segments by region, purchase behaviour and cost, there have been three dominant forms of device

(a) Evolution of market and services

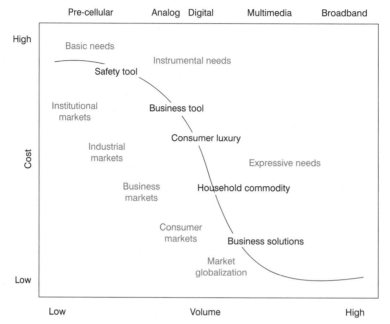

Initially, the wireless was synonymous with emergency services. In the 1980s, the analog cellphone penetrated business markets. In the 1990s, the cellphone became a household commodity. During these phases, the function of the phone shifted from basic needs to instrumental and expressive needs

(b) Impact of commodification, competition and price erosion

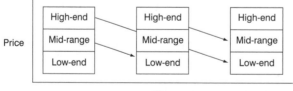

All new features and functionalities are vulnerable to imitation and competition. Over time, economies of scale and scope allow brand leaders to employ high volume in order to cut costs. Products and categories that were once a privilege of the few become affordable to all. At the same time, yesterday's high-end devices take, for instance, colour displays and digital cameras – turn into today's low-end products.

Figure 7.3 Mobile networks and handsets

segmentation with mobile devices: segmentation by technology, lifestyle and functionality. A fourth one – experience – is emerging. These layers of segmentation – technology, lifestyle, functionality, experience – are not disruptive or mutually exclusive, but evolutionary and parallel (see Figure 7.4). As price pressures have mounted and as technology and lifestyle segmentation have become table stakes in the business, vendors have been pushing single-purpose handsets, ie optimized functionality. Subscribers, however, are looking for value-added services and new experiences (see Box 7.1).

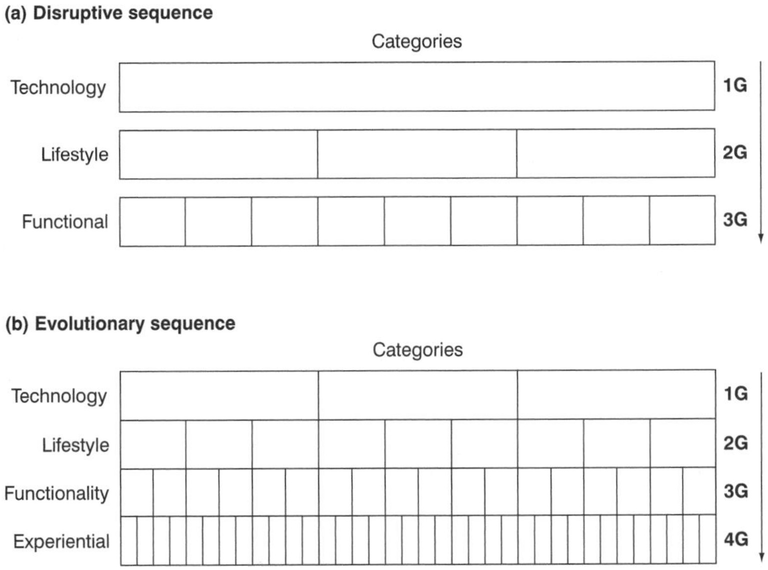

(a) Disruptive sequence

Categories

Technology			1G
Lifestyle			2G
Functional			3G

(b) Evolutionary sequence

Categories

Technology			1G
Lifestyle			2G
Functionality			3G
Experiential			4G

Today, mobile business is moving away 'from the business of ears to the business of eyes.' Along with technology, mobility is driven by marketing. Successive *technology* generations (a) may be disruptive and discontinuous, but *markets* are sustaining and continuous (b). Mass marketing is giving way to growing complexity and increasing novelty – new forms of segmentations, new market niches.

Figure 7.4   Two logics of segmentation

Box 7.1   FROM FUNCTIONALITY TO EXPERIENCE

In the new mobile world, cellphones are becoming extensions of the body. 'Seamless mobility is converging on the person,' argues Geoffrey Frost, Motorola's brand steward who was promoted to senior vice president of marketing in 2003.

'People can access voice, media and data-rich services wherever they are, everything from their favourite music to their kids' whereabouts to the condition of their homes and the shortest route to real time traffic. Look at a map of that and put the person in the centre and look at their environment and all the spaces in their lives, at home, at work, in their car and just out in the world in general. It requires you to do certain things in terms of the device that you carry, and embedding intelligence in the environment, making smart cars and homes; smart atmospheric that can fuel smart devices.'

From features and benefits to enhanced abilities

In the technology sector, cellphones have historically been perceived as amalgams of features and functionalities. Traditional marketing – 'feature & benefit' (F&B) marketing, as experiential marketers call it – has only reinforced the tendency to look at the identifiers of these devices rather than seeing them from the standpoint of a human being – that is, as extended abilities. These are the drivers of 'Moto-isms' that have become the lingua franca at Motorola. Things are 'Moto-morphed' boldly. (See Figure 7.5.) It is a world not unlike Apple's iMac. It brands extended abilities.

'I think of cellphones as ability amplifiers,' says Geoffrey Frost. 'They enable us to realize the dreams of science fiction. When I talk to someone who's just using the cellphone as a phone, it is indistinguishable from the ability to hear and speak at a distance. That is an old human dream. If you look at what we can do now with camera phones, how is this different from the ability for me to see what you're seeing three thousand miles away?

'As we're taking the push-to-talk over cellular, you can push buttons and talk to several people simultaneously. Soon we'll take it even further and you can push a button and several of your friends can see what you're seeing. You'll have the ability to monitor and control your home from the device. It won't be long before someone can ring my front doorbell in Chicago while I'm here in New York City talking with you and I'll see who it is; and if it is the delivery guy, I can push a button and let him in.'

Experience segments

'What are the new experiences that these abilities create?' asks Frost. 'A good way to size markets is to divide the world into segments of people. Another way is to focus on experiential or circumstantial segmentation, which are different kinds of things that you like to do. For example, you could argue that there is an experience segment called 'at the edge of civilization'. If you are a rich person, you might be in a segment that takes you to Aspen going skiing every year, or a segment called "I don't have a lot of money and I have a camper." The experience involves a device that will keep me in touch well beyond the range of conventional civilization.

'Take the teen segment. They are very gregarious, very extroverted and club-oriented and explore experiences. In those circumstances, you may want to share with your friends what you are seeing and where you are. You may want to show off a little bit. If you go back to the 1970s, you may remember the glowing hoops. Now you can almost do techno-kinetic, sound-sensitive jewellery out of these devices that you wear around your neck. You can also set it so that it's got lights and various configurations and considerations that you can set to respond to the base beat of the music. We've put a few of these out in Japan, China and elsewhere.'

To Frost, the point is not necessarily the youthful age of these early adopters, but openness to new experiences. Enable the experience, and they will come. 'I'm not saying that you should go after kids only. Say there are two million white-collar people that carry Blackberries. You could argue that, in one segment, what matters is efficiency, productivity and connectivity. However, those users may also like cool designs and games. One of the biggest markets for games actually consists of business guys. I tend to look at those segments as less adaptive in terms of people and more at different aspects of a person. Experiential segmentation helps you to see things differently.

'No one knows where the money is in this business,' says Frost. 'Remember when NTT DoCoMo decided to transform their handsets into US $700 colour screen miniterminals, and the conventionalists said that it was never going to take off until you get those prices down. Guess what happened? Teen girls in Japan showed up with US $700 to buy these terminals. Or take the sneakers. There was a time when people weren't willing to pay more than US $25 to buy a pair of sneakers. But if it was Air Jordan, you'd pay US $125 and stand in line at five o'clock in the morning to wait for your pair.

Source: the author's interview with Geoffrey Frost, chief marketing officer, Motorola, Inc, 30 June 2004.

Moto is after the *sensory* experience. "OHMYMOTO" is part of it, as well as "MOTOLIBERA" and "MOTOGRAPHIC". But to understand Moto as about sex would be a mistake. It's about experience. If the experience is sexy, that's a different story.

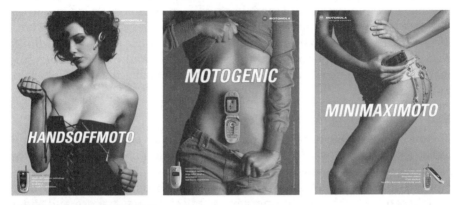

MP3MOTO, SURROUNDMOTO

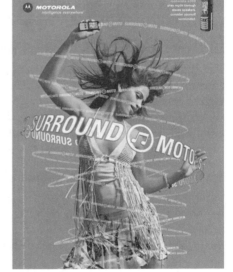

Source: Motorola, Inc.

Figure 7.5 Moto-morphing things

Segmentation by technology

Historically, technology was the basis for segmentation until the early 1990s. This base went hand in hand with low penetration. Technology and price drove the business. In this kind of segmentation, function rules over style. What matters is what the phone can do. In the 1980s, variations of Motorola's brick dominated the product portfolios, primarily in the business markets, and to a small extent in high-end consumer niche segments. Today, price and performance capabilities continue to dominate technology segmentation.

Low end: cheap entry-level phones

Today, the low-end cellphone segment means cheap entry-level phones with a small screen, small-to-medium size and weight. These phones are targeted to new users, the pre-paid market and those with lower disposable income. In the past few years, industry leaders like Nokia and smaller players like LG have increased their models in the low-end segment, partly because of the declining cost structure in China, but also to expand a foothold in India, emerging markets in Latin America and Asia, and in transitional economies in Eastern Europe.

Mid-range: growing replacement market

The mid-range segment provides for more mature users and particularly the replacement market, which has escalated with saturation. These models offer *more*; more features, more ergonomic designs, larger displays (for instance, Nokia 8310, Samsung A800). Mid-range has also given rise to a set of functional mobile devices, including games, MP3 players, camera and video phones. With the shift toward segmentation by functionality, this category has witnessed a shift from the candy-bar form to more diverse shapes and designs, particularly clamshells and colourful devices.

High end: wealthy early adopters and professionals

The high-end segment targets wealthy professionals, early adopters in the consumer markets and business users in the corporate market. It is characterized by two categories. Many affluent and business users tend to go with style phones (Nokia 7650, Samsung V200), just as corporate users and early-adopter techies have been targeted with bulkier models (DoCoMo's 3G FOMA phones optimized with the latest features and technologies).

Smart phones: high-end consumers, business professionals

Since Apple's legendary Newton project in the late 1980s, both mobile vendors and IT enablers have struggled to create the first popular mass-market smart phone.[6] Typically, smart phones have larger display, the form factor and more features, from the Orange SPV to the popular Sony Ericsson P800. As a category, the smart phone is essentially a phone with PDA functionality, whereas PDAs are seen as PDAs and only secondarily as phones. The early smart phones provide content and web browsing. They employ standard and new operating systems and protocols (Pocket PC, WAP), while synchronizing with other devices (desktops and mobile phones). Producers tend to depict smart phones as a separate category, but from the standpoint of the marketplace they are high-end mobiles, because of the price factor. The subset has great growth and expansion potential (see Box 7.2).[7] Still, despite large R&D efforts and making unprecedented concessions on the look and feel of its software, Microsoft's first smart phones hit the US market only in autumn 2003. Nokia's 7710 widescreen smart phone followed in spring 2005.

Box 7.2   SMART PHONES: THE MICROSOFT VISION

'The ITU Telecom conference in late 1999 was a watershed event for our company,' says Ed Suwanjindar. 'It was there that Bill Gates outlined a vision for connecting people to information and each other through a great software experience.' As lead product manager in the mobile devices division at Microsoft, Suwanjindar is responsible for marketing a range of new software for intelligent mobile computing devices. The division is focused on developing software for targeted device categories, including the Windows-powered pocket PC and smartphone.

'As we got engaged in the wireless landscape, we realized that it's a global industry and built our organization accordingly,' says Suwanjindar. 'We've been doing market research, and watching people and customers all over the world, in Stockholm to Hong Kong and Bangkok, from London to Miami, in order to understand how people use mobile devices. 'We have tried to learn what are the key scenarios, how people interact with their phones, and taking those lessons and applying what we know about software and data experiences.'

Great software, loyal customers

Ever since Apple's Newton in the late 1980s and the first Palms in the early 1990s, Microsoft had been exploring opportunities in the hand-held market. As a business proposition, the mobile business became attractive only later. 'Prior to 1999, there was work on Windows CE,' says Suwanjindar. 'Those products weren't wireless-enabled scenarios. 'Those were basically PC-through-hand-held scenarios. It was around early 2000 that hand-held devices became more prevalent, and people wanted to have mobile PDAs. We identified with the potential opportunity to connect with a growing customer base and to provide a great mobile software experience. That's when we began to deliver new software products.

'The Pocket PC was the first milestone. The next wave of opportunity followed with the convergence of voice and wireless data devices. In the past, we had asked ourselves, 'How can we add wireless to the existing software experience?' Now we went further, 'How can we build software with wireless capability?' That's when we started building software specifically for phones. When we looked at the wireless landscape, it was pretty clear that this was an entirely new market with very steep projected growth for smart devices. When we say "smart", we are thinking about devices that you can add software to, so that people can have a rich online and offline experience. We saw this as an opportunity of hundreds of millions of units and an entirely new market for software platforms and applications. So we began to think about extending the reach of Microsoft infrastructure, applications, services and end user experiences to mobile subscribers.'

At Microsoft, the software experience is considered critical to develop attractive and differentiated services, which drive the marketplace. 'Certain fundamentals apply to network service providers, whether they are fixed-line or wireless; or represent analog, digital or multimedia networks. Their business challenges remain constant. They must acquire new subscribers and retain existing ones. They must find ways to deliver new and differentiated applications and services to their subscribers. The technologies that empower the strategies change; but the business fundamentals remain the same. We continue to cooperate with both our operator partners and developer communities. If you have great applications that motivate people to use wireless data on their devices, you may have services that capture subscribers in a very "sticky way", to use an old dotcom term.

'We have an internal saying, "Fixed network usage drives wireless addiction." The idea is that certain things that people find interesting on their desktops become addictive experiences when they are able to take advantage of them on mobile. They recapture moments that would otherwise be lost. So if you're sitting in a train station waiting for the next train to arrive, or standing in the grocery line at the checkout, or waiting for a hotdog at a baseball game; if you use those moments to do really mundane things like deleting e-mail or texting, that can be a really powerful experience.

'Today, a lot of these experiences are associated with things on PCs, but people have begun to do things solely on mobile devices. We believe that the true and complete customer experience is a composite of the two. It reflects both the PC and internet world and the things that people have begun to do solely on mobile devices.'

Source: the author's interview with Ed Suwanjindar, lead product manager, Microsoft Mobile and Embedded Division, 8 April 2004.

Struggle for smart phones

In the mid-1990s, then-CEO Bill Gates assigned 300 Microsoft staffers to create a stripped-down version of the Windows PC operating system, which became the basis for the Pocket PCs by Hewlett-Packard, Dell and others. Gates was looking ahead to when hand-helds would converge with mobile phones, transmitting data through the air as easily as the spoken word. Determined to avoid the PC makers' price competition, Nokia and its rivals, including Ericsson and Motorola, formed a venture (Symbian) to develop their own operating systems for smart phones.

At Microsoft, the Pocket PC division began to work on licensing deals with the second-tier mobile vendors. However, as the cellphone software was essentially the same as the Windows CE for hand-held computers, it had too many features and was too complicated for mobile users. In 1998, the Microsoft mobile devices team decided to design a new cellphone operating system. Meanwhile, the first handset partnerships stumbled, with a fraud lawsuit and the smart phone's poor sales and short battery life. These problems were coupled with negotiations with operators and new vendors, which demanded tailored software. As Microsoft compromised, the US $300 Motorola phone, released in October 2003, met with better reviews. Altogether, manufacturers shipped 459,000 Microsoft-based smart phones in the fourth quarter of 2003, which was far behind Symbian's 2.36 million but enough to move ahead of phones that used Palm and Linux software. Microsoft set its faith on corporate sales, as with hand-held devices. Since corporate buying could amount to 25 per cent of the smart-phone market, Microsoft hoped to take 80 per cent of that segment. Symbian, however, was challenging the software giant – in the marketplace and courts.

By August 2004, Symbian had widened its lead against Microsoft in the race to dominate the global market for software used in high-end handsets. Software supplied by Symbian controlled 41 per cent of the personal organizers and smart phones shipped worldwide in the second quarter, compared with 37 per cent in the same quarter a year before. Microsoft's share remained steady at 23 per cent, while the share of PalmSource fell to 23 per cent from 31 per cent.

Sources: Menn (2004), Pringle (2004b), Steinbock (2002).

Other devices

Since the late 1990s, there has been growing consolidation and convergence in other portable devices as cost-conscious manufacturers have sought to meet customer needs. Today, the key categories comprise PDAs, handheld PCs, tablets and notebooks.[8]

- Besides calendars, address books and other organizing features, *mobile PDAs* are thin and lightweight, and have colour screens (such as Palm, Casio and HP). Unlike 3G laptops, they are less expensive, and offer less powerful solutions. The segment comprises two kinds of devices. The first provide wireless connectivity through add-on modules (Handspring, Visor). The second offer PDA devices with embedded connectivity (Sagem WA3040, Trium Mondo).[9]
- With *notebooks and tablets*, wireless connectivity has been enabled by modems, and more recently by integrated solutions. Operating systems include Windows, Windows CE and Linux. Providing similar functionality as notebooks, tablets allow all input to be done via the screen. As hybrids of notebooks and PDAs, the magazine-size tablets have been employed in e-books.
- Essentially mini-desktops, *hand-held PCs* support portable office facilities, providing a lightweight, pocket-sized alternative to a full-sized notebook (such as HP Jornada 820 and Sharp Mobilon). Because of their similar functionality, the distinction between low-end notebooks and hand-held PCs is becoming blurry.

Segmentation by lifestyle

Lifestyle segmentation evolved with the digital transition in the 1990s. It emerged with rapid growth and saturation. New categories, segments and styles drive the business. In lifestyle segmentation, it is (the user's personal) style that reigns over (the handset's technological) function. What matters is not just what the phone can do, but what it represents. Despite increasing competition and brand fatigue, Nokia remains in the forefront of lifestyle segmentation. Around 2001–3, Nokia developed its product category matrix, which can be illustrated by six style categories (basic, expression, active, classic, fashion and premium) and five application categories (voice, entertainment, media, imaging and business) (Figure 7.5). Different players have different segmentation strategies, but certain categories recur in these strategies.

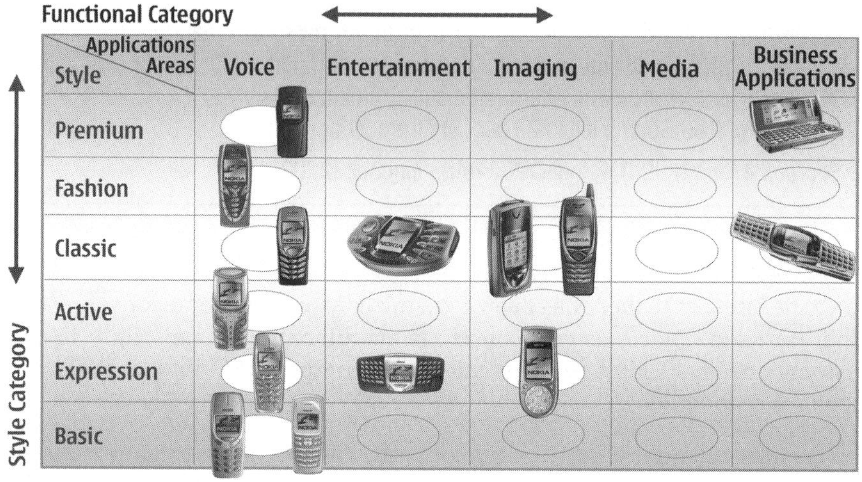

The matrix helps to identify potential new products in each cross-section between style and function. For different models to be successful, Nokia thinks they must be differentiated from one another in terms of features, functionality and design. Where Nokia employs the matrix to dominate the categories, rivals exploit it to challenge the industry leader and to establish a foothold in niche segments.

Source: Nokia Corp.

Figure 7.6   Nokia's product category matrix

Generic: the common denominator

This is the Ford Model T of the style market. As the 'all in one' mobile device, it provides the generic options in voice and data. It offers basic characteristics that are common to all lifestyle categories. It is the common denominator. Since it reflects the greatest volume of devices, it is also the most competitive space, from the early efforts (the first generation WAP phones, Microsoft's smart phones, Qualcomm's pdQ) to later models (Siemens ME45, Samsung SPH-i330). It favours large brand players that can generate low margin, but high volume on a worldwide basis. Conversely, it provides niches for smaller players that focus on small volumes but high margins.

Entertainment: media potatoes

These devices emphasize larger colour displays and cameras. They have heavy focus on multimedia content. Because of its very nature, the category has attracted not just leading mobile players, but established consumer electronics giants. Along with Nokia, Sony Ericsson, Sony, Panasonic (Matsushita), Samsung and Siemens were among the first to enter the segment, hoping to leverage their existing capabilities in movies, music and games. The segment offers many devices for a single use, including game playing, sports, music and video. Take, for instance, the issue of colour. In 1999, some Japanese 502i series models were equipped with colour displays. By late 2000, a wealth of colour content was available and virtually all new models came with colour displays. The 503i series was equipped to handle Java, which allowed the content producers to offer a wealth of new applications.

Youth: cheap and chic trendsetters

Where generic and entertainment segments are defined by the use function of the device, the youth segment is defined by time and price. As early adopters of new technologies and kingmakers of 'cool', young demographics are vital to vendors and operators. The segment is highly differentiable and provides a significant entry point. It accounted for the SMS explosion in the late 1990s, while boosting the penetration and usage rates in the advanced markets. It is likely to play a key role in instant and multimedia messaging. Starting with Nokia's changeable covers, customization by the vendors and personalization by users has been very typical of this segment, particularly with ringtones. With its chat pack, messaging features and key chain-like adornments, the slim and compact Motorola T191 and many other models have pushed hard toward increasing personalization.

Fashion: style over function

Originating from the style-conscious high end, this segment draws from the fashion business. It emerged at the end of the 1990s, with the introduction of Nokia's 8860 which made Nokia's chief designer Frank Nuovo the trendsetter to follow at Vogue. The fashion phones (Nokia 8910, Siemens Xelibri, Motorola V70, Samsung A500) are not an entry point, like the youth segment, but closer to the entertainment segment. Representing the purchase of the second or third handset, they reflect the replacement market. With business phones, function rules over style. With fashion phones, style reigns over function. With business phones, it is what the phone does that counts; with fashion phones, it is how the phone looks that really matters. Many fashion users seek for lower-cost replicas of high-end designs. But the segment has also given rise to an intriguing luxury niche, with the launch of Nokia's Vertu, which has been followed by DBTEL's diamond phone, Samsung's high-end strategies, and Sony's Qualia offerings.

Business: function over style

The business segment is all about excellence and high data capabilities; about a single device for many uses. Function reigns over style. It is definitely what the phone can do that counts. In large corporations and small and medium-sized businesses, the business handset is a productivity tool, from Palm and Blackberry to the Nokia Communicator and Microsoft's smart phones (Samsung's -i700, or Orange SVP). The leading vendors, operators and IT players have targeted the largest clients across industries, but the corporate space also provides new opportunities to small entrants, from tailoring devices to tailoring services. Moreover, certain industries have a great need for specific sub-categories, from travelling business professionals (who have a need for multimode mobile devices) to industrial firms (which need rugged devices and high-end industrial data collection).

Segmentation by functionality

Since the late 1990s, the industry has given rise to entirely new applications, because of the rapid cost decline, increasing bandwidth, and the convergence of mobility and information technology. Segmentation by functionality concentrates on single-purpose phones, with one dominant function, such as games, data, messaging, music and so forth. Augmenting technology and lifestyle segmentation, this kind of segmentation is complementary and driven by optimization. What matters is not just what the phone can do, but how well it can do whatever it does. The early single-purpose handset market has been dominated by Nokia. Currently, many of these handsets are targeting the youth market (teenagers and adolescents), even though much of the youth market is expected to be absorbed by other segments.

Imaging: mobilizing digital images

In 2002, EMS and MMS provided a powerful boost to imaging, while the camera handsets arrived hand in hand with colour displays (see Box 7.3). The first-generation phones offer a built-in small digital camera or have the ability to snap on a camera attachment. In comparison with photographic digital cameras, the camera phones provide relatively low resolution. Sharp and J-Phone introduced the first camera phone (J-SH04) in November 2000. By January 2004, some 60 per cent of mobile phones in Japan were camera phones, and in 2005 almost all mobile phones will be camera phones. Top-range models had two megapixel cameras and autofocus, which pose increasing challenges to the imaging industry.

Box 7.3 THE BIRTH OF THE IMAGING ERA

'We felt very much alone,' says Juha Putkiranta. 'People had little faith in imaging.' It was November 2001 and Nokia had just launched its first handset with an integrated digital camera. Putkiranta, chief of the imaging business unit, had no doubts that camera phones would take off. But sceptics thought the mobile devices were just over-priced gadgets. 'The idea of imaging functionality coupled with the cellular functionality was still very new,' he recalls.

Rewind to 2000

The mad rush to the imaging frontier had been initiated in 2000. 'We didn't have the capabilities yet,' recalls Putkiranta. 'Original equipment manufacturers (OEMs) sold us the package. The first imaging products were launched in Japan, primarily by J-Phone (today Vodafone Japan). Then Nokia brought out an integrated camera into the market. The 7650 provided a major push in the marketplace to deploy camera phones. (See Figure 7.6.) It was barely 150 grams. It has a full-graphics colour display and a Series 60 platform. Image capture had 640 x 480 resolution. Phone display is used as a view finder. Photo album had a 3.6 MB dynamic memory for images, calendar, phonebook, messages, and add-on applications. Since those days the functionality has penetrated very rapidly.'

Then came the second phase. 'It happened with a significant increase in quality, original capabilities that characterize global phones. The quality migration from the camera industry has begun. Megapixel cameras are now in the mass market in all continents. At the same time, we see other convergence phenomena at work in other parts of the value chain.'

Costs and quality

'I had two concerns,' he acknowledges. 'First of all, I knew many people thought the mobile devices were too expensive, over-priced gadgets, as it were. Then there was the concern that the quality wasn't sufficient for users to accept the phone. In both cases, we proved sceptics wrong faster than even we anticipated. In effect, the quality response was pretty strong. Subscribers saw the value quite quickly. And when the unit sales took off, the costs declined fast.'

A week after the Nokia 7610 with a megapixel camera was introduced, Nokia's CEO and chairman Jorma Ollila spoke in the general meeting in Helsinki, in March 2004. 'Imaging is, at the moment, the most important mobile multimedia application. Camera phones became mass-market products in 2003 with more than 70 million units sold worldwide. Nokia has been one of the first companies to bring high-end imaging devices to the market.' (Ollila, 2004). That month, seven mobile vendors announced new models with megapixel cameras, shooting pictures with a million points of resolution; three times more than the current camera phones, and comparable to digital cameras a few years back. At US $400–600, they were still further away from the mass market, but volume sales would force a substantial price decline over time.

Success

In 2003, sales of camera phones exceeded 84 million units worldwide, twice the purchases of conventional digital cameras. Consumers were intrigued by the convenience of having a point-and-shoot camera always available. In 2004, the camera phone sales were expected to double, to 169 million units (about 25 per cent of all handsets), while consumers would snap some 29 billion photos. By 2006, the sales would more than double again, up to 380 million.[10]

As the volume sales exploded, mobile vendors established a solid foothold in the low-end imaging segments, while digital camera makers retreated to protect the high-end segments. They were also joining forces. Nokia, for instance, allied with Kodak to launch worldwide thousands of kiosks in stores, which accept digital photos from CDs, memory cards or via wireless connections and print photos for 40 cents each.

Nokia also launched an assortment of gizmos that help consumers enjoy their photos at home without a PC, including Nokia Image Album – which Putkiranta has termed a 'digital shoebox for snapshots'. Today, the idea of imaging functionality coupled with the cellular functionality is an integral part of the look and feel of the mobile device.

Source: the author's interview with Juha Putkiranta. SVP, Imaging Business Unit Multimedia Business Group, Nokia, 1 June 2004.

The Nokia 7650 phone has an integrated digital camera. It allows the user to store, download or send pictures to a friend as a multimedia message (MMS).
Source: Nokia Corp.

Figure 7.7   Introduction of the Nokia 7650 (March 2004)

Messaging: business and SMS

Bulkier than typical phones, these handsets are focused on the messaging function. They incorporate features such as SMS/EMS, MMS, a built-in or clip-on camera, larger colour screen, large keyboard or Qwerty keyboard, large memory capacity, WAP and data services. In business markets, many single-function handsets have been inspired by RIM's Blackberry and even older messaging/e-mail devices (such as the BlackBerry 7510). In turn, the BlackBerry 7700 Series of wireless hand-helds allows business professionals to access e-mail, applications and an integrated phone, all from the palm of their hand. Nokia's entry model in this space was 5510 text-messaging device, which has been superseded by the messaging portfolio, including the Nokia 6822 phone.

Games: from Nintendo's Game Boy to N-Gage

These handsets are focused on the gaming function, incorporating attributes such as pre-loaded games, larger colour displays, Java, a joystick, data services and unique game-play designs. Vendors were intrigued by the potential of the gaming devices as a subset of the 'entertainment' lifestyle segment, as well as a potential disruptive force in the traditional video game market. Around 2003–4, the gaming space was 'hot', stimulating traditional producers and developers (Nintendo), consumer electronics giants (Sony's

PlayStation), IT concerns (X Box), even Hollywood studios (for more on mobile games, see Chapter 6). Intense rivalry, however, posed significant challenges to new mobile entrants, such as Nokia, Motorola and others.

Music: downloading ringtones

As early as December 1999, NTT DoCoMo introduced in Japan the 502i series, which added support for downloading ringtone melodies. The innovation created a huge market for downloadable ringtones. These handsets are focused on the music function, incorporating attributes such as a mobile music player for MP3 and AAC files, stereo FM radio, digital recorder, Java and data services. By 2004, many handsets already provided a built-in FM radio, polyphonic ringtones and MP3 support. Because of Apple's iPod, the category was 'hot', but as consumer electronics giants were following in the footprints of the pioneers, intense rivalry was bound to depress excess profits. In the music-focused handsets, Nokia's entry was the 3300 phone. In addition to Kyocera (whose KURV entertainment device featured user-changeable 'smart skins'), the segment has been targeted by Sony Ericsson, which will sell music-playing mobiles under its Walkman brand, while working closely with Sony Connect and Sony BMG, its music division, on content.

The early emphasis on messaging and imaging handsets may reflect experimentation rather than endurance. In the long run, these devices may be consolidated with multi-function portfolios, which will be shaped by user needs rather than product development potential.

Segmentation by experience

In the 1990s, the mobile industry became obsessed with generational technologies, argues Motorola's marketing chief Geoffrey Frost. The focus was misplaced. It should have been about the new technology enhancements to the abilities that the industry was creating for users. The differentiation is no longer just in the devices, but increasingly in the experience of using those devices (see Box 7.4). It is not just the *device* (say, the 'razor-thin' Moto RAZR V2) that users find intriguing, but the *experience* of this 'thinness' (until, of course, the uniqueness of that experience is imitated and competed away).

Experiential segmentation first evolved in the most advanced Asian markets toward the end of the 1990s and, in the European and US lead markets around 2002–4. This base has accompanied high penetration, increasing usage and globalization. In this kind of segmentation, function and style are table stakes. What matters is not just what the phone can do or represents, but what kind of experiences it can provide to the user. The new customers are sophisticated and informed. They want the best technology that fits their needs. They want the greatest style that fits their style. But they also want multi-sensory experiences through the branded product and services.

Box 7.4   THE WORLD ACCORDING TO MOTO

'In the World Trade Organization riots in Seattle, there was a photograph of a policeman wailing away on a protestor with his baton and the protestor had a bat in his hand. A journalist noticed that both were wearing the new Nike batting gloves. As he interviewed them and asked why they chose this product for street rioting, the kid turned to him and said, "Because it's the real deal man!"'

'If you think that you are going to chase cool, you will fail,' says Geoffrey Frost, Motorola's marketing wizard. 'You have to figure out what's the right thing to do and what's different. If you do it really well, it generates a real buzz around a product.' The most fundamental lesson Frost took from Nike to Motorola is that cool is a 'by-product of something very real'.

From Nike to Moto

Before joining Motorola in 1999, Frost was global director of advertising and brand communications for Nike, where he oversaw brand strategy, advertising, direct marketing and Nike.com. Highlights from his experience at Nike include Michael Jordan's 'Frozen moment' and Tiger Woods' 'Hello world' and 'I am Tiger Woods' campaigns.

'Paul Galvin, the founder of Motorola, named this company according to the words "motor car" and "Victrola", which became Motorola,' recalls Frost. 'Motorola took the large Victrola. It was miniaturized and bolted to the dashboard of the car. That was the first car radio and it created a new kind of experience, a mobile experience. Drawing from this rich history, "Moto" is about rediscovering and reinventing the language.'

'Be all that you can be'

Nike's footwear and Motorola's mobile devices are used by youthful demographics. and both draw from innovation and fashion. Both have a physical form factor, but that is only part of what they are. This is typical to both Nokia and Nike.

Excellence, or 'to be all you can be', is not something that is typical to Olympic heroes only. Think of the Nike mission, 'To bring inspiration and innovation to every athlete (if you have a body, you are an athlete) in the world.' And then think of Motorola's concept of 'intelligence everywhere'. It is something that is no longer reserved only for the astronauts that Motorola once prepared to land on the moon. It belongs to everybody, just like your mobile device – 'the device formerly known as the cellphone'. This is not your father's Motorola. It is driven by the quest for cool.

Quest for cool

'In the 1930s, Paul Galvin was almost turned down by a board of directors because he believed that there would be World War II and that the wireless would play a key role,' says Frost. 'Motorola researched new ways to miniaturize the hand-held, which led to the Walkie-Talkie, the precursor of the mobile phone. In the 1970s, AT&T said that only car phones were possible, but Motorola came up with the first portable phone. That's the kind of heritage we've got. It's about creating the right things, not just need points but possibility points.

'For a company like Motorola that has been around for three quarters of a century,' says Frost, 'the temptation is to try to make things cool. The challenge is to try and figure what are the right things to do. That's how things were done initially.'

At Nike, the dilemma was how to stand out in a commodity business. It's not that different in Motorola's business. One of Frost's first moves was to dump Leo Burnett Worldwide and McCann-Erickson Worldwide, handing Motorola's US $400 million-a-year ad budget to Ogilvy & Mather Worldwide, which has created arresting and whimsical commercials. What speed has meant in Nike, communication means in Motorola. In both cases, functionality goes hand in hand with style that's 'cool'.

Genealogy of communication

At Nike, each product can trace its roots back through the company's family history – to the people, innovators, designers, tinkers, builders, athletes, coaches, teams and consumers who inspired its predecessors. Innovation and inspiration follow from this 'genealogy of speed'. At Motorola, Frost seeks something similar following the company's genealogy of communication. Cool is also about co-creation, working with the users – and sometimes beyond the users.

'The famous American circus impresario P T Barnum, once said, "What if you give the public what it wants and the public doesn't want it?" People cannot imagine what they have never seen before, so the definition of a great product idea is something that people cannot imagine, have never heard of and can't live without. Everybody wishes there was a neat answer to that question. A lot of what we do is to imagine that some of the new experiences that we've created are validated and right. We do it co-creatively with users.

'Seoul, Korea used to be quite backward,' says Frost. 'Now it's one of the hippest towns in the world and very advanced in technology. A lot of people dismissed NTT DoCoMo's early success, arguing that it stemmed from Japan's low internet penetration. The reality is that if you can travel in and out of these environments, you'll often find that a compelling new experience that happens in one place is suddenly immensely attractive in other places. But it's not a simple grid.'

Michael Jordan's heel

'At Nike, we were not a bunch of people up there designing sneakers, we were into sports. We did not hire athletes to promote our products. We asked athletes to become partners in creating our products. Once, Michael Jordan was trying out the latest version of shoes, working on the next year's product. We had a tiny factory out in Oregon where we make prototypes. So he comes over to the designer and says, "You know, the heel is higher than is right for me." The designer says, "No, no, it is exactly right, really." Michael Jordan wasn't persuaded. We finally took it back to the lab and measured it and sure enough we found out it was 1 or 2 mm to the height of the heel. This co-creative aspect of dissolving the barriers between the creators and the consumers is the only way to proceed. Then the question becomes, "How do you organize to do it?"

'It requires engagement, a transparent organization that breaks down the walls and lives in and out of the world of service," says Frost. Outside his cramped office, walls have been torn down to inspire collegiality. He has flung open the doors to the outside world to hear what customers want and to exploit new ways of designing, producing and selling handsets.

Source: the author's interview with Geoffrey Frost, chief marketing officer, Motorola Inc, 30 June 2004.

With features, it is what the product can do that matters. With image, it is what the product represents that counts. With functionality, optimal performance is the prime objective. With experience, it is what the consumers feel, think and do in relation to the product that counts. In the first two cases, the marketer's focus is on the device itself; in the last one, it is valued only instrumentally as part of a richer experience, not in and of itself.

Interaction maps

Instead of branding the product as experience, the focus can be shifted from customer experience to experience innovation. Some marketers have developed 'interaction maps' to visualize what the interaction is currently and the experience it gives rise to. The objective is to create an experience that is aligned with the brand (Raeghi and Calder, 2002).

Customer experience management

Still another approach is customer experience management, 'the process of strategically managing a customer's entire experience with a product or a company'. This involves several steps, such as analysing the experiential world of the customer; building the experiential platform; designing the brand experience; structuring the customer interface; and engaging in continuous experiential innovation (Schmidt, 2003: 17).

With experience, marketers tend to combine products, services and places into a multi-sensory brand encounter, which may be recurrent or involve extended contact with the brand.[11] Experiential marketing does not render obsolete either technology or lifestyle segmentation, but occurs within and across those categories and segments that these two approaches have made possible. It is focused relationship marketing.

TOWARD WEARABLES

In the past, the handset was named by its underlying technology, as the cell-phone in the United States, or as the bulky device one carried, as evidenced by the French *le portable*. In Japan, it is *keitai denwa*, a carried telephone, or simply *keitai*. In China, it is *sho ji*, or 'hand machine', but the early mobile was better known as a *dageda*, which literally means 'big brother big', in reference to the triad bosses of Hong Kong cinema who were often seen to carry mobiles before the use became widespread. In the 1990s, the Finnish Nokia dominated handsets, which came to be called *kännykkä*, which really refers to an extension of the hand, as in something longer than a hand. This was a shorthand for intelligence within the reach of hands, a notion that Motorola soon trademarked as 'Intelligence everywhere'.

In the past, the terminal was at the heart of the mobile experience, which was confined to ears (voice communications), except for the SMS capability. Today, this sensory experience is being enriched as 'portables' are turning into 'wearables'.

Wearable intelligence

In April 2002, Sprint launched the first wearable cellphone in the United States, with a screen to display personalized greetings such as 'Wassup?' and 'How ya doing?' To match mood, one just had to change the decorative side panels. The US $149.99 phone, which weighed just 3.7 ounces, was made by the Korean mobile phone maker LG. Despite the size of an ice cream sandwich, it was bundled with games and wireless web access. In January 2003, Bill Gates announced the launch of smart wristwatches designed to receive and display continuous, up-to-date information through the use of a new nationwide wireless communication technology – and it was accompanied by others.

Wristomo

Making voice communication easy from anywhere, NTT DoCoMo worked in collaboration with Seiko Instruments to launch the Wristomo in May 2003. The first ever mobile phone to take the form of a wristwatch, it features a black and white display and has four buttons for easy control and the input of mail messages. The wristwatch came with a standard accessory kit including battery charger, cushioned pad and adjustable wristband.[12]

Nokia Imagewear

In September 2003, Nokia unveiled a new product group – Nokia Imagewear. Combining style, design and wearability with easy to use technology, these products provide unique and new ways for users to express themselves. The first products in the series are the Nokia Medallion I and II and the Nokia Kaleidoscope I. 'Technological innovations are now making these small, intelligent, wearable accessories possible,' says Frank Nuovo. 'Nokia intends to lead and shape this exciting new mobile lifestyle as it emerges over the next few years' (Nokia, 2003c).

NTT DoCoMo: FingerWhisper

By mid-2004, cellphones were already concealed in watches, jacket lapels, even earrings. NTT DoCoMo was pushing the limits even further. Worn on the wrist, the FingerWhisper is being developed at NTT DoCoMo Yokosuka R&D Center. It utilizes the human hand as part of the receiver. The watch-like terminal converts voice to vibration through an actuator and channels this vibration through the bones to the tip of the index finger (Figure 7.7).

Today, the concept of ubiquity lends itself to placing interfaces in the surrounding environment. The wearable terminal offers an alternative solution, with people carrying the interfaces and sensors. Initially, the mobile experience was about voice only; with content and other services; it will shift from ears to eyes, as well. At the same time, the experience will grow more enriching and tactile – thus preparing the way toward experiential innovation.

The FingerWhisper is a new kind of wearable telephone handset that utilizes the human hand as part of the receiver. Worn on the wrist, this watch-like terminal converts voice to vibration through an actuator and channels this vibration through the bones to the tip of the index finger. By inserting this finger into the ear canal, the vibration can be heard as voice. NTT DoCoMo calls this process the bone conduction receiving mechanism. Since the microphone is located on the inner side of the wrist, the posture of the user's hand, when using the terminal, is the same as when using a cellphone.

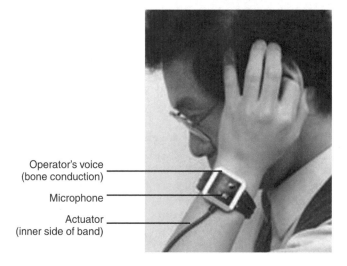

Operator's voice (bone conduction)

Microphone

Actuator (inner side of band)

Source: NTT DoCoMo, Inc.

Figure 7.8 FingerWhisper

Part 3

Mobile business services

8

Mobile marketing and consumer behaviour

Until the early 1990s, both technology innovation *and* marketing innovation in the mobile business took place in the United States. Today, mobile innovation is split across the world. The emerging mobile marketing and consumer behaviour reflect these new realities. The first advanced mobile marketing campaigns were initiated in Europe and Scandinavia, Japan and Korea, even in the growth markets of China and India – and only then in the United States.

THE MOBILE MARKETING BUSINESS

The origins

It was only with the early 1990s and the transition to consumer markets that the key industry participants – mobile vendors and operators – learnt to market their products and services.[1] By the end of the decade, the industry's problem was an inflated faith in marketing prowess. Today, advanced markets have been penetrated and saturated; with maturation, usage has become the new benchmark for success. Hypergrowth is more typical to emerging markets, where penetration strategies reign. According to the projections from the Kelsey Group, Ovum and Durlacher around 2002, wireless advertising revenues were expected to reach between US $16 billion and US $23 billion by the year 2005. These projections were up from estimates of US $210 million for the industry in 2000 (Carat Interactive, 2002). The new medium promised personalized, localized, interactive and immediate marketing opportunities, at least in the long term (see Box 8.1).

Box 8.1 SCIENCE FICTION OR REALITY? A DAY IN MOBILE LIFE

Flytxt is one of the leading mobile marketing service providers. It was co-founded by Pamir Gelenbe, who is consistently disappointed by the lack of sophistication of today's mobile users, especially given what is possible with a mobile phone. Here is his typical day – via the mobile-enabled life:

03:30

Awoken in the middle of the night by a picture message, which has been triggered from my home in France. It has an alarm system that detects motion, takes a picture and forwards it to my phone. It drives my girlfriend mad, especially because it's been set off by a stray cat! I promise myself to organize a trip home; it's been months since I've seen my aunt who lives nearby.

07:00

Three and a half hours later, I'm woken up again. I've downloaded my favourite song, Christina Aguilera's 'Beautiful', as a true tone and set it as my alarm. Funnily enough, it's less and less my favourite song every day.

07:30

I'm going to a developers' forum on Java applications this morning in Cambridge. As usual, I've left thinking about how I'm going to get there until the last minute. I check out the train times on my phone. The next train leaves in 30 minutes. I can just make it if I get my skates on. Before logging off, I automatically send a text to my phone, which I check again on my way.

08:07

Making my train by the skin of my teeth, I haven't had time to buy a paper for the journey, so try to get comfortable in my seat and settle into today's top news stories on my phone.

08:20

Already restless, I activate Bluetooth on my handset. In doing this, I automatically transform into a secret spy. I can identify other Bluetooth-enabled handsets in my carriage. One of the cool things you can do with Bluetooth is challenge other handset owners to multi-player games. With GPRS-enabled handsets, you literally have a world of gamers to choose from!

Although I'm a gamer, I have another motive for activating my Bluetooth. It also means that I can send messages to other enabled handsets, completely anonymously. When I'm feeling extremely mischievous, I send bizarre images, which confuses the hell out of people! Most people leave their Bluetooth activated and not everyone knows what it is, so they have no idea where they've come from.

This time, however, I've underestimated my compartment companion. I surreptitiously Bluetooth an unusual photo I keep of a cow baring its teeth to the user, sitting somewhere within a 10-metre radius of me. To my surprise, 30 seconds later I receive a Bluetooth back. They've Bluetoothed me a mooner! My expression must have given me away; I spot someone who's been hiding behind a newspaper close by begin to shake with laughter.

An unbelievable coincidence – it turns out to be someone I attended lectures with at college, on his way to the same seminar. Technology makes the world a scarily small place.

08:45

Before pulling into Cambridge station, my acquaintance remembers that the cab queues at the station are long, so he goes to his phone's Directories and books a local cab. It costs 50 pence, but we're in a cab as we step off the train, and arrive at the seminar on the dot of 09:00.

13:00

The seminar turns out to be worth the trip to Cambridge, and when I step outside, I discover it's a gorgeous bright autumnal day and decide to walk back to the station. I get directions from my phone by plugging in the postcode from the seminar invite printout. Another 50 pence in the pocket of the mobile operator, but I console myself with the thought that the pricing model for these services has to change one of these days, and feel virtuous that it's exercise and I'm saving money on a cab fare.

13:30

On the train on my way back I get a call from a friend who I haven't been in touch with for ages. Feeling the prankster in me coming on again, I decide not to answer immediately, but to use a new voicemail technology that I've downloaded to my phone to play another trick. The software allows you to listen in to the message as it's being left and also interrupt the speaker, if you want to speak to them. It's a handy piece of kit, especially if you're like me, and have handed out your mobile number too many times. As my friend is leaving a chatty message, I interrupt, pretending to be the answer machine, adopting my well-rehearsed robotic voice. I manage to completely freak him out for a few moments, but then he guesses what's going on. He's smart and I guess he's known me for too long.

14:30

Planning my next holiday as I walk back from the tube station, I go to the Time Out 'City Guides', one of the choices on my menu bar and go to Nice, France. I check out the blurb and the photos before going to the eating and drinking section – my favourite pastime. Then straight to Lastminute.com to book flights. It crashes a couple of times, but I finally get there.

15:30

I touch base with my colleagues before replying to e-mails. Although I check e-mails on my handset, I prefer to reply to them from my computer, otherwise it takes three times as long.

17:00

Halfway through the afternoon, I give myself a teatime break and play my favourite game on Game Arcade, 'Marcel Desailly'. After choosing my team line up, I (France) play Senegal and whip them into shape, finishing 2 goals to nil.

21:00

After getting down to a few hours' serious work in the office, I head for home. As a joke for my girlfriend I download an application from vibelet.com, which transforms my handset into a vibrator! There are more than the obvious advantages of being a technophile.

Source: Gelenbe (2003a).

For a century, US marketers, the great creators of mass marketing and brand building, dominated marketing activities worldwide, from Coca-Cola and Procter & Gamble to General Motors and General Electric, Intel and Microsoft. Today, however, innovations may emerge in a number of cutting-edge locations worldwide. The world's greatest marketers remain headquartered in the United States, but mobile leaders do not.

In the 1990s, internet marketing was pioneered in the United States, while most of the pioneering interactive agencies first surfaced in New York's Silicon Alley and California's Silicon Valley (Steinbock 2000). Mobile innovation has thrived in the GSM-driven Nordic countries and CDMA-driven South Korea, both of which lack scale and large, trendsetting marketing and media industries. Service innovation has flourished in Japan, but this success has proved hard to export worldwide. Much of the pioneering marketing service innovation has taken place in the United Kingdom. At the same time, the bold campaigns of relatively few agencies in China have attracted many blue-chip corporations, because of the massive scale of the marketplace.

Chinese burritos – via SMS

'Certain mobile data services are still dominated by text messaging, which is different from Europe and the States,' says David Turchetti, CEO of 21 Communications. 'It's used as a means of prompting consumers to a point of sale or to some desired action. It's not used as a branding medium. For example, when Kentucky Fried Chicken was launching a new product, they had a whole media mix around this product called the Lao Beijing, like an old Beijing Chicken Wrap, a kind of a Chinese burrito. Ogilvy was doing the advertising campaign, and we were invited to do mobile marketing. It entailed prompting consumers to download a coupon on their phones, which they would then take into the point of sale and actually show at the register to get a discount.'[2]

In the past, US marketers pioneered worldwide marketing campaigns. Now multinational marketers are pioneering worldwide mobile campaigns in advanced markets, such as Japan and Korea, and emerging markets, such as China and India. Based in Shanghai, 21 Communications provides digital and wireless solutions for media and marketing. Its clients include Philips, Johnson & Johnson, Lufthansa, Cigna Insurance, PricewaterhouseCoopers and Adidas.

'The mobile phone will surpass the internet PC, just because so many more people will have phones in China than those who have PCs,' says Turchetti. 'In Japan and Europe, SMS took off as a novel, cute, fun and flirtatious way to communicate. In China it was because of cost-effectiveness. Even today many in China only use SMS; they don't use the voice function at all. If you call them, they will cut you off before they pick up. They will hang up on you, then send a message saying, 'Who are you, what do you want, how can I help you?' Then they expect to continue the dialogue over the SMS. In Europe people can afford expensive communications, in China they can't.'

Marketing services and the mobile value chain

During the early 1980s, national telecom monopolies still dominated the industry value chains. Today, the value chain is dominated by mobile vendors and operators, IT enablers, and, more recently by content providers. A vital community of marketing services providers supports the delivery of mobile marketing campaigns with specialist services. In the early stages, some of these providers focus on technology development, others on marketing services; over time, the players will consolidate. For now, the key players comprise marketers, marketing agencies, mobile specialists and operators (Figure 8.1).

Marketers

To marketers, mobile marketing is an evolving medium, which presents great opportunities in customer relationships, via extraordinary reach, highly targeted campaigns and depth in customer intimacy. Mobile channels pose substantial challenges, including business and legal risks (privacy, spam), but potential rewards outweigh perceived risks. The long-term prospect of trans-lating mobile campaigns into point-of-sale instruments provides a powerful incentive even to sceptics.

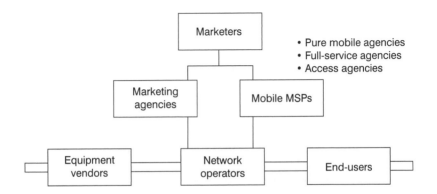

Figure 8.1   The role of mobile marketing service providers

Marketing agencies

Despite their slow entry into the business, traditional agencies have steadily increased investments in mobile campaigns across Europe, cooperating with other players in the emerging value chain. Providing expert services in marketing communications, marketing agencies develop broad media and marketing service plans, which now include mobile communication.

Mobile marketing service providers

These service providers specialize in mobile marketing. For now, they have conducted most mobile campaigns, individually or in cooperation with marketing agencies. Mobile specialists support agencies' creative ideas with appropriate mobile approaches. Marketing agencies have used a variety of contractual agreements to cooperate with service providers, while diversifying risk.

Operators

In the emerging mobile marketing value chain, operators market their own services in consumer and business markets. They also offer network access for mobile campaigns, which is seen as an opportunity to raise average revenues per user (ARPU).

In addition to these basic business models, other efforts reflect increasing specialization in demographics (youth markets), sectors (media), research and databases. A distinction has also been made between pure mobile agencies (small creative interactive agencies behind the early campaigns), full-service agencies (managing the full mobile marketing value chain, including technology and client-service teams), and access providers (which offer direct connections to operators) (Gelenbe, 2003b). In the long run, consolidation will turn mobile marketing services into the functions of a few leading marketing agencies and many niche players.

MOBILE MARKETING SERVICE INNOVATION

The mobile marketing space is still emerging. Almost all existing formats of user connectivity have been driven by SMS, and certain categories are still being tested. Mobile communication should never be a stand-alone channel, or an aggressive promotional tactic. It should be used to extend the presence of a company or product into an additional channel. The key is integration. Companies with a physical presence (a physical store, a catalogue, even a website) can leverage mobile media to extend their presence to be anywhere the user is at any time.

Dispelling the myth of the Starbucks latte discount ringing your mobile device

Due to the limitations of physical size and bandwidth of existing mobile devices, advertisers face the challenge of communicating a message in a limited space. For this reason, we will see a return to the sponsorship days as we saw in the early days of television and radio, where content of interest to the user will be 'brought to you by …'. As devices evolve and bandwidth increases, so will the clutter of wireless advertising, and marketers will begin to get much more creative and perhaps increase the entertainment value of their messages (assuming users accept this advance). As with all other media, advertisers will be forced to break through the clutter with more appealing, captivating messages.

The cliché vision of the future of wireless advertising is a wireless device ringing as a user walks by a Starbucks to offer a 20 per cent discount on a latte. This will never be practised for the following reasons:

- Starbucks would never attempt this annoying tactic as it would receive tremendous customer backlash such that would not be outweighed by increased sales from the promotion.
- In the same vein, Starbucks is an established brand and will not risk tarnishing itself with such a controversial effort. It will, on the other hand, invest in a locator device that will allow customers to locate (pull) the nearest retail shop through a locator database, ultimately leveraging location-based technology.
- In the event that any user wanted this 'service', he or she would opt in by signing up with the coffee shop or a provider such as Vindigo. By definition, these subscribers would be some of the organization's best customers (probably most profitable), so Starbucks would have little need to offer them a discount – these customers are Starbucks regulars and will react to media such as signage.
- Based upon the fact that there are thousands of Starbucks retail outlets nationwide, a wireless device would be in constant notification mode when its user was driving through any major metropolis. Again, this is the role of signage.

While Starbucks will not push out these sorts of discount notifications aggressively, it will invest in a service to allow its customers to locate the nearest outlet, and has already announced the ability to take pre-orders from wireless devices. Use of pull marketing will allow users to determine when they are interested in interacting with the coffee chain on their terms. Starbucks will surely offer these customers discounts and promotions on new or ageing items, such as 'Try our new x-rated coffee drink, the Naughtte Latte'.

Source: "The Future of Wireless Marketing", Carat Interactive, 2002; the author's interview with Barry Peters, VP Relationship Marketing & Evolving Media, Carat Interactive, April 26, 2004.

Toward the late 1990s, SMS first demonstrated the promise of mobile marketing, even if the technology infrastructure did not enable more sophisticated services. Today, mobile marketing is moving from the niche of the pioneering professionals into a core channel for the mainstream marketing industry. In late 2003, the Mobile Marketing Association defined mobile marketing in the following way:

> Mobile marketing is any form of marketing, advertising or sales promotion activity aimed at consumers and conducted over a mobile channel. Methods of communication for this type of marketing include voice files, SMS, MMS, WAP messaging, Java, SyncML and video and audio messaging.

> (MMA, 2003)

As the mobile channel provides a direct link to customer intimacy, it also underscores the threat of privacy violation, spam and the need for an industry code of conduct.

Marketing and mobile services

In the mobile space, marketing services are dependent on the current stage of technology development and service innovation; in practice, simple voice and SMS capabilities. Over time, mobile marketing shall deploy new mobile services (see Chapters 3–6):

- **rich voice:** marketing using voice communications, including simple or rich voice, and videophones;
- the **internet:** marketing using mobile internet, intranet/extranet access, in relation to mobile portals, banners, interstitials and the like;
- **messaging:** marketing deploying location-based services, people communications, such as SMS, MMS;
- **content:** marketing relying on information, entertainment, transaction, and databases.

With increasing bandwidth, greater cost-efficiencies and performance capabilities, the transition from voice to data is rapidly enabling new mobile services (see Table 8.1).

Because of their extraordinary reach, intimacy and interactivity, mobile devices offer an ideal venue for customer relationship marketing. For now, mobile marketing campaigns remain constrained by the available bandwidth, efficiencies and performance capabilities. However, with the transition from voice to data, the subsequent arrival of broadband cellular as well as new technology alternatives, these campaigns will evolve rapidly and grow quite sophisticated in the very near future.

Mobile relationship marketing

Mobile marketing can be understood as just another new channel, though – during its infancy – a trendy one. Ideally, customer relationship marketing provides real-time customer service by developing a relationship with each customer through the effective use of individual account information. Based on accumulating knowledge about each customer, companies can then customize market offerings, services, programmes, messages and media. In order to optimize the opportunities in customer relationship marketing, it must reach customers, develop and retain customer relationships (Figure 8.2).[3]

Penetrating markets, reaching customers

In this phase, the marketing task is to attract and identify mobile prospects and customers. The point is not to go after everyone, but to identify those that count and then go after them.

Developing and deepening customer relationships

At first, the task is to segment customers in terms of their needs and value to the marketer, in order to focus on the most valuable customers in terms of:

	Push	Pull
Multiple response	• Mobile distribution • Interaction initiated by a message to the user • User response required; multiple interaction loops • Dialogue, higher involvement • Creative design, imaginative interaction, apps to deal with dialogue • Opt-in database of mobile numbers	• Often media other than mobile (TV, etc) • Interaction initiated by a message by the user; multiple interaction loops • Code/number for the user to text to; participation in competition, voting, etc on other media • Dialogue, higher involvement • Creative design, imaginative interaction, apps to deal with dialogue
Single response	• Mobile distribution primary • Interaction initiated by a message to the user • May require a user response • Low involvement • Simple design and interaction	• Often media other than mobile (TV, etc) • Interaction initiated by a message by the user • Code/number for the user to text to; participation in competition, voting, etc on other media • Low involvement • Simplest form, requires just a single respond/acknowledge loop

Source: Based on Nester & Lyall (2003); White Papers and studies by FirstPartner, Flytxt, 12snap, Mobliss.

Figure 8.2 Building deep relationships: mobile matrix

Table 8.1 Mobile marketing services

Service	Characteristics	Notes
Content		
Information	*Trend toward 'TV-style' marketing*	Higher forms of content-driven
Entertainment		mobile marketing require high-speed
Transactions		networks and devices, as well as
Databases	↑	sophisticated mobile marketing
Internet		
Internet	Footnote link (linked ad)	Limited space; linking is critical
	– Competitions, special offers, etc	Perceived as spam-like irritation;
	Interstitials	graphics may slow mobile use
		Niche use, limited space
	Search listing (brand presented among top results)	
	Portal listing (brand listed in operator menu)	Recognizability, visibility
	Downloading (ringtone, icon, game) after SMS invitation	Cost factor; requires user sophistication; early phase success in youth markets
Messaging		
MMS	Most SMS formats may be used for MMS	Rich format; higher costs (will decline over time); requires critical mass for network effects (viral marketing)
LBS	User receives SMS or MMS message based on location	Emerging technology; privacy issues; cross-national differences; requires prior opt-in by users; may cause user backlash
SMS		
(push)	Sending SMS to targeted users	Typical to promotions; requires rewards for users to react; perceived as spam; regulation pressures
(pull/push)	Requires user opt-in (users text to a number to receive alerts)	Alerts on promotions, headline news, etc; content costs, perceived value for users; permissions-based database for other campaigns
(pull)	After promotion on other media (radio, TV, press, internet, etc) SMS used as a response venue Competition formats ('text to win')	Response rates high (but typical to early adoption phases); integration potential with other media / channels
(pull)	User sends SMS to a number to request a call back Call back	Feedback method for traditional media advertising (magazines, TV, outdoors); on internet callback options have proved useful
Voice		
Voice guidance	User responds to a campaign or TV show and phones to a number for voice registration / competition User follows guidelines (responds to a number to receive a code or to leave a message)	Common to TV shows and competitions; free / premium calls and length of number rental to be considered Premium charges; efforts to prolong user calls; regulation pressures

lifetime value (net present value of all future profits coming from purchases), margin levels and referrals, less customer-specific servicing costs. These preliminary efforts – customer segmentation and customer value – allow the marketer to interact in the right way with the right customers, learn more about their individual needs over time and thereby deepen the relationship.

Retaining and growing customers

Having attracted and identified appropriate customers and prospects and kept customers via segmentation and value, the marketer can begin to customize products, services and messages to each customer, individually.

In customer relationship marketing, winning companies are those that excel in acquiring, retaining and growing customers, via marketing activities and databases.

The role of marketing activities

Companies that know how to build attractive customer bases excel in customer-driven marketing activities. They know how to identify and attract appropriate prospects and customers. They know how to:

● segment these customers and focus on the most valuable groups;
● build marketing relationships with individual customers;
● deepen such relationships through the use of accumulated databases;
● customize products, services and messages to individual customers (Peppers and Rogers, 1993).

The role of databases

Winning companies also know how to collect information, build customer databases and apply database marketing. These databases comprise both consumer and business services.[4] They also play a central role in the new mobile services (for instance, NTT DoCoMo's i-mode and FOMA).

Mobile solutions provide an intimate way to support relationship marketing. Over time, the basic principles of relationship marketing – attracting, retaining and sustaining customers – will be accompanied by increasing sophistication in mobile services. 'Say, I'm walking in the street and see a billboard, it's about a car I'm interested in and has a Wi-Fi hotspot. I send an SMS to it and receive a small clip on the car into my mobile,' says Ami Hasan, a Finnish brand visionary. 'It's intriguing, but the long-term vision is still blurry. Coupled with the internet, the mobile is like the world's largest library, but the lights are not on.'[5] The secret is to figure out what the users will look for.

Privacy issues and permission marketing

If attempts to employ an aggressive hard sell in traditional mass marketing or segmentation have become self-defeating, parallel efforts to extend top-down push into the mobile space are doomed.[6] Mobile devices are interactive, immediate and highly intimate. These devices are not just something we use; they are something we *are*.

Since the late 1990s, trade associations have been proactive to deter privacy threats in the mobile space, by stressing best practices in managing consumer privacy. In the absence of user permission, efforts to invade the mobile space will be perceived as efforts to violate personal intimacy.

Intimate interruptions can be detrimental to the brand, the reputation and integrity of the agency and marketing service providers, while mobile operators know only too well that customer backlash translates to increased churn. The first indicators are not positive. While there are more than 160 million cellphone users in the United States, a tiny percentage of cellphone users are receptive to such marketing. In 2004, only 20 per cent of US cellphone users had received a text ad via cellphone. Of that group, 9 per cent said the ad bothered them, while another 9 per cent said they 'just deleted it'. Only 2 per cent said they had received an ad that was 'relevant for me'.[7]

FROM CAMPAIGNS TO DIFFUSION

According to conventional industry wisdom, mobile marketing is often portrayed as a toolbox of mobile technologies, from SMS and ringtones to alerts and video streaming. Similarly, in the early days of the internet, many technology marketers were so swept by the potential of emerging technologies that actual marketing activities were ignored. In reality, technology solutions *enable* marketing, but are no substitute for marketing.

Mobile marketing campaigns

Integration

Until recently, most mobile campaigns could use only SMS messaging, which is constrained to text and 160 characters. Despite the inherent limitations of SMS, it has proved very effective and generated high brand recall and response rates, particularly in the youth markets.

Mobile innovation provides new venues for relationship marketing, as evidenced by push and pull campaigns, and by hybrid campaigns. Typically, these campaigns have been launched by sending a message to the target user segment or by messages using other than mobile media (such as television, radio and leaflets).

More often than not, mobile relationship marketing is part of a broader campaign, and it is often subject to integrated marketing communications. In mobile campaigns, marketing messages are delivered to the user's mobile device. In a provider-driven campaign, the messages are pushed to the user; in a user-driven campaign, the initiator is the user who pulls the message, typically in response to information on other media (such as television, magazines, newspapers or flyers). In these campaigns, the delivery and reception of the messages is handled by computer systems, with little or no manual intervention.

Push campaigns

In push campaigns, marketing services are delivered directly to the user on the mobile device. In such campaigns, the service provider initiates communications. A push campaign is predicated on a list of targeted users with a marketing message that is compelling and preferably interactive. One of the first large-scale on-pack campaigns was carried out in the UK for Cadbury by FlyTxt and Triangle Communications.

Simple and complex messaging campaigns: pull via mobile (Cadbury 'Txt'n'Win')

Objectives:

Cadbury was faced with the problem of teenagers spending pocket money on mobile phone cards instead of Crunchies and Fuse bars. Cadbury needed to drive sales, rejuvenate the brand amongst younger audiences and accumulate intelligence about chocolate-eating behaviour in an effort to reinvigorate sales and better target consumers.

Flytxt products employed

Flytxt Labs bespoke development.

Solution

- Flytxt and Triangle Communications developed a major competition to run on chocolate wrappers, inviting consumers to 'Txt'n'Win'.
- Cadbury launched this first SMS based on-pack promotion on 65 million chocolate bars.
- Consumers were invited to 'Text'n'Win' when they bought any of the 10 leading Cadbury brands including Crunchie, Caramel, Time Out and Cadbury's Dairy Milk.
- Each bar of Cadbury's had a unique code which consumers sent in by SMS to see if they won a prize.
- There was more than £1 million in prizes to be won across the 10 participating brands. Prizes included 100 chances to win £5,000 cash and many more opportunities to win widescreen TVs, Sony Playstation 2s, DVD players, Palm Pilots and CD compilations.
- The promotion was groundbreaking, and it is still the biggest SMS-based sales promotion campaign ever carried out.

Results

- Cadbury received more than 5 million messages from the 'Text'n'Win' game.
- This equates to a response rate of 8 per cent.

> - The campaign gave Cadbury crucial and revealing data on consumer behaviour. The intelligence gathered allowed Cadbury to learn when people are most likely to eat chocolate and if there really is a special Friday feeling about Crunchie.
> - Cadbury enjoyed a strong Christmas and Dairy Milk increased its market share.
> - The final three months of the year saw chocolate sales volumes return to growth.
> - Shares in the group rose by 5 per cent, as investors were impressed with earnings per share rise of 16 per cent. The group saw turnover rise by 21 per cent to £5.52 billion.
>
> **Client testimonial**
>
> At the time of Cadbury's full year results, John Sunderland, the Group's CEO commented about the campaign: 'It gave sales a big lift at a time when the confectionary market has been pretty flat.'
>
> **Awards**
>
> No 1 Wireless Marketing Campaign, *Campaign*.
>
> *Source:* Flytxt Ltd 2004.

With push campaigns, brands and agencies have been compelled to develop an opt-in database of mobile numbers, which is a mandatory requirement in EU countries. In the past, push campaigns have had relatively high response rates (over 12 per cent, nearly double typical direct marketing channels), but these figures should be assessed with caution. During the early days of the internet, marketers discovered comparable phenomena with web marketing, but such rates did not prove sustainable. Often, they are typical of the fervent experimentation stage, when the medium still has novelty attraction.

Pull campaigns

In pull campaigns, the user requests a message (a phone call or a mobile message) from the service provider. In such campaigns, it is the user who initiates communications relating to the mobile marketing campaign. In the early years, some campaigns were set up to collect consumer profiles through the mobile media channel or to enrich information on existing consumer profiles with mobile data. In early 2001, 12snap, for instance, concluded a deal with McDonald's Germany to build a customer database of mobile numbers and handle ongoing promotions. The one-year campaign consisted of two stages. The first relied on a non-mobile approach, whereas the second relied on the mobile device. Flyers were distributed inside the restaurants for customer data capture. Customers then received an SMS confirmation of their registration to 'McSMS'. A database of more than 450,000 customers resulted from this opt-in. Thereafter customers were entertained with SMS and voice-based entertainment applications, such as:

- create your own burger;
- a 'shout into your mobile' competition;
- drive a Formula 1 car during the McRacing weeks;
- BigXtra logo download;
- guess the artist by listening to a sound snippet.

The campaign drove customers to the restaurants and had a positive effect on brand building. It became part of McDonald's marketing mix.

Single and multiple-response campaigns

In the past, single-response pull campaigns were the first mobile experience for many brands and agencies. Today, multiple response pull campaigns request user participation through various incentives, including games, ring tones and icons, and coupons. As mobile marketing joins the mainstream, rivalry for user attention will intensify.

Just as most mobile marketing campaigns can be grouped into push and pull campaigns, interaction may be based on a single or multiple response. In the past, a single response was often used to experiment with the new medium. This is giving way to more sophisticated campaigns, which rely on multiple response and characterize efforts to build and deepen relationships over time. If single-response push campaigns represent a simple mobile marketing campaign, multiple-response pull campaigns provide greater complexity, even with the current primitive technologies (Figure 8.4). Currently, most mobile campaigns are based on texting, the simplest form of messaging. Over time, the novelty and complexity of these campaigns may escalate dramatically, with combinations of rich voice, intranet and extranet access, location based services coupled with SMS and MMS, as well as content, from information and entertainment to transactions and databases.

Both push and pull categories have a role to play in mobile marketing. The former is typical to promotional campaigns, whereas the latter is characteristic of relationship development. The full spectrum of mobile message formats is relatively broad.

The success of American Idol

'With mobile, our philosophy is to be a one-stop shop, which means text messaging, mobile gaming, using Java Brew, ringtones or graphics,' says Brian Levin, CEO of Mobliss. 'Media companies and content suppliers want to go wireless. They don't care about the devices. They just want to reach people. For us, that has meant great opportunities – certainly with *American Idol*, but also with the work we've done with Coca-Cola and Nike.'[8]

In 2002 Mobliss, an Index Group company and leading developer and distributor of mobile media, marketing and entertainment content, took the remote control out of the hands of viewers and replaced it with a telephone. It engaged viewers with the same event on two different but complementary media. 'That's the key, to handle the intersection of two industries, technology and telecom, you've got to prove that you have the ability to deliver technology in an efficient fashion,' comments Levin. 'It is also important to handle Hollywood and Madison Avenue, especially for us since we're based in Seattle. For Mobliss, the big thing was landing *American Idol*.

Landing *American Idol*

'We had just licensed *Family Feud* and *The Price is Right* from Freemantle,' recalls Levin. 'They told us about their UK show called *Pop Idol*, which they were bringing to the United States as *American Idol*. At the time, there were dozens of reality shows and nobody knew which one was going to be big. *Survivor* was strong, but it could go either way.

'Shortly after our meeting, I flew to the UK for a conference. I arrived really late, but even at midnight there was this line around the block next to the Virgin Store. "What's going on?" I asked. "That's the guy who won *Pop Idol*," I was told. "His single is going on sale at midnight." I mean, *wow!* That was an indication that we were getting into something big.

'We had a good relationship with AT&T Wireless here in Seattle. So we started talking about *American Idol* and tried to get them to do it. We didn't do voting during the first season, but they decided to create mobile content around the show, including SMS and WAP. They called us because they knew we'd do it quickly. We implemented the programme within two weeks of notice. It was successful, and with the next season, we did full voting, which was then unheard of in the United States because most people didn't know anything about SMS at the time.'

The watershed

The year 2002 marked the first major interactive wireless programme delivered by a US television network when the fans of the Fox Television program *American Idol*, produced by FremantleMedia North America and 19 TV Ltd, passed through an opt-in process to receive news alerts about developments on the programme and news about contestants. Wireless subscribers on all major US networks participated in this programme.

'The problem is that SMS is really an accidental success,' says Levin. 'That technology was not meant for what it's being used for now. And in the case of broadcast television it poses a special difficulty because when Ryan Secrest gets on and says, "Hey, everybody vote now," the network can't handle all the simultaneous traffic. We spent countless months and man-hours working with AT&T to create enough capacity to handle the peak message flow with 2,300 hits per second. That's very difficult and high-risk because if we miss a vote, that becomes a huge issue. So we've got to make sure that the voting process is secure and that if something goes wrong, we still have every vote stored from every show ever aired.'

Fox's record-breaking show captivated some 40 million viewers in summer 2002. It allowed fans to text vote and give 'thumbs up' to their favourite rising superstar. Text voting added a new dimension of interactivity to a show already anchored in audience participation. Along with the broadcast network, carriers also gained. While they realized long-term benefits from increasing user awareness, acceptance and adoption of data-based mobile services, the sustained spike in text messaging brought about by on-screen prompts opened the taps on the messaging revenue stream. *American Idol* was the watershed event. Mobile technology enabled mobile services, which proved critical in building and deepening customer relationships.

Leveraging the brand

During the third season of *Idol*, Mobliss helped process more than 13.5 million text messages, including fan mail, sweepstakes entries, trivia and votes from AT&T Wireless customers. Earlier in 2004 Mobliss released 'American Idol – The Wireless Game' to extend viewers' experience of the hit television programme. 'Over the last three seasons of *American Idol*, we have witnessed an explosion of interactive television in the mobile marketplace,' contends Levin. 'Text voting in conjunction with *American Idol* and the overall success of the show has contributed to bringing mobile media into the mainstream.'

From the second season to the third season, Mobliss and AT&T Wireless witnessed an 80 per cent growth in the text messages sent in conjunction with *American Idol*. Viewers are now more likely than ever to participate in mobile calls to action. Interactive mobile components are driving awareness and extending the experience beyond the actual broadcast.

Enabling viewers to vote by text messaging is a key interactive element of the show, in each of the 30 countries where the local versions of the *Idol* brand have been produced. '*American Idol* was really the model case of success in the United States,' says Levin. 'Unlike in European countries, it also required us to handle interactive television activity in three large time zones. On the surface, it seems so easy to get a text message, but it can be real complex in the back.'

The experience was not critical just because the US marketplace had been behind European and Asian developments, but because it demonstrated that traditional mass marketing and personal (mobile) marketing do not have to be mutually exclusive. In effect, the two can be highly complementary.

Mass marketing and personal marketing

In the early 1990s, Don Peppers and Martha Rogers began to develop a new frame of reference for marketing: a paradigm based not on mass markets, but on markets of one customer at a time. This paradigm did not spring from the imperatives of assembly-line manufacturing, but from the possibility of computer-controlled, customized production, individualized distribution, and addressable, interactive commercial media. 'The old paradigm, a system of mass production, mass media and mass marketing, is being replaced by a totally new paradigm, a one-to-one economic system.'[9] These voices were augmented by the advocates of integrated marketing communications:

> Mass marketing was invented to sell standardized mass-produced products to a similarly standardized, undifferentiated mass of consumers… Enter a new age of advertising: respectful, not patronizing; dialogue-seeking, not monologuic; responsive, not formula-driven. It speaks to the highest point of common interest, not the lowest common denominator.
>
> (Schultz, Tannenbaum and Lauterborn, 1994: 5, 13)

While the original ideas may have been quite subtle, the net effect was not. The differences between mass marketing and personal marketing have often been magnified beyond recognition. Individualized production, distribution, promotion and advertising, and media have been perceived as the antithesis of mass production, distribution, promotion and advertising, and media. Where mass marketing has enabled only one-way messages, the argument goes, scale economies and market share, personal marketing has enabled possible two-way messages, scope economies and the share of customer spend.

Mass marketing and relationship marketing do differ, sometimes even dramatically. But as mobile marketing indicates, they are complements, not substitutes. Because of its reach and intimacy, mobility has extraordinary potential in driving audiences to mass media and marketing, while building and deepening customer relationships.

Mobility as a cross-media experience

According to Anssi Vanjoki, executive vice president of Nokia, mobility is much more than 'just another outlet'. It is the glue that will tie together different media. 'It will be a cross-media experience, personal media,' he says. 'Small multimedia device can be cross-media for magazine, you can have a POS camera that takes a bar code read, which automatically drives you more information, promotion or discount into your device. You can make a dull magazine page alive so that it's connected to the net. It is the mobile device that makes it possible. It's a cross-media platform.'[10] The decline of mass markets is not just a threat to mass marketers. It is also an opportunity, argues Vanjoki:

> We should define what we mean by mass marketing. Perhaps we should use the term volume marketing. The marketing efficiency comes from the volume of what you do. However, the mobile messaging that you do is more tailored and has higher personalization. It's high-volume but also highly differentiated. If you put an ad to a magazine, maybe you're using demographic information, or your market is well defined by the readership of that magazine. Perhaps you can get up to a 70 per cent hit rate of your segmented target audience. But it means that 30 per cent is wasted. With personal marketing and with permission marketing, you know that there's no waste.

Innovation adopter categorization

In the bestseller *Next*, Michael Lewis recalls a visit to Finland, the promised land of mobile:

> It wasn't until I traveled to Finland that I realized that there was a deeply serious commercial precedent for an unseemly interest in children. Oddly enough, a Finnish company, Nokia, had come to dominate the mobile phone business to the point where pretty much everyone now agreed that the Finns would be the first to connect mobile phones to the Internet in a way that the rest of us would find necessary.
>
> (Lewis, 2001)

The Finns' fascination with mobiles is culturally intriguing, but kids are not that different across countries. Nor is the early adoption of innovations a peculiarly Finnish phenomenon. In the United States, tweens, the earliest adopters of all, have driven the use of mobile (see Box 8.2). In fact, these issues are neither new nor exclusive to the technology sector. They have been explored in diffusion research for more than a century, even if the frameworks on the adoption process derive from the 1920s.

Diffusion and user acceptance

According to service marketers, 'customers participate in service production in a way that they do not with the production of goods, so acceptance of new technologies is much more critical in service industries' (Dabholkar, 2000). This acceptance is also a trade-off because it means loss of human interaction, the learning of new skills and the assumption of some liability. Conversely, the more these perceived costs can be reduced, the faster will be the process of diffusion. Such acceptance is predicated on the interplay of technology and market innovation.

Technology innovation

For mobile media, this requires interoperable service enablers, appropriate content development environment and tools, optimization of video content for mobile consumption, readiness of infrastructure equipment and mobile devices, billing and charging capabilities, as well as digital rights management for enhancing content services. As evidenced by the rapid growth of SMS, success requires service interoperability between market participants.

Market innovation

For business models, acceptance of mobile media services requires development of the value chain, simple and affordable pricing, licensing agreements with content owners, as well as service interoperability between market participants.

Box 8.2   MOBILE TWEENS

'Nickelodeon has always been an interactive brand. Enabling kids to vote for the Kids' Choice Awards via their cell phone provides yet another layer of interactivity that empowers kids with cutting-edge technology that is relevant to their everyday lives,' says Paul Jelinek, vice president of new media business development at Nickelodeon.

In 2003, Nickelodeon's 17th Annual Kids' Choice Awards was seen by nearly 12.5 million people and 26 million votes were received for the show. In March 2004, Mobliss announced it would provide wireless text messaging to enhance audience members' interactivity with the tween version of the Academy Awards. For the first time, kids could vote for their favourite choice in all 15 categories, while they were watching the show on television.

Tween power

'Nickelodeon Online is really a misnomer, this is truly a new media group, focused on online wireless and television convergence with those screens. Our whole vision for the new media group is about focusing on the consumer and their relationship to those screens from an interactive media standpoint. Wireless was not always part of that vision.'

With a buying power estimated to reach nearly US $41 billion by 2005 and influence over US $74 billion in family spending each year, it's hardly a wonder that marketers of consumer goods are pulling out all the stops to reach the lucrative 'tween' market. Defined as youths between the ages of 8 and 14, tweens have landed squarely in the middle of corporate America's radar screen. Old enough to start earning a little money of their own and have a say in what Mom and Dad buy while they're shopping, tweens represent a potential gold mine for marketers. But they also present a challenge: a tween is a mass of contradictions.

Consider the conflicting developments kids at this age face: an emerging sense of independence balanced by still-strong ties to parents; a strong desire to be cool and stand out, yet not be considered by peers as an outsider; one foot still in childhood and the other making initially tentative and then bold steps toward teendom. This is not an easy path for marketers to navigate. Yet with a certain understanding of and insight into this key demographic, a savvy marketer can stake a claim to mind and wallet share of the tween consumer, and, more importantly, his or her parents (E-Letter, 2002).

Growing up mobile

'From Nickelodeon's brand perspective, we have more than 50 per cent of 2–11-year-old kids' viewing time in the United States. We are the number one cable and satellite television rated network for the last eight years running in terms of total 24-hour average ratings. ESPN, CNN, all of those companies don't match up to us in terms of 24-hour ratings. Kids are watching a disproportionate share of television, and they are watching Nickelodeon a disproportionate share of time.'

With the transition from voice to data services, particularly interactive messaging, the youthful adopters have grown, well, ever younger! Take, for instance, Nickelodeon's everGirl, which integrates a website, pop music and a customized line of apparel and accessories to create a healthy lifestyle brand that allows tween girls to explore who they are and what they want to become.

Nickelodeon is the number one entertainment brand for kids in the United States, with television programming and production in the United States and around the world, plus consumer products, online, recreation, books, magazines and feature films. Nickelodeon's US television network is seen in 88 million households and has been the number one rated basic cable network for more than eight consecutive years.

In the United States, most kids grow up with Nickelodeon, and spend their teens and adolescence with MTV – another Viacom property – and other popular programming, years before their adulthood. The challenge for Nickelodeon was that the new channel was not pioneered in the United States.

US brand, international early adopters

'I was trying to find ways for Nickelodeon to connect to its audiences in a much more integrated way,' recalls Jelinek. 'Mobile communications and cell phone usage was a big source of usage interactivity and potential business opportunities as it related to US opportunities.

'Around 2002, Nickelodeon's focus in the new space became more refined, when a group of MTV Network business development and strategy people decided to focus collaboratively on an overall wireless strategy for our business in the United States.

'When we got together as a group two and a half years ago, it was actually a very good time for us to be doing that business development because in the US the market for wireless penetration was not fully penetrated; it was maybe 30–40 per cent. The segment that was growing and was underserved was the youth area, which was exactly the market that MTV and Nickelodeon wanted to serve, particularly MTV. You also knew that the youth market was underpenetrated and that was the market most likely to consume content and data over cell phones.

'It was important to us because we're primarily an advertising-driven company by and large, and we knew that if we wanted to get into that space in a much more aggressive way, this was a very good opportunity to approach carriers to develop integrated content/advertising partnerships with potential distributors.'

In July 2002, at the heart of Times Square, Virgin Mobile USA unveiled its national, youth-focused cell phone service and its multi-year strategic partnership with MTV Networks. The deal provided for exclusive wireless content and consumer products from MTV and VH1, and additional wireless content from Nickelodeon and CMT. Nickelodeon wanted to focus on one large carrier relationship, which could help drive a significant amount of advertising revenue and content licensing revenue to the company.

'We ended up with a long-term partnership with Virgin Mobile, which was a very good complement for MTV because it was targeting that 18–24-year-old demo very succinctly. For Nickelodeon, they were primarily interested in Nickelodeon for certain types of brand and content that appealed to that older youth segment, like Sponge Bob branded content. We were non-exclusive with them which allows us to think through a much more elaborate strategy for carriers in the US.'

Source: the author's interview with Paul Jelinek, VP, new business development, Nickelodeon Online, 13 May 2004.

User acceptance

To attract the user, the new services must be compelling. Similarly, service activation and discovery must be simple and user-friendly. To achieve user acceptance, the marketing mix must succeed:

- *Promotion and advertising: attraction.* Users gravitate toward what they find intriguing, and often need time and persuasion to learn 'savvy' in using mobile media. Once the interest has been aroused, successful usage will support the launch of complementary products and services in the future.
- *Distribution: convenience.* Even if users are interested, acceptance will not materialize if service activation and discovery is complicated. Consequently, the right device settings should be preconfigured or installed over the air.
- *Pricing: affordability.* Another precondition for user acceptance is appropriate, simple and affordable pricing, which matches the perceived value of the services.
- *Product: compelling content.* The world is full of content. Initially, novelty may compensate for few products or trivial content, but only compelling services ensure sustained usage amid alternative offerings from television, cable, publishing and games.

In addition to the 'traditional 4P' considerations that permeate any marketing effort, these service companies need to manage the 'three new Ps' (see Chapter 2). The industry players need to manage the personnel and customers who are involved in the mobile service experience (experiential marketing), the physical aspects of the service (design), and the process by which the service is created and delivered (ease of use).

Innovation adoption categories

Classic marketing approaches focus primarily on demographics and socioeconomic indicators, whereas diffusion research incorporates a focus on innovation adoption as measured by time, or the length of adoption. The adoption of an innovation usually follows a normal, bell-shaped curve when plotted over time on a frequency basis. When the cumulative number of adopters is plotted, the result is an S-shaped curve. The same adoption data can be represented by either a bell-shaped (frequency) curve or an S-shaped (cumulative) curve (Figure 8.3).

With market expansion, the model has led to refinements, including the idea of a 'chasm' – situated between the early adopters and the early majority – that the companies must overcome to reach the mainstream market.[11] In marketing, the focus has been on how the market forces behind the technology adoption lifecycle necessitate shifts in marketing strategy and tactics for succeeding in each stage of the cycle. For instance, Forrester Research combined lifestyle, psychographic and technology indicators to study the adoption processes as entire industries migrated online.[12]

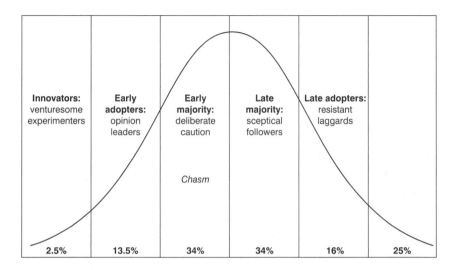

Innovators: venturesome experimenters	Early adopters: opinion leaders	Early majority: deliberate caution	Late majority: sceptical followers	Late adopters: resistant laggards
		Chasm		
2.5%	13.5%	34%	34%	16%	25%

Innovators. Interest in new ideas prompts them out of local peer networks and into more international social relationships. Prerequisites involve substantial financial resources and complex technical knowledge. They must also be able to cope with a high degree of uncertainty. These are the 'cell gurus' that opinion leaders tend to follow. They form a very small market niche, but it is critical; it is through innovators that new innovations trickle into the market.

Early adopters. Early adopters are localites and possess the greatest degree of opinion leadership. The early adopter is considered by many as 'the individual to check with' before using a new idea. This category decreases uncertainty about a new idea by adopting it. By the late 1990s, the early adopters featured in most marketing campaigns that sought to establish new cell innovations in the market. These campaigns emphasize 'coolness' and the 'next big thing'.

Early majority. The early majority adopt new ideas just before the average member of a system. They interact frequently with their peers, but seldom hold positions of opinion leadership in a system. This category is large and makes up a third of the target population. Since early majority members tend to deliberate for some time before adopting a new idea, marketers seek to speed up the adoption process.

Late majority. The late majority adopts new ideas after the average members. They make up another third of the population. The pressure of peers is necessary to motivate adoption. Relatively scarce resources require most uncertainty about a new idea to be removed before the adoption. Marketing campaigns tend to stress cautious values – certainty rather than uncertainty, safety rather than risk, proved solutions rather than bold experiments.

Late adopters. Late adopters or traditionalists are the last to adopt an innovation. They have little or no opinion leadership and are the most local in their outlook. The innovation–decision process is lengthy. Resistance may be entirely rational, as their resources are often highly limited. Since this category tends to represent lower socioeconomic strata and opposition to innovation, it hardly features in the marketing campaigns.

Figure 8.3   Innovation and diffusion: innovation adopter categorization

These ideas have been embraced by the mobile leaders in the 1990s. The new entrants and challengers (Nokia among vendors, Vodafone amid operators) were the first to employ new marketing strategies – just as they first had to devise tactics to cross the chasm from barely profitable niches to lucrative mainstream markets. In Nokia's marketing strategies, the diffusion framework has enabled the vendor to tailor appropriate approaches to penetrate the mass consumer markets. The diffusion framework has also served as a roadmap to the operators.

Mobile adoption categories

In the 1990s, Nokia distinguished between three categories of users (business, adult and youth). These were coupled with innovation adopter categories: high flyers (innovators), trendsetters (early adopters), posers (early majority) and social contact seekers (late majority). In this way, user segmentation has served as a basis for prioritization and selection (Table 8.2). Meanwhile, operators began to develop the changing market with SMS, new applications and picture messaging services. As existing services prepare users for future service offerings, they also become accustomed to the ease of use and speed, gradually adapting these into their habits worldwide (see Box 8.3).[13]

Table 8.2   Innovation and diffusion: mapping early-adopter opinion leaders

1st Level 2nd Level	Business High flyers	Posers	Adult Posers	Social contact seekers	Youth Social contact seekers	Trend setters
Key characteristics	Business driven, heavy users, look for services that increase work efficiency	Significant business use. But the mobile is important also for personal life. Being trendy is more important than improving business efficiency	Mainly personal use, like to impress others, and to be trendy	Personal use, can stay ages on the phone. Contactability is very important	Under 25 years, personal use, can stay ages on the phone. Being member of contact network is valued	Under 25 years, not necessarily heavy users, but like to impress others by using fancy services
Adoption	In the 1st wave	In the 2nd wave	In the 2nd wave	In the 3rd wave	In the 3rd wave	In the 1st wave

The six early-adopter segments represent only the key opinion leaders. They do not represent the entire potential 3G customer base. Rather, the assumption is that the mass market will follow these key groups.

	Attract new users	Keep existing users	Increase market visibility	Increase off-peak traffic	Increase peak traffic
Business high flyers	Information services with rich, possibly location-based content	Lifestyle bulletin boards Corporate VPN Wireless office solutions	Travel manager	Personalized news services with rich content	Intranet and extranet browsing File download Video conferencing
Business/ posers	Booking and ticketing Loyalty programme services	Corporate VPN Wireless office solutions	Personal assistant	Internet browsing Multimedia messaging	Intranet and extranet

Source: Nokia Corp.

Box 8.3   THE ASIAN MOBILE MOMENTUM

'In Japan and Korea, the mobile media markets have been in a state of flux,' says Dave McCaughan. 'There's a lot of experimentation. It's comparable to the 1940s in America and the introduction of television. As the programming shifted from the sponsor model to commercial breaks, it was initially pretty crude. If you try to commercialize any new medium, it will take a long while to develop.'

After nine years as research director with McCann-Erickson Australia, Dave McCaughan took on a new role as consumer insights director for the Asia–Pacific region in January 1996, based in Bangkok. With continuous programmes, he enables McCann clients and staff to understand the changing Asian consumer marketplace, particularly a number of key new youth research projects in the Asia-Pacific.

'But we've already seen dynamic changes and rapid growth, particularly in the cutting-edge Asian markets. Mobile phone has become a major medium.'

Early adopters

'In Japan and Korea, the adoption rate has been driven by the youth demographics, from the ages of early- to mid-twenties,' says McCaughan. 'They like to spend time with their peers. They tend to be people who spend all of their income on themselves for entertainment, clothing and so on. They are followed by the teenagers who pressure their parents into buying the technology for them. We've seen manufacturers quickly moving into that area.

'In some other Asian markets it is the business people who buy into the medium first. If you look at a market like Sri Lanka or the Philippines, they are among the most advanced worldwide in the mass use of the SMS messaging.

'Mobile communication took off in those markets,' says McCaughan, 'because land-based telephone systems weren't available, or were too expensive and too slow. In a market like Sri Lanka, if you wanted to get a land line it would take about six to eight months between application and the actual delivery of the service. Whereas the mobile service you could get immediately, and bypass having a land line altogether. In many of the developing Asian markets – everywhere from India and the Philippines, to certain regions in China, which witnessed a dramatic take-off of the mobile markets in the mid-1990s – many business people use mobile phones to supplement or replace land lines. The adoption rates also took off for personal use, to stay in touch with friends.'

'The 21st century's cigarette'

'In the Japanese marketplace, 80 per cent of housewives have mobile phones that they use daily,' McCaughan says. 'The use of the mobile phone many times a day is considered normal. It's not the case that people use it when they're bored. Rather, they adopt it as a normal part of behaviour. One person I interviewed put it best by saying that "The mobile phone is the 21st century's cigarette." It is what you do to fill time.

'Japan has been the most advanced market in terms of services for half a decade, but it is being taken over now by Korea. For the past few years, Korea has produced the most advanced technology. Now it has become the leader in services as well. The mobile phone has probably changed what "hanging out" means to people. You can now hang out with people any time and anywhere, without actual physical contact.'

Personalization

'The big thing in the most advanced markets is personalization. You can see it in Korea, which is leading in new service introductions. People really are using the mobile phone as a way of expressing themselves.

'Psychologically, we don't really know well whether people are personalizing the phone for themselves or for others, just as we don't yet understand what this all means or how important it is. There are also cultural differences that complicate efforts to understand the meaning of personalization. The difference between riding the subway in Shanghai, Seoul or Tokyo is that, in Korea and Japan, nobody talks, people are constantly on their mobile applications but they never actually talk. In Shanghai or Hong Kong, the story is very different. Over there, people spend a lot of time talking.

'The difference has to do with cultural norms. In Hong Kong, the environment is much louder than in Japan. It affects the way people treat and use mobile technology in public. There's also some cross-over in terms of the way one personalizes. Is it what others can see and hear, or is it about what you can see and hear? Take, for example, the use of toys that you can tie on to your mobile phone. You can see that usage more in certain markets than in others. It is more a sense of I want the world to see how I've individualized my mobile phone, as opposed to what I've done to my screen to individualize it for myself.'

Fashion as adoption driver

In addition to cultural determinants, there are some other things that drive adoption. Today, individual technology attainment is less about technology and more about being fashionable. 'I need the new Nikes in the same way as I'm going to need a new cellphone,' says McCaughan. 'It's the thing to do. It's what I see on television. If there's an analogy between the mobile phone and the cigarette as a way of passing time, you can look at the mobile phones as being similar to the recent coffee revolution. It was not a coffee technology that brought about a lifestyle change. Rather, coffee is now seen more as something of a lifestyle enhancement because it's perceived as more fashionable. That's what drives the growth of mobile technology.

'Look at iMac. Its success was not driven by the development of new software, but great design. With mobile communication, adoption is more driven by cosmetic rather than technology features. More people want the latest thing not because of new software development, but because of soft features – in other words, designs.'

Source: the author's interview with Dave McCaughan, director of strategic planning, consumer insights, McCann-Erickson Asia–Pacific, 13 May 2004.

9

Mobile business services

Mimicking the evolution of consumer services, the changing mobile business services reflect new capabilities in rich voice, the internet, messaging, personalized content, mobile media and entertainment. Traditional enterprise solution providers have rushed to the marketplace, but so have mobile enterprise solution providers. With consumer services, the markets have been globalizing since the 1990s. With business services and enterprise solutions, US big business continues to play a central role.

EVOLUTION OF MOBILE BUSINESS SERVICES

With the transition from voice to data, service innovation is diffusing into the consumer markets. Concurrently, a parallel transformation is sweeping across business markets. Historically, business markets and services have played a critical role in mobile innovation, from the creation of the first customers, emergency and industrial services, to business services and vertical markets. Today, these services are rapidly globalizing.

First business customers

Between the late 1890s and 1910s, Marconi pioneered the first institutional and business market in the wireless. His customers ranged from the maritime sector to governments and shipping interests, national telecom monopolies and large insurance businesses. The evolution of the wireless industry was initiated in business markets, not in consumer markets.

From emergency services to industrial services

As the mobile momentum shifted from Europe to the United States, the US police departments pioneered AM communications. During the Second World War, US defence forces embraced FM communications, which were commercialized in the post-war era, particularly in industrial services. Through this pre-cellular phase from the 1920s to 1970s, mobile services were still relatively primitive, focusing on emergency and industrial dispatch services. They were also being tested in high-end consumer markets (MTS, IMTS).

Cars, corporations and customized devices

With analog cellular from the early 1980s to early 1990s, the price tag of the car phone restricted users to business professionals who could absorb the cost as a business expense, or to consumers who enjoyed relatively high disposable incomes. The cellphone was considered a 'toy' for the exclusive CEO set. At the time, market research by AT&T and Ameritech indicated that the cellular would remain a niche for years to come. But as unit prices fell and receivers became transportable or portable, the ranks of business subscribers opened even further. Assumptions about a limited user base proved groundless:

> Cellular telephones started to appear in the hands of plumbers, repairmen, reporters, construction foremen, real estate brokers and others for whom constant linkage to another location was critical to business. In spite of the relatively high price tag common to new technology, the efficiency of wireless had begun to sell itself to a broader slice of the business community than had been anticipated by the industry's marketers (CTIA, 1994: 57–58).

Globalization of consumer market services

It was the transition to digital cellular in the early 1990s that truly shifted the momentum from business markets to consumer markets. At the same time, mobile innovation migrated to the Nordic countries and Japan. In the United States, corporate professionals discovered personal digital assistants by Palm, Handspring and RIM, and, in 2000, PocketPCs by Microsoft and Compaq. Unit volumes, however, were low. As PDA manufacturers sold 10 million units annually, mobile vendors were selling hundreds of millions of cellphones (Steinbock, 2002: chs 13–14).

By 2003, US services/health care and government represented almost 50 per cent of the overall vertical markets in the United States. Coupled with retail/wholesale trade and manufacturing, these four great segments accounted for more than 80 per cent of the total. Understandably, US-based IT enablers sought to extend their digital leadership into the mobile space (see Box 9.1).

Box 9.1   TOWARD MOBILE WINDOWS DEVICES

The rise of Microsoft's mobile activities, including mobile enterprise solutions, is 'one of the untold stories', acknowledges Douglas Dedo, marketing manager for enterprise strategy in Microsoft Windows Mobile Division. 'Some projects started in the early 1990s, when laptops became increasingly popular and manufacturers started to go into smaller digital mobility. Customers liked the mobility of the laptop and found it liberating. But they also wanted a smaller package, longer battery life, just as they wanted it to turn on and off instantly.'

'At Microsoft, the two early projects took place in the late 1990s. They were attempting to make a smaller version of the PC operating system. Both of those projects failed because the architecture of the PC software was designed for a desktop.'

Windows CE

'Microsoft had to create an extended operating system to target this kind of a device. That's when we really began working on the Windows CE operating system. It took us a few years before we were able to finish. In 1996 we created the hand-held PC software platform using the Windows CE operating system. We also saw businesses trying it out in more and more mobile situations. As we saw pharmaceutical companies buying thousands of devices, as well as government agencies and financial institutions, we realized that these devices met a significant level of interest in the business world.

'About the same time, Palm created the connected organizer, an even smaller device. So we started working on projects where we could create devices that would fit in your pocket. That meant going after the PDA class and creating phone-sized devices.'

Complete solution

'Our approach is the same Microsoft took for the PC. That is, to create a software platform and an ecosystem of business partners to fill in the different needs for a complete solution. As with the PC, we've created the Windows mobile platform for these devices and then work with the device manufacturers – Motorola and Samsung and PDA manufacturers, such as Hewlett-Packard, Dell and Toshiba – there are over 30 of those. We also work with system integrators, and many others.

'The business model is the same, with one significant difference. Historically, we have not had a PC or laptop with a phone built into it. But with these new mobile devices there is a desire to marry a phone capability with computing functionality. With a phone capability built into our platform, we now have a new business partner. These are the global operators, such as Verizon Wireless, AT&T Wireless, Orange and others. We're working with more than 50 operators in over 25 countries hoping to make these devices available all over the world to a broad range of customers in a business context as well as individual purchasers. We are focused on creating a mobility ecosystem.'

From data to mobile

'Initially, Microsoft built computers as PC stand-alone devices. Over the 24 years that PCs have been around, Microsoft has gone from internet productivity to ethernet productivity to Wi-Fi and Bluetooth productivity over these different mediums. Incorporating a phone to a PDA is a lot simpler exercise for someone who has extensively been working with data than it is for someone who has been working with a voice communications device and is trying to move into the data arena.

'You are dealing with a very complex world when you are trying to bring in data to the equation. That is one of the reasons why the global operators have been pretty excited to work with Microsoft. They have spent a lot of money on their data networks and they see that we have expertise with the data side of the equation. Orange was one of our earliest smart phone partners. Their average revenue per user is increasing by an average of 25 per cent for the additional data that the users are able to get out of it.'

Flexibility

'The model we are following is a business partner-based model. It provides flexibility. SAP is one of our partners for creative solutions to enterprise customers. We also work very closely with system integrators, such as Accenture, HP Services, Gemini and others. This model allows you to externalize the services in the current system and put the data into a format that can be consumed on new mobile or computing devices that the original system was not designed for.

'A simple example is Dollar Rent-A-Car. With the new operating model, they have gained a lot more flexibility in terms of where they can make reservations available, just as they now can work with new business partners to capture new business.'

Dynamic content

Dedo considers the transition from basic service innovation to advanced dynamic content, including mobile media, as incremental rather than disruptive. 'It's hard for people to conceptualize such changes without real-life examples. You have seen cameras going into cellphones now for some time but there are also cameras that have gone into PDAs, both plug-in and embedded integrated cameras. When they first came out people thought of vacation time, but it is really a very powerful business tool. Insurance companies are taking pictures of damaged vehicles and property, doctors are taking pictures of patients for a second opinion and more research. Public safety takes pictures of crime scenes and you are getting this information widely and much quicker.

'Multimedia is a very valuable business tool. When we move into the video space there are many business roles where graphical information is actually very important, for example people doing field service or air conditioning repair or other types of heavy machinery.'

Source: the author's interview with Douglas Dedo, marketing manager for enterprise strategy, Windows Mobile Division, Microsoft Corp., 27 April 2004.

Mobile multimedia pioneers in business services

NTT DoCoMo's service innovation

Initially, the success of i-mode was based on pioneering in the Japanese consumer markets. The business interest came as something of a surprise, says Takeshi Natsuno:

> From mid-2000, we saw a conspicuous number of purchases of hundreds, thousands, or even tens of thousands of phones at one time. Those were clearly bulk purchases by corporations… We thought there might be some corporate demand, but, when we looked into it, we found far more corporate use than we had expected.
>
> (Natsuno, 2000: 104)

Soon the operator was dedicated to creating i-mode business partnerships with leading companies in various industries around the world. i-mode was also seen as a cost-efficient solution. 'If you want to provide a special PDA for your employees, you must put in a lot of money,' acknowledges Natsuno. 'A PDA costs US $400–500. If the cellphone can do the PDA's job, then employees can buy the phones on their own. In Japan, consumers led the corporations to the i-mode. Consumers were the first adapters, corporations followed.'[1] Similar trends prevail in Europe and North America.

As a business tool, i-mode provides numerous efficiencies. Salespeople can gain mobile access to company databases, managers maintain voice, image and text contact with field staff, and marketers can receive accurate feedback in real time.

Sales support for a medical equipment manufacturer

In medical technology, Medtronic is a world-leading company, providing lifelong solutions for people suffering from chronic illnesses. Before using i-mode, the Medtronic salespeople had to contact the office by phone and verbally check information. The i-mode service has considerably eased the burden on the salespeople, enabling them to check and update schedules and sales information by accessing the corporate database, industry news and information at any time. By enhancing the sales process, i-mode increased the efficiency of business.[2]

Since 2001, NTT DoCoMo's high-speed FOMA has supported mobile intranet access, real-time monitoring with video playback, and mobile business-to-employee functions. Benefiting a wide range of businesses from manufacturing to construction, and from retail to trading, FOMA allows companies to respond to customer needs, streamline business processes, restructure operations, and adopt new working styles.

Videophones in insurance contract reviews

Starting in August 2003, American Family Life Assurance Company of Columbus (AFLAC) began to test a service for life insurance interviewers. FOMA is used to confirm the health and identity of insurance contract applicants. In the past, interviewers conducted the interviews in person. Results were sent to the Underwriting Department at headquarters for final decisions. With remote interviews, life insurance interviewers in the Tokyo Underwriting Department conduct the interviews. This allows for faster reviews and decisions on contract applications – as well as significant cost reductions in temp fees, travel expenses for interviewers, administration and training fees.[3]

Vodafone's Mobile Office

In Europe, services such as Vodafone Live! and Mobile Office from Vodafone are based on customer propositions that have been packaged together for a specific target market. 'Office was basically developed in parallel with Vodafone Live!, with the same development and management teams,' acknowledges Thomas Geitner, chief technology officer, who played a critical role in both. 'Evolution has been slightly different, but the guiding principles have been comparable.'[4]

During these parallel initiatives, Vodafone had to rethink its role as the leading service provider in the rapidly changing industry value system. 'We had to figure out how we could mobile-enable Lotus and Microsoft Office. These were very complicated issues. Then we could finally go to companies to present our stuff and meet the CIOs, and tell them that we had a mobile-enabled version of Microsoft Exchange. You know what they'd say? "I'm surprised you are coming to sell me the Office."'

The parallel work enabled the developers of the Mobile Office to draw from the concepts and lessons of Vodafone Live!. 'We focused on what we can do and sell well to the customer,' recalls Geitner. 'If the propositions looked too complicated, I could only say, "Go back and return when you can say everything to the customers in three minutes." If it can't be done, it won't sell. Ease of use and sellability were the key behind the Vodafone Mobile Connect Card. Customers wanted quick, easy and secure access to their company networks and existing office applications. To eliminate the usual IT manager and end-user frustration associated with configuring laptop PC data cards with hardware and IT systems, Vodafone created a complete customer solution.'

Ironically enough, neither of these two great pioneers has a dominant role in the greatest 'must win' market, the United States, where carriers such as Verizon Wireless and others have been pioneering mobile enterprise solutions (see Box 9.2).

Box 9.2   ENTERPRISE SOLUTIONS – VERIZON WIRELESS STYLE

'US firms lead in the enterprise solutions space,' says Cindy Patterson. 'Every Fortune 1,000 company wants to make more money. They do that by making their employees more productive.' As vice president of enterprise data sales for Verizon Wireless, the 16-year veteran of the telecom industry oversees a sales group that develops data services on both a horizontal and vertical market basis.

Verizon Wireless has distributed its sales force over 19 different regions of the United States. While teams of salespersons and data engineers work on specific enterprise accounts, reps are deployed wherever they are needed. 'We leverage people across the accounts and go to where the business is happening. We're the Fly Team.'

Wireless Office

Wireless Office is Verizon's basic suite of general and customized services targeted at corporate accounts, including mobile voice, internet/intranet access, e-mail, personal information management and other features for corporate users. Among more specific solutions, the company offers Wireless Sync corporate e-mail synchronization software, which it made certain works across all kinds of data services and combined voice/data handhelds.

Wireless Office was launched in spring 2004 as Verizon announced commercial deployment of next-generation cdma2000 1X EV-DO (EVolution, Data Only) in its Washington DC and San Diego markets. Though many of the Wireless Office services are usable on Verizon's broadly deployed RTT (real-time technology) data networks, the real value of the initiative will be triggered by Verizon's push into high-speed EV-DO networks. These enable applications such as high-resolution video and workgroup collaboration that could be targeted at vertical industry markets or even specific enterprises.

Verizon sees Wi-Fi as a complement to the wireless network. EV-DO is the carrier's critical resource. 'It opens up the door to a broadband-like experience,' notes Patterson.

Get IT on board

How does the enterprise solutions business work at Verizon Wireless? 'A lot of companies make decentralized decisions when it comes to buying wireless services,' Patterson says. 'But the corporate customer's IT department must always be involved. Otherwise, there will be problems in implementing the solutions.'

After the IT department is on board, the Verizon team works closely with IT to choose the right solutions and devices for the departments and employees. As IT managers are often overwhelmed by the range of data devices available on the market, Verizon must conform to an IT manager's requirements to standardize on few devices. 'It can take from 60 days to six months to standardize on a device, depending on the size of the group using it and how customized they want it to be,' Patterson says.

Because of the PDAs and Blackberries among corporate users, Verizon has expanded its catalogue of data devices as part of its Wireless Office strategy. The carrier now offers the BlackBerry 6750 and PocketPCs from Kyocera and Samsung.

Vertical solutions

Around 2003, Verizon Wireless decided to go after seven different vertical segments, where it saw the greatest need for mobility solutions, including financial services (banking and insurance companies); industrials (manufacturing, mining and construction); distribution (retail and wholesale); transportation (travel and transportation, airlines, package delivery); health services (health care, pharmaceuticals, hospitals); utility, media and entertainment; and federal government.

At first, the reps focus on the business unit that oversees employees who travel regularly or work remotely. But different industries require different approaches. 'With financials,' comments Patterson, 'we focus on e-mail and personal information management. They go for the executives and their sales forces. They want their information pushed out to mobile workers, wherever they happen to be. In this space, we also see the emergence of two vertical applications, claims adjustment and wireless ATM. The third factor that's emerging in this space is the point-of-sale base.

'With utilities, we've been working a lot on field-based applications, telemetry, and system control data applications. With industrials and manufacturing, we've deployed ruggedized devices. Using Wi-Fi in the building and wide area network outside, they want to be able to scan the inventory as it is leaving the manufacturing facility and to track it through the distribution process until it gets to its destination. They are also using automatic vehicle location services to track the delivery fleet.

'In health care, we work with a number of pharmaceuticals to wirelessly give them access to large amounts of data. In distribution, we're working on a number of large deployments with consumer packages to these companies so that they can have their sales people in retail stores capture information. In transportation, we cooperate with packaged goods companies or companies that make large deliveries to corporations. With federal government, we're providing many agencies access to critical information and regular applications, such as e-mail and PIM field.

'We're working with hundreds of companies to deploy vertical and horizontal applications,' says Patterson. 'With diagonal applications, we run apps so that they work correctly on a smaller screen, such as a PDA. With these Fortune 1,000 accounts and government accounts, there are really three different types of categories of applications – vertical, horizontal and diagonal – within the seven vertical segments.'

Differentiating offerings

When Patterson's team sells a solution to a customer, they sell the network, but their partners might also sell the device to the customers directly, or they might sell software applications directly to the company, or the system administrator will charge directly to the company. Patterson's sales team has Fortune 1,000 accounts assigned to them. 'We are really out there to sell the Verizon wireless network, but we're also acting as consultants and pulling together all the necessary components for a customer.

'When we go out to a Fortune 1,000 customer, we try to figure out what are the different opportunities and needs within their business, what are the problems they are trying to solve, and where we can bring productivity to their business. Then we work on bringing in partners that can help them deliver an end-to-end solution to the customer.'

What attracts customers to the carriers is the customer service that the operators provide before and after the sale of the network. Moreover, financial stability is crucial. 'With its parent, Verizon is the sixteenth and twenty-sixth largest company in the world. Financial strength makes customers feel secure.'

Source: the author's interview with Cindy Patterson, VP – enterprise data sales, Verizon Wireless, 29 April 2004.

BUSINESS SERVICE INNOVATION

From digitization to mobilization

In the 1990s, the rise of the internet enabled digitization, but the digital world was still stationary. Today, mobility enables digitization anywhere and any time. In addition to redefining business services, mobilization has had three broader consequences: the conversion of (physical) paper to (online) forms, wireless broadband in corporate markets, and the new generation of multi-function mobile devices.

From paper to mobile forms

In the past, paper-based activities have been replaced with digital forms. Before the arrival of PCs, the substitution was confined to narrow business markets and technology segments. As PCs proliferated in homes and offices, digitization accelerated with word processing and spreadsheets, which drove consumer lifestyle and business productivity. With analogue and digital cellular, voice communications still reigned over data. Today, data reigns over voice, and paper-based activities are converting to digital forms-based mobile applications. These substitutions comprise simple paper-to-forms conversions and more complex value-to-forms conversions (see, for example, Dedo, 2004).

Cost-driven mobile conversions

In cost-driven conversions, mobile devices often support process engineering efforts. Typical examples include reducing operational costs, data collection time, improving customer response times, or shortening the cycle time. For instance, GMAC Commercial Mortgage managed to reduce the time it took to process commercial loans from 90–120 days down to 10 days or less with a project that was completed in three months by three people. The productivity gain was realized by process re-engineering that converted a serial paper-based process to parallel tasks, which was supported by electronic forms on a Pocket PC.[5]

Value-driven conversions

Additionally, mobile solutions enable organizations to collect high-quality and more complete data with electronic forms which can generate cost savings and new revenue possibilities. In this case, the goal involves not just cost efficiencies but increasing buyer value as well. Take, for instance, the changing restaurant experience. Located in Hawthorn, Victoria, Kudos Restaurant and Wine Bar is a modern 140-seat restaurant, and a pioneer in using mobile communications to enhance the value of increased customer satisfaction. Its ability to advise customers of current menu and wine label availability, combined with the improved accuracy of orders, has substantially enhanced the customer experience and encouraged repeat business.[6]

Wireless broadband

Since the end of the 1990s, the role of broadband wireless has rapidly accelerated in the mobile industry. In the corporate markets, new broadband technologies – Wi-Fi, WiMax and alternative options – are seen as new growth engines. To IT enablers, such as Intel and Microsoft, these technologies represent an extraordinary opportunity to establish a foothold in workplaces, at home and in hotspots (such as hotels and convention centres). Wireless local area network (WLAN) enables business people to stay connected as they move throughout the corporate campus, easily tapping into the resources of the wired network (see Box 9.3).

Empowering health care with wireless productivity

McKesson Corp. has a rapidly growing healthcare business reaching upwards of US $57 billion per year in annual sales and a highly mobile workforce of 24,000 employees. With Intel's assistance, McKesson standardized on notebook PCs based on Intel Centrino mobile technology and desktop PCs based on Intel Pentium 4 processors. To maximize mobile productivity, the company deployed WLANs at several sites. Now employees can respond to customers and colleagues faster. Keeping PCs current contributed to lower total cost of ownership (TCO) and enhanced productivity, customer responsiveness, user satisfaction and profitability (Intel, 2004).

From single-function devices to multi-function devices

In business segments, mobile devices are about excellence and high data capabilities. Function reigns over style. In most business organizations (large corporations and SMEs), the handset is primarily a productivity tool. However, different functionalities matter in different industries.

Upgrading custom devices

In the late 1990s, consumer markets transitioned from entry-level phones to replacements. Still, many business segments remain dominated by custom devices, which are used, for example, by people providing field-based services, delivering packages and keeping track of stock on store shelves or in warehouses. As support and maintenance costs are growing, replacing these older devices with more powerful handsets may significantly reduce the overall cost of ownership and provide a more flexible platform for mobile

Box 9.3 TRANSFORMING INDUSTRIES

'Starting in 2003, mobile computing has become a top agenda item with chief executives and chief information officers. Meanwhile, rising numbers of cellphones and PDAs have the CIOs wondering about security issues and asset management,' says Deborah S Conrad, vice president of Intel's sales and marketing group and general manager of Intel's solutions market development group.

Mobile momentum

'Some companies have gone mobile by putting mobile laptops in the hands of their employees and doing about 20 per cent of their business mobile, including insurance and real estate agents. Things are really changing. As laptops became less expensive and were cheaper to maintain, the trend caught on rapidly, due to cost effectiveness.

'With the momentum of the wireless mobile systems, Intel wanted to participate in the development of this new technology. As mobile devices proliferated so rapidly, senior executives and information officers started a discussion on what to do with the increasingly demanding mobile environment. This has created an opportunity for end-to-end solutions that have a mobile component. Typically, emerging markets do not have much legacy systems, whereas maturing markets have a lot of existing equipment and investment.'

Mobilizing point of sale and point of care

Mobile solutions have been particularly attractive in two industries. 'Retail and health care have gone mobile for similar reasons. In retail, mobile computing has enabled a better point of sale and better customer reach. In health care, we've seen a definite rise in health care professionals wanting to improve the point of services at the patient level.

'Historically, retail has been very slow moving to this new technology. With the introduction of mobile devices, they now have an end-to-end opportunity to overhaul the entire customer experience, distribution and inventory. Procter & Gamble or Wal-Mart can deliver customer information in real time, in New York City and Detroit, due to their wireless network. In health care, if you are a doctor and you are in a patient's room, you can reach into your notebook computer and get much information about the patient's case.'

Mobilizing construction

'Construction companies put information in ruggedized notebooks for their workers and supervisors. They claim tremendous efficiency because it makes their jobs easier. The use of walkie-talkies is eliminated and they can collaborate better, for example, comparing designs or sending electronic photos and contents around a huge massive construction site. It's all done in real time and wirelessly.

'These industries really benefit from wireless technologies because they are working with real-time problem solving, adjustments of design or manufacturing material. They can get quickly to real-time decisions because they put a mobile computing environment in place.'

Source: the author's interview with Deborah S Conrad, VP, Sales and Marketing Group; Director, Solutions Market Development Group, Intel Corp, 26 April 2004.

business solutions. In some organizations, the cost savings associated with modernizing legacy devices and infrastructure may pay for the entire project. Potential areas for cost savings include lower costs in hardware and software development, and lower wireless service charges.[7]

From consumer markets to the business sector

Emulating the categorization of consumer services, mobile business services can be classified into four broad groups of connectivity:

- rich voice;
- the internet (mobile internet, mobile intranet / extranet);
- messaging (location-based services, people communications, such as SMS, MMS);
- content (including information, entertainment, but also transactions and database).

Though predicated on continuous presence, the service categories include offerings even for intermittently connected applications.

Intermittently connected applications

Because of physical limitations (well-shielded buildings or geographic sites) or legal restrictions (affecting for example hospitals and aeroplanes), mobile users may not always have access to wireless connectivity throughout their work day. In the absence of connectivity for cellphones or wireless LANs, certain solutions must be self-contained on a mobile device with the capability to swap e-mail, data and business transactions when intermittently connected. Among other things, these solutions enable shorter development time and higher performance, reduced field service errors, as well as improved sales force productivity and enhanced customer service (Dedo, 2004).

Voice

The traditional mobile voice offering includes features such as operator services, directory assistance and roaming. With multimedia cellular, these simple voice offerings can be augmented with rich voice communications, providing advanced voice capabilities (such as voice over internet protocol (VoIP) and voice-activated net access). By spring 2005, wireless voiceover IP was beginning to occur in the business market. Over time, the service will also include mobile videophone and multimedia communications. The videophone service, for instance, gives clients and customers an initial view of products, maintaining closer ties between office and field operations, or simply talking to a colleague.

Corporate use of advanced videophone capabilities

Itoki is a corporate interior design company with a nationwide sales force that makes efficient use of NTT DoCoMo's high speed FOMA service. In the past, the company used digital capabilities to offer remote access to the corporate local area network (LAN), while deploying digital cameras to take pictures. These were then transferred onto notebook PCs for sending via digital cellular. The process was time-consuming because a large volume of data had to be transmitted. With FOMA, salespeople can gain rapid access to the corporate LAN and retrieve useful information in minimal time. Efficiency is increased, expenses are streamlined, and the company is better able to respond to market needs.[8]

The internet

In addition to enhanced voice services, multimedia enables connectivity to the internet. This means mobile internet access for consumer markets as well as mobile intranet/extranet access for business markets. Business services offer secure mobile access to corporate LANs, virtual private networks (VPNs) and the internet. These services include mobile access to desktop applications (e-mail, contact lists, spreadsheets, corporate management systems and so on), internet access and mobile access to the intranet and/or extranet portals.

Overall, mobile intranet/extranet access requires more sophisticated interfaces to the enterprise portals and shifts in marketing strategies. Target segments comprise mobile workers, including sales and marketing professionals in communication-intensive industries such as finance, transportation and insurance. Other frequently cited industries include utility, transport, health care and public safety.

Enhanced dispatch management

Otsuka Shokai sells office equipment and offers after-sales support. Some 5,000 calls are received from customers each day, and when repairs are required, operators have to arrange orders with 1,200 engineers located in 220 offices nationwide. Before using the i-mode system, operators received repair orders by phone, faxed them to service support centres nationwide, and called the centres to confirm receipt of the order. The assigned engineer then called the customer to arrange a time, and upon completion of the job the engineer returned to the centre to make a report. The system was inefficient and made scheduling very difficult. With i-mode, the support centre can dispatch the engineers and send repair details directly to mobile phone, while repair reports can be sent to the support centre. Additionally, the company is able to keep records of the repairs made by the engineers in a database.[9]

Messaging

Over time, increasing adoption of multimedia cellular and broadband technologies is expected to promote business use of messaging. Business users represent high-end segments that evolve faster than consumer markets. Time is of the essence for corporate users, and presence helps them save time and communicate more efficiently (Nokia, 2001a: 5). Through people connectivity, mobile networks enable not just a text-based short message service, but also the richer multimedia messaging service. Instant messaging allows the users to send short and simple messages that are delivered immediately to online users. MMS contributes to lifestyle through sharing and entertainment, but it also enhances productivity in business markets.

Notification-based solutions

In some businesses, key milestones and metrics are monitored daily. Notification-based solutions are required when the data points fall outside the acceptable operating range for the business or when a change happens to the organization. The longer the delay in notification, the higher the potential cost is to the business. An automated notification-based approach can simplify administrative tasks. Deployed mobile solutions that use automated notifications have included sport scores transmitted in real time, as well as real-time information for real-time decisions and more time for customers (see Table 9.1) (Dedo, 2004).

Fleet management and location-based services

Location-based services (LBS) refer to business and consumer services that enable users or machines to find other people or machines, and/or enable others to find users, just as they enable users to identify their own location. A key characteristic of these services is localized content, which may include information such as local weather reports, news, hotel and restaurant information, traffic and travel reports, navigational services, telematics and mobile commerce. For instance, Qualcomm's FleetAdvisor system offers a robust fleet management solution for private fleets of all sizes.[10]

Personalized content

Initially, the i-mode aggregated services comprised four sub-categories: information, entertainment, databases and transactions. In business services, the focus is on information, which is often complemented by databases and transactions, even entertainment (sales, presentations, demonstrations).

Information

In business, the information sub-category – news updates, weather, local information – is particularly important and can be customized to match user requirements, in terms of business and geographic segments.

Table 9.1 Examples of notifications and the mobile workforce

Engineering	An elevator, farm machinery, large household appliance, or other pieces of equipment need to be serviced or approach warranty deadlines.
Financial investments	Changes in the market have reached a level for purchasing or selling certain securities or financial instruments. Notification when a customer executes a trade or opens a new account. The financial advisor can then contact customers and be proactive in understanding their needs.
Government	The homeland security alert status level has changed, the Amber Alert system has been activated, new warrants for someone's arrest have been issued, or a crime has been reported. A system that sends alerts of bridges that need inspecting because of flood and other weather conditions or accident damage. Parking violation devices sending alerts to police personnel can aid in consistent enforcement of parking laws as well as enable recovery of other unpaid tickets or stolen vehicles.
Healthcare	In a hospital environment this could be a patient emergency, a lab test result becomes available (especially if it is out of the normal bounds for the test), the Centre for Disease Control has issued a new alert for an outbreak in some part of the world, or a prescription has expired which requires a refill.
Hospitality	A manager of multiple hotel properties needs to know occupancy rates to determine advertising levels and promotions on a continuing basis.
Insurance	Policies that are coming up for renewal or claims that need to be investigated.
Manufacturing	The raw materials on hand are not enough to satisfy the current order rate, a piece of equipment or cell controller in the manufacturing process has stopped functioning, or a supplier is unable to deliver a product on time. Alerts can also be sent when machinery or vehicles need regular scheduled maintenance, reach a warranty replacement date, or are scheduled for obsolescence.
Pharmaceutical	A participant in a drug trial needs to be notified it is time to take medication and fill out a form.
Real estate	New properties have come on the market, typically through a multiple listing service, that match a client's specifications.
Retail	Inventory is low and needs to be restocked at a retail outlet or a vending machine.
Sports	Immediate results transmitted from a sporting event.
Transportation	An aircraft has landed that needs to be serviced, a package is available that needs to be picked up, or a ship has arrived that needs to be unloaded.
Utility	A rupture has occurred in a pipeline, a generator is running low on fuel, a transformer is malfunctioning.

Source: Dedo (2004).

Entertainment

In mobile consumer services, this category is currently known for down-loading, games, media and trivia. But it too allows for a wide variety of business applications, from product demonstration to promotion.

Database

This category comprises vital business services, including telephone directory, city guides, dictionaries, delivery status inquiries, and so on.

Transactions

This category includes banking, securities trading, credit card information, ticket reservations and shopping. Like directories, transactions are vital to business services.

These categories have proved popular in consumer markets from Japan to Europe and the United States. In addition to contributing to lifestyle, they add to productivity in business markets. Take, for instance, market updates. Launched in January 2001, NTT DoCoMo's i-appli service uses the Java platform for consumer electronics and built-in devices, and i-mode's extended library. The service provides dynamic content, including stock prices and charts, which can be automatically updated, while the colour display keeps track of stock movements of particular interest.[11]

Reducing transcription costs

In Kingsport, Tennessee, Holston Medical Group made electronic medical records (EMR) available on Pocket PCs, which has resulted in over US $2.4 million in research funding for the next three years. It is expected to produce annual savings of US $24,000 per physician by eliminating transcription costs. Small Pocket PCs fit the needs of a mobile health care provider by offering quick access to a broad range of patient, medical and insurance data and transactions.[12]

Mobile media and entertainment

In the past few years, dynamic content has been heralded by several industry developments, including colour displays and ringtones, JAVA-enabled terminals, higher speed, digital camera capabilities and mobile e-commerce. As multimedia cellular proliferates and broadband wireless follows, the new infrastructure will enable dynamic mobile content. With its FOMA service, NTT DoCoMo has pioneered many of these categories, along with SK Telecom, Vodafone and other trendsetting carriers. Among other things, mobile media will comprise MMS still pictures and animations, video messaging (or video MMS), video streaming and video download, 'See What I See' (SWIS) or real-time person-to-person multimedia communication, video telephony and broadcasting.

MMS still pictures, animations and video messaging

In the pioneer markets, the evolution took off with MMS still pictures and animations in the second half of 2002. With video messaging, users send or receive a multimedia message, which contains a video clip, to a mobile device from another device or an application. In business markets, mobile video unplugs and complements current messaging services.

Video streaming and download

Mobile users may view video content in several ways, typically via downloading or streaming with NTT DoCoMo's (i-motion and V-live services, respectively). The latter, for instance, can be used in remote monitoring for training and security purposes, while other services can be deployed for video-conferencing (Visualnet).

SWIS

SWIS refers to real-time person-to-person communication where one person is sharing what he or she can see with another. It is based on a concurrent voice call, coupled with a video session to share content. In business markets, it can be employed as a conferencing tool by individuals on the internet, to chat, e-mail, perform file transfers and so on.

Video telephony

Video telephony is the mobile version of internet telephony. Through video telephony, the mobile user can make or receive a video call, which allows the user to see and talk to the other person. With NTT DoCoMo's FOMA, the videophone service allows subscribers to speak to each other face to face. In a business setting, the service allows salespeople to talk to customers, while accessing a corporate database.

Broadcasting

With high-bandwidth channels and high transmission speeds, digital broadcasting can provide a wide variety of cost-efficient content, such as television services, to mobile users, including businesses.

Business content services

During the past five years, the i-mode usage has shifted toward entertainment and free internet services. With consumer services, these were the popular categories in 2003: ringtones/standby screens (37 per cent), entertainment, games/horoscopes (39 per cent), information (12 per cent) and transactions plus database (12 per cent). With business services, one might expect a reverse trend: a focus on information, transactions plus database.

ENTERPRISE SOLUTIONS PROVIDERS

In the early days of business computing, companies used to write their own software to control their business processes. Since many of these processes occur in common across various types of businesses, common reusable software provides cost-effective alternatives to custom software. Since the 1990s, enterprise resource planning (ERP) systems have provided management information that seeks to boost the productivity of companies.

The rise of enterprise resource planning systems

The ERP companies design, develop, market and support software for automating the process of managing enterprise functions such as accounting, human resources, order processing, scheduling, distribution and inventory management.

Material requirement planning

ERP systems originate from material requirement planning (MRP), which was first introduced in the 1970s as a computerized approach to planning and obtaining the required materials for manufacturing and production. It relied on mainframes as the main source for input and processing. As a result, application processing occurred centrally on the mainframe. The user devices were 'dumb terminals' with display memory but virtually no processing power.

Manufacturing resource planning

In the 1980s MRP expanded from management of materials to plant and personnel planning and distribution planning, which grew to MRP-II (manufacturing resource planning). Although it was a broader concept, it relied on mainframes in conjunction with LAN to input and access information. Because it utilized powerful desktop computers and LANs, along with client server applications, data became decentralized. With increasing decentralization of organizational data, departmental computing environments emerged with local control.

Enterprise resource planning

In the 1990s the development of ERP was driven by efforts to harmonize the functioning of the entire company, through decentralized data and local organizational autonomy. ERP relies on WANs (wide area networks), which allow coordination of activities globally. Many companies have found the appeal of such integrated information systems irresistible. Several functions – including purchasing and manufacturing, distribution, forecasting and sales – have greatly benefited from a variety of ERP systems in the past few years. In parallel with ERP, the 1990s witnessed the rise of supply chain management (SCM) and customer relationship management (CRM), which reflect efforts by firms to manage coordination with customers and suppliers, as well as extended enterprise systems.

ERP and its discontents

Today, an entire industry has formed around ERP software. The key players are SAP, Microsoft and its Microsoft Business Solutions, PeopleSoft and Best Software. Others focus their offerings on specific industries (Intuit in personal finance), operating systems (Red Hat in Linux), globally (SSA Global Technologies), to SMEs (Best Software), specific vertical industries (Lawson Software), or outsourcing (chinadotcom Corp.) More recently, the ERP players have been augmented by solutions providers focusing on CRM, marketing and sales software. The boundaries between ERP and CRM are blurry.

Successfully implemented, ERP links financial, manufacturing, human resources, distribution and order management systems into a tightly integrated single system with shared data and visibility across the business. By streamlining data flows throughout an organization, these commercial software packages, offered by vendors like SAP, promise dramatic gains in a company's efficiency and bottom line. The bad news is that ERP systems can also be expensive, complex and notoriously difficult to implement.[13] The main reason for the failures involves business issues:

> Companies fail to reconcile the technological imperatives of the enterprise system with the business needs of the enterprise itself. An enterprise system, by its very nature, imposes its own logic on a company's strategy, organization, and culture.
>
> (Davenport, 1998)

Unlike computer systems of the past, which were developed in-house with a company's specific requirements in mind, enterprise systems are off-the-shelf solutions. They impose their own logic on a company's strategy, culture and organization, often forcing companies to change the way they do business. Competitive advantage from IT can result and be sustained where IT is applied in a way that is carefully tailored to a company's unique way of competing versus rivals. Where that is not the case, competitive advantages are more likely to be lost than captured.

Mobile enterprise solutions providers

By taking the network out of the office, portable devices – mobile phones, laptops and PDAs – contribute to productivity by mobilizing the office, supporting the real-time enterprise, enabling full collaboration in the field, improving corporate communications and the balance between work and lifestyle.

The benefits require the business to overcome traditional barriers to widespread deployment, which include the cost perception, the proprietary nature of the technology, complex management requirements and lack of security. Today, the barriers are falling because core technologies are becoming more affordable, standardized and manageable. Concurrently, the necessary support services to combine full e-mail and secure remote access capabilities on fixed or mobile devices are becoming widely available. The business case can now be made with better prospects for an appropriate return on investment (ROI).[14]

While enterprise solutions providers are extending their capabilities to mobile space, mobile solutions providers are extending their capabilities to enterprise space. Both are attracted by an estimated €37 billion market (see Figure 9.1). The basic offerings comprise advanced voice, personal information management, access to e-mail and the internet, network integrity and security. Today, three broad mobile groups in particular compete for mobile enterprise space worldwide: equipment manufacturers, operators and IT enablers. The generic strategies of these strategic groups tend to differ, because of their different positions in the industry value chain.

Vendors

Among equipment manufacturers, the key players are the US-based Motorola and Qualcomm, as well as Nordic vendors such as Nokia and Ericsson. While both the latter have exploited GSM technology to capture leadership, Ericsson's focus is on network equipment and telecom markets, whereas Nokia's has been on mobile devices and consumer markets.

Evolution of enterprise mobility

2005	2006	2007	2008
Mobile office	**Mobile workforce**		**Mobile enterprise**
• Mobile e-mail breaks 5% penetration	• Mobile e-mail goes mainstream		• Single user interface, seamless voice over wireless and roaming
• Multi-radio device pilots	• Volume multi-radio devices		• Mobile device used by white collar workers 65% computing time
• Corporate vs. personal use policies emerge	• Emergence of integrated mobility servers		• Mobility servers to volume
	• +50% devices issued by IT departments		
	• 40% corporate apps have mobility element		

Addressable market

Enterprise mobility professional services €4.4 billion	Business voice, business smart phones and converged €25 billion	Maintenance and support services €1.6 billion
	Mobility infrastructure €6 billion	

Source: Projections by Nokia and industry sources.

Figure 9.1 The enterprise solutions addressable market (2004)

Operators

With operators, Vodafone is one of the few truly worldwide players. The role of Verizon Wireless, and other US-based operations, has been paramount in the United States, the centre of worldwide corporate markets. Other trendsetting players include NTT DoCoMo and SK Telecom (advanced mobile services).

IT enablers

Microsoft, Intel and IBM are all US IT leaders, but their business mission and mobile activities are quite different. Intel has focused on infrastructure investments, Microsoft on software applications and IBM on system integration through its emphasis on pervasive computing (see Box 9.4).

CORPORATE MARKETS

By 2000, there were some 65,000 transnational corporations (TNCs) operating in the world. These multinationals make up some of the most important corporate markets for enterprise solutions worldwide. Not all country markets and organizations play an equal role in corporate markets. Until recently, the role of the United States has been paramount. This fact has substantial implications for mobile enterprise solutions.

The world's most valuable companies

In 2001, there were a total of 7.1 million business establishments in the United States. Some 86 per cent of these companies had under 20 employees, whereas only 1 per cent – the largest US corporations – had more than 1,000 employees. In 2000, corporations represented 20 per cent of 25,000 business firms, while accounting for more than 85 per cent of the business receipts of all business firms (Statistical Abstract, 2003). Among these corporations, multinationals tend to invest most in innovation and reflect the greatest scale and scope worldwide.

One way to assess the world's largest multinational companies is to rank them by market capitalization. This is the basis for the Financial Times Global 500, which provides an annualized snapshot of the world's largest companies. Historically, US multinationals have dominated the FT Global 500. Penetration enables value activities, which in turn make possible business success. But there is no simple translation from the potential of value activities to actual success. On the other hand, the great size of certain countries – including China and India, Mexico and Brazil – does underscore their great long-term market potential (see Figure 9.2).

Box 9.4   IBM'S MIDDLEWARE SOLUTIONS

'Enterprise customers are looking to mobilize access to applications on many devices across many platforms,' says Letina Connelly who leads the worldwide strategy and marketing efforts for IBM's Pervasive Computing Division. Since 2003, the 'Big Blue' has launched several products and partnerships designed to help businesses deploy wireless services across a range of devices and networks. With an open standards-based architecture, these include strategic alliances with Nokia, Sony Ericsson, Wavecom and Alcatel.

'The ability to access core enterprise data on any device, anywhere, any time, can produce ROI results,' says Connelly. 'The problem is that most enterprise customers have a variety of devices and network protocols. These challenges start to become an inhibitor.'

IBM is creating a 'seamless ecosystem' in the wireless space. 'We are working with device manufacturers, including Nokia, Palm, Ericsson and Sharp, to put software on their devices to allow this to happen quickly.'

Middleware for device diversity

IBM started the pervasive computer division at the end of the 1990s. 'From the very beginning it was our view that more and more IT transactions will be migrating toward non-desktop based IT technology. We wanted to position IBM well in the wireless space. Workforce mobility is something that we have developed for a while. You could argue that companies like Symbol or Intermake were doing exactly that, especially with field force automation. Those are the kind of capabilities that you have with Hertz, when you go to park the car and you are asked to sign a device. Those are very specialized devices.

'Over time, these companies have basically built their own applications hardwired to a device. They are not in the business of building operating technology or middleware technology. They are now starting to use more standard technology which provides more flexibility and allows them to concentrate on the application.'

International differences

'In Europe, the use of smart phone and SMS in the corporate context has become more popular than in the United States. The phone isn't necessarily used for transactions or with placing an order, but it did allow the business to handle more efficiently and effectively. Companies want mobility and a mobile workforce, but different devices require different techniques.

'Japan and Korea are very consumer oriented. They are rapid adapters of the "next big" devices, as well as new wireless technologies, such as smart phones, camera phones and so forth. In the corporate context, the adoption has been much slower. Korea has the highest broadband penetration, some enterprise adoption and is perhaps more consumer-oriented. In the business world, relationships are a significant driver for the way business works in Japan. Corporate culture is still hierarchical, but it is changing.'

Source: the author's interview with Letina Connelly, director of strategy, Pervasive Computing, IBM, 18 May 2004.

Figure 9.2 FT Global 500: Market capitalization (US$ billion) and number of companies

Mobile solutions and company size

With the advent of 3G and high-speed wireless connectivity, companies of all sizes are streamlining their operations, increasing worker productivity and achieving a compelling return on their investments. Still, communication and IT service needs vary across industries and enterprises, in terms of solutions and services, customization and integration, IT skills and decisions (see Table 9.2).

Small companies

Small companies favour off-the-shelf solutions. Services may be hosted, and limited to voice and e-mail communication and basic office applications.

Table 9.2 Communication and IT needs vary by enterprise size

	Small	Medium	Large
Solutions	Off the shelf	Local IT vendors	Full range
Services	Hosted	Some	Full range
Customization	–	Low	High
Integration	–	Low	High
IT skills	Low	Non-core	Core competence
IT decisions	–	Short-term	Long-term

Because of their small size, there is often little or no need for customization and integration. Internal IT skills are low, whereas IT decisions are tactical and short-term rather than strategic and long-term.

Medium-size companies

Local IT vendors provide solutions for medium-sized companies, which often rely on specific enterprise applications. The level of customization and integration is usually low. IT skills may be non-core, but the companies seek to run services themselves, instead of outsourcing them. IT decisions tend to be tactical and short-term.

Large corporations

Large corporations have a long-term IT strategy, which usually shapes their communication and IT needs. Today, many consider IT skills a core competence. The level of customization and integration is high. Most if not all employees enjoy a wide variety of services and solutions.

Unlike small and medium-size companies, large corporations tend to rely on a wide range of solutions and services, while favouring high-level customization and integration.

Industry characteristics

The size of the enterprise does not always define its service and mobility level. The industry in which the enterprise operates also has an effect on the degree of use of vertical applications. Although a logistics or IT consulting enterprise could be small in size, it might use very sophisticated enterprise-specific applications. When process efficiency or customer experience is the critical requirement needed to compete in a particular industry, companies often use a wide range of vertical applications such as CRM and ERP (Figure 9.3) (Nokia, 2003d). In large companies, SMEs, public sector and non-profit organizations, service and mobility needs vary in terms of companies, industries and employee usage profiles.

Three waves

In the US corporate markets, the wireless data segment is barely a decade old. It evolved toward the end of the analog era. Initially, implementations were done by large corporations, such as Federal Express, that could afford to deploy their own private networks and the expense of having individualized, custom solutions crafted for them. At the time, industry-specific applications were the order of the day (Diercks, 2003). With digital transition, the market shifted to consumer and horizontal applications, such as e-mail. By the late 1990s, the business was rapidly specializing and globalizing. With the multimedia transition and the new broadband wireless options, providers focused attention again on delivering industry-specific solutions, in the quest for new

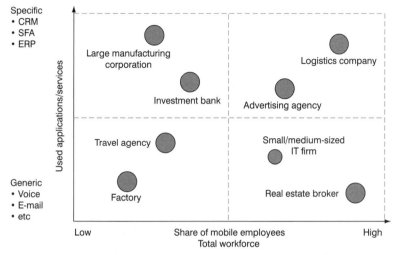

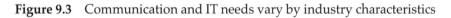

Source: Nokia (2003d), with minor modifications.

Figure 9.3 Communication and IT needs vary by industry characteristics

sources of growth and revenues. The undertaking was not easy because these applications were already available in-house. Still, users needed assistance in extending them, to make them accessible wirelessly to mobile employees.

Key vertical markets

The 'mobile office' is no longer reserved to the upper echelon of corporate users, as an increasing number of companies take advantage of the promise of high-speed mobile connectivity. Companies across industries have deployed mobile solutions, and this adoption of enterprise data solutions will continue. In the United States, the critical vertical markets include:

- manufacturing;
- transportation;
- utilities;
- retail/wholesale trade;
- government;
- services/health care;
- finance, insurance and real estate ('FIRE').

According to a 2003 study of these US vertical markets, services/health care and government represented almost 50 per cent of the overall vertical markets in the mobile business. Coupled with retail/wholesale trade and manufacturing, these four great segments accounted for more than 80 per cent of the total. Some of the earliest adopter industries – transportation and utilities and the FIRE sector – have put wireless data to broad use. With the health care industry, current implementation remains limited. Other vertical markets –

manufacturing, government and retail/wholesale trade – are large, but have been slower to implement the technology on a broad scale (Diercks, 2003).

Currently, most mobile data implementations rely on the cellular network, and often on private company networks, with less use of messaging and other technologies. In the future, these companies continue to be excellent prospects for public WLAN services. End-user companies are focusing more attention on notebooks with wireless modems in the future. The wireless data market has shifted back to focus on vertical markets, where needs are diverse and often complex. Solutions must be tailored to meet each individual market's requirements.

Employee usage profiles

Whether they work for large multinationals, small start-ups, public agencies or non-profit organizations, employees tend to need a fair number of basic services during the work day. In order to develop appropriate services, it is thus vital to understand the service needs of individual employees (see Box 9.5).

Service needs

As communication needs play a great role in business, it can be useful to distinguish between peer-to-peer communication services (voice and messaging communication) and customized services (the internet, content).

Communication services

In business, communication services comprise voice (simple and rich voice) and data-based communication (SMS, MMS and so on).

Customized services

Customized services may include phonebook, calendar, generic office applications, connectivity to enterprise intranet and extranet, as well as various enterprise specific applications, including CRM or SCM applications.

Generic voice, e-mail and office applications are called horizontal applications, while enterprise-specific tailored solutions are known as vertical applications (see Table 9.3).

Mobility needs

Just as service needs vary by employee and over time, so does the need for employee mobility (see Figure 9.4). Some employees stay at the same location throughout the working day, whereas others may have frequent domestic or international business trips. At the broadest level, employee needs for mobile services may be low, medium or high.

Box 9.5   MOBILIZING THE ENTIRE WORKFORCE

In October 2004, Nokia launched its Enterprise Solutions business group, which was located in Westchester, New York. 'We do have a strong customer base with a strong and well known product, so we're not unknown to corporate customers,' says Mary T McDowell. 'Getting more awareness and building more credibility for our solutions is definitely part of the challenge.'

As a 17-year veteran of HP-Compaq, McDowell has a track record of success in building new business. As senior vice president and general manager of Nokia Enterprise Solutions she is responsible for Nokia's complete line of enterprise products and solutions, which include its mobile business device range as well as security and mobile connectivity solutions.

Collaboration is the key

'Nokia's success in the enterprise market clearly depends on our ability to work strategically with the right players,' McDowell says. 'IBM has helped us out in a number of dimensions. Their software groupings and application capabilities give us access to their sales force because they don't have a competing device. Most partnerships are not monogamous so you must maintain your competitiveness.'

Nokia's collaboration includes industry leaders such as IBM, Cisco, Symantec, Computer Associates, Oracle, Hewlett Packard, SAP and many others. 'We will definitely be collaborating with Verizon and Vodafone and other larger operators. We're present at several layers of the IT stack, but Nokia needs to be competitive at each layer, alone or in collaboration. There is probably some tension between the IT and telecom vendors. But there must also be strong collaboration between direct manufacturers, application vendors, operators and integrators to pull the pieces together.'

Extended mobility

'There's a desire to maintain some heterogeneity in solutions. Companies don't necessarily want everything to be a Microsoft product. People want to use Excel and Word and we support those formats on our Communicator devices.'

Bringing extended mobility to the enterprise is one of Nokia's three key strategies and the objective of Enterprise Solutions. The group focuses on mobile business devices and providing IP network perimeter security (firewalls and VPN), secure mobile connectivity (remote access VPN and content) solutions.

In February 2004, Nokia announced a new enterprise-grade Communicator platform, as well as new alliances with leading enterprise players. 'In the previous launch attempts in the United States, the Communicator did not have the right frequency and support and so it never really caught on. This time, we'll have the right support and also incorporate wireless LAN, which is a much stronger requirement in the United States than in the European market. It can be a true alternative to a laptop for certain types of travel. The volume product today is the messaging devices and then our smart phones, such as the 6600. Over time, you'll see more enterprise-specific smart phones.'

Boosting productivity

'Every company, regardless of size, business philosophy or geographical location, will benefit from mobility,' says McDowell. 'Nokia's approach is to take the best in mobility and marry it with the best of the IT world.

'In the past, enterprise mobility was something that people tried to solve by themselves. Today, more and more companies see the need to solve it in a much more systematic and cost-conscious kind of way. Rapid adoption is typical to industries that employ knowledge workers. In addition to telecom, for example, the finance sector has been very important. We also look at industries that have large field forces and that lend themselves to automation. The evolution is proceeding from mobilizing horizontal mobile applications to the next level, where the focus is on more complex business processes that may have more of a vertical dimension.'

Mobilizing people

Nokia already sells a full range of complete mobile voice, connectivity, and security solutions to businesses and institutions. 'In any organization, there are different types of users ranging from the high-end power user to the basic user,' McDowell says. 'Business mobility solutions to date have really only penetrated the high end-user community, which represents less than 5 per cent of the average workforce.

'With a variety of devices, networks, operating systems and applications, the majority of companies lack general mobility guidelines or a comprehensive management system. The diverse needs of the enterprise customer aren't easily met by a 'one size fits all' philosophy. Nokia offers a holistic gateway and device platform-based approach, where we can deliver both real productivity enhancements for users, and cost control and security for IT. The best way of mobilizing people is to leverage the device they already have in their pocket, the mobile phone. Having a specialized device for daily use tends to create a lot of expense and a lot of support for the company.'

Carrier benefits

Beyond the enterprise customer, Nokia believes mobile operators stand to gain the most when business mobility takes off. Carriers will benefit from a larger addressable market, increased average revenue per user, compatibility and interoperability, roaming and interconnecting networks, different service and alliance models, and higher device volumes. Operators will also be the clearinghouse to deliver a single bill and service level.

Nokia business optimized devices, enabled with e-mail, PIM (Personal Information Manager) and calendar functionality, provide operators with an opportunity to significantly expand the emerging mobile e-mail market while growing the overall market. 'Enterprises are demanding mobile services,' says McDowell. 'Wireless access to corporate networks, the emergence of broadband and wireless LAN, the maturity of new wireless devices such as the Nokia 9500 Communicator, the market maturity of technologies and services are all converging into a clear opportunity for the entire business mobility ecosystem. This is a tremendous opportunity to unlock business mobility for Nokia and its partners.'

Source: the author's interview with Mary T McDowell, SVP and general manager of Enterprise Solutions, Nokia Corp, 27 May 2004.

Table 9.3 Employees need a multitude of services

Voice	Voice (simple or rich voice calls in the office or on the move)
Internet	E-mail (e-mail to PC or mobile phone); PIM (calendar, phonebook, contacts); business connectivity (access to intranet/extranet/internet from PC/laptop/mobile phone)
Communication	Messaging (voice, text, multimedia, instant messaging)
Business Processes	Office applications (Notes, MS) and company specific vertical applications
	Value activities

Low mobility needs are typical to employees who stay in one place through most of the day, such as assembly line workers in a car plant, call centre service employees or fast-food store employees, whether in Detroit, Bangalore or Disney World, Florida.

Medium mobility needs characterize employees, such as academic professionals and managers in assembly plants, whose needs tend to alternate between non-mobile and highly mobile. For instance, employees in a university campus prefer to use a PC or a laptop in their office, but may also need mobile communications as they move from one place or meeting to another.

High mobility needs are typical to people who spend more than one day of the work week outside their office or home site, from sales professionals to cab drivers.

Similarly, the degree and type of mobility required by users varies. For instance, the mobility profile of telecommuters differs from that of business travellers.

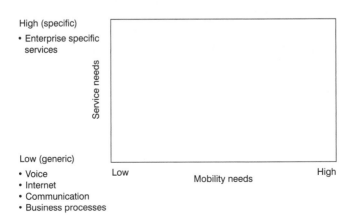

Figure 9.4 Two axes: service and mobility needs

Developing mobility profiles

By combining the estimated service and mobility needs, it is possible to develop employee profiles, which help to understand the needs of individual employees. Service needs and mobility needs can be combined into employee profiles. These enable a better assessment of the needs of individual employees.

Vendor postures

Mobile vendors such as Nokia and IT enablers like Microsoft have developed mobility profiles to better understand the needs of the business end-users. The Nokia profile focuses on mobile usage profiles, whereas Microsoft's illustrates mobility scenarios based on a variety of devices (see Table 9.4).

Operator postures

As operators develop strategic postures for addressing business customers with mobile solutions, they too need to assess the service and mobility needs of individual employees. Uniform packages – a single device with similar services for everyone – is no longer sufficient. Today, multiple ownership is a reality in many workplaces. Also, most employees are not yet mobile, despite increasing mobilization. The mobile employees are often considered the most valuable employees in an enterprise, and by mobilizing services beyond voice and messaging, operators can offer significant efficiency gains to companies. For operators, this means higher levels of average revenue per user (ARPU) and more mobile data in the network.[15]

Developing mobile service offerings

Mobile operators should define their mobile service offering for businesses according to the size of the company, the nature of the industry, and the service and mobility needs of the employees. An incremental approach is to start with smaller companies, which are characterized by high mobility but limited service needs. Since operators have historically been strong in horizontal services, such as voice and messaging, they could package boosted e-mail to these companies. The same services can be expanded to larger corporations, especially those looking for outsourcing opportunities. Mobilizing vertical applications, such as CRM, is more complex and will in most cases require close partnering with system integrators and IT and software companies in order to provide an end-to-end solution.

With each company, there are a number of end-users with different needs. By combining end-user segmentation with enterprise segmentation, operators can build a high-performing portfolio of mobile business solutions that meet these needs – even as they must ensure the highest possible customer satisfaction and return on investment.

Table 9.4 Two axes: service and mobility needs

Nokia's Approach	Microsoft's Approach
Nokia's seven profiles illustrate different service and mobility profiles.[1]	Microsoft's mobility scenarios comprise four generic service and mobility profiles.[2]

Low Mobile Usage

These are *at site workers*, who spend most of their time in the same place. They can be divided into two segments, according to their PC usage. *At site desk workers* rely on PC (e-mail, basic office applications) and phone in work. Their mobility is low. They may serve in call centres and research organizations. *At site talkers* may only have a fixed phone and they share or do not use a PC at all; but they are more mobile than the at-site workers (eg, salesmen in an electronics store).

Low Mobile Usage

Corridor warriors are knowledge workers who spend much time away from their desks, eg, healthcare professionals and managers who travel less than 20 per cent of the time and are usually dashing from one meeting to the next. They require access to information and applications, ad-hoc collaboration with colleagues, and a paperless environment. The Tablet PC was the form factor for corridor warriors, coupled with Pocket PCs or Smartphones.

Medium Mobile Usage

Campus workers are white-collar employees in medium or large corporations. They have a PC/laptop, a fixed phone and a mobile handset. Although they work mainly in their workplace, they also travel regularly between sites or travel domestically and internationally. Their job description alternates between heavy computing and heavy communications.

Medium Mobile Usage

These comprise *telecommuters* and *data collectors*. Telecommuters worked at home at least one day a week, often accessing corporate resources from a home computer by using a broadband or dial-up connection, or leaving the office only occasionally. *Data collectors* are field service employees in a variety of vertical industries (eg, delivery drivers, warehouse employees, and insurance claim adjusters). They are away from their desks more than 80 per cent of the time. Windows Mobile-based Pocket PCs provide many vertical-market applications for them.

High Mobile Usage

These comprise four sub-segments. All are highly mobile, but use different services. *Mobile talkers* use their phones with intense loyalty; they do not leave home without it. Typically employed in sales and coordination, these users see their mobile phone as a talking device. *Mobile messengers* also take advantage of text messages and e-mails to deliver or confirm information. They extend from sales team managers to truck drivers. What makes *mobile multitaskers* different from mobile talkers and messengers is that basic voice or messaging services are not sufficient for them; they use frequently enterprise specific applications, such as CRM or warehouse database applications. *Mobile specialists* form the narrowest category. Their profile is distinctive in that they often have a laptop connected to an enterprise intranet or to a specific application, and they may also send substantial amounts of data while mobile.

High Mobile Usage

Road warriors travel frequently, spending up to 80 per cent of their time out of the office. Whether they are corporate executives, members of a mobile sales force, or field representatives, they need robust hardware and software on the road. They have a broad choice of mobile devices from which to choose. They tend to use their handheld devices for calendaring, e-mail, and travel planning, so they can back up their primary computers with a Pocket PC or Windows Mobile-based Smartphones. Their information is with them regardless of whether they're in a taxi, waiting for a flight, or on the go.

---

[1] Nokia (2003d), Nokia for Business: Meeting the mobility and service needs of employees, White Paper, Nokia Networks, 10/2003.

[2] Honeycutt, Jerry (2004), Windows XP Professional, Windows Mobile 2003, and Office Professional Edition 2003 for a Mobile Workforce, Microsoft Corp., March 2004.

10

Strategy and mobility

In the late 1990s, distorted market signals gave rise to the notion of the 'twin drivers' (the internet and mobility), which justified high valuations in the two high-growth markets. Concurrently, many argued that the internet rendered strategy obsolete. In reality, a disconnect prevailed between fundamentals and valuations. Instead of market signals, it would have been more prudent to pay attention to economic value. Whether driven by new technology or new markets, first-mover advantages do not suffice in and of themselves; they must be translated to sustainable competitive advantages. The winners will be those companies that can dynamically master new technologies, while pioneering new markets with new products and services. They know how to align mobility – and more broadly, information technology – with strategy.

FROM MARKET SIGNALS TO ECONOMIC VALUE

With the rise of the internet and the hypergrowth of the mobile markets, valuations went through the roof. As Jeremy Siegel put it in *Stocks for the Long Run*, 'Although the prices of Internet stocks seemed nonsensical, many of the leading brokerage firms and investment houses sought to justify these valuations by almost metaphysical reasoning' (Siegel, 2002: 148–49).

In the 1990s, many presumed that the internet would render the old rules about companies and competition obsolete. That may have been an understandable reaction to market developments, but it led many new dotcoms and incumbent industry leaders alike to bad strategic decisions. These decisions eroded the attractiveness of their industries, while undermining competitive advantages (Porter, 2001). About the same time, something similar took place with many mobile leaders and small mobcoms in Western Europe (Steinbock, 2003c).

Twin drivers

By the mid-1990s, the internet boosted valuations. It was the 'next big thing'. The romanticized Silicon Valley was depicted as the engine of new capitalism. Europeans had lost the game, Americans triumphed. Japan was still in recession, the emerging 'China phenomenon' was ignored. After the internet boom, still another cycle of technology-driven hype followed. Now the 'mobilization' of the internet was portrayed as the 'next big thing', and the Old Country substituted for the United States' high-tech Mecca. European-based mobile leaders were determined to bring the benefits of the convergence of the internet and mobility to the markets.

The dreams of limitless market growth in the wireless sector climaxed with the soaring market valuations. 'If the cell-phone business is your investment of choice, you may have staked out a good spot,' commented *Business Week* in August 1998. 'Nokia and Ericsson are both great companies at the forefront of a growing market. If you can't decide between the two… Buy 'em both' (Stone, 1998). About a year later, *Fortune* seconded, noting that Nokia's stock 'goes bananas, up almost 2,000% in five years… It's a great story, and one that will probably continue for a few more years ' (Guyon, 1999). By spring 2000, CEO Jorma Ollila and President Pekka Ala-Pietilä spoke about the 'twin drivers' of the industry: 'We are using the twin drivers of the Internet and mobility to break through the limits of time and place' (Ollila and Ala-Pietilä, 1999).

Before the meltdown of mobile valuations in 2001, Nokia's market capitalization soared to US $260 billion; in August 2002, it was US $54 billion. Although it fared better than most of its rivals, business was no longer about dreams, but about 'making best execution an asset' (Ollila and Ala-Pietilä, 2000). With the bust of the stock market, the slowdown of the technology sector, the eclipse of the telecom boom and the inflated 3G licence auctions in Europe, the competitive environment looked very different.

Twisted dreams

Until the WAP debacle and 3G licence auctions, European mobcoms exhibited many characteristics of the dotcoms in the United States. In both cases, the proliferation of small start-ups in the emerging technology segment led to artificial businesses, which were competing by artificial means and boosted by opportunistic capital. In both cases, a period of transition gave rise to ideas that new rules of competition had replaced fundamental business realities. In both cases, too, as market forces played out, capital withdrew (Bensche and Ritter, 2003).

In the early stages of the roll-out of an important new technology, market signals can be unreliable. New technologies trigger fervent experimentation, but they are seldom economically sustainable. In the emerging phase of innovation, heavy experimentation can cause technology providers to prosper, irrespective of whether the respective technologies prove to be successful or are flawed. Market behaviour may not reflect business fundamentals. With the US dotcoms and Euro mobcoms, signals from the stock market were untrustworthy at best. Distorted revenues, costs and share prices were coupled with unreliable financial metrics. Traditional measures of profitability and economic value were downplayed (Porter, 2001).

Historically, technology businesses, including wireless stocks, have significantly contributed to four peak periods of high price relative to earnings – during the 20th-century technology boom (driven by the wireless bubble), the radio boom (driven by wireless communications), the post-war conglomerate boom and the millennium boom (reinforced by the twin driver myth) (Figure 10.1)[1]

Like the internet, mobility is an enabling technology. It may be used in most industries and as part of most strategies, wisely or unwisely. It can provide companies with greater efficiencies, differentiation and new opportunities to compete, or combinations of all three. The key question is not whether to but *how* to deploy mobile technologies. The true challenge is to create economic value, which involves two fundamental drivers that influence profitability: first, industry forces, which determine the profitability of the average competitor, and second, sustainable competitive advantage, which allows a company to outperform the average competitor. These two underlying drivers transcend any specific technology or line of business. They prevail increasingly worldwide, but may vary significantly by industry and company.

MOBILITY AND COMPETITIVE ADVANTAGE

During the internet boom, technology-based advantages were often associated with competitive advantages. Yet this identity is seldom automatic. Take, for instance, the many forms of mobilization. Mobile asset management allows field service engineers to access relevant business processes anywhere and any time to solve maintenance issues. Mobile field service enables field service engineers and technicians to react quickly to customer problems. Mobile sales support provides for salespeople who need to perform revenue-generating tasks quickly and productively. Mobile procurement empowers mobile staff to manage the entire procurement function, from price comparison to ordering. Mobile time and travel give mobile employees access to human resource functionality, including time and travel management. These have been termed five mobile strategies that create business value (Kalakota, 2004).

These forms of mobility, however, are examples not of mobile strategies, but of mobile adoption. During the early phases of mobile transition – or any new enabling technologies – the first movers may well enjoy substantial superiority

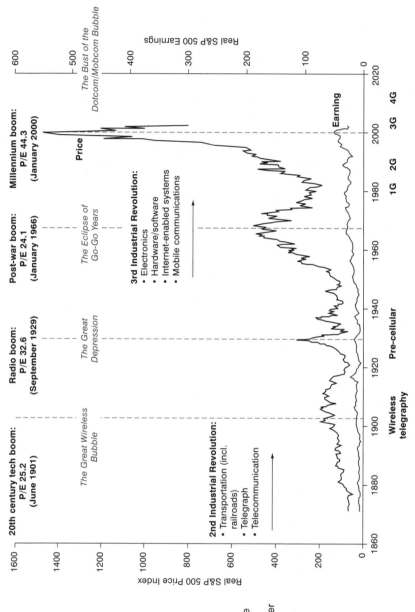

Figure 10.1 Valuation peaks, 1871–2000

over competitors, through efficiency or differentiation or both. But these advantages are often difficult to translate to sustainable competitive advantage. When competitors catch up, pioneer benefits typically dissipate. In fact, they are examples of mobile conversions: that is, the mobilization of physical and virtual value activities. There are many others, and they are all driven by the economic logic of the business. They may be necessary to compete, but they bring no assurances of winning the competition.

All companies perform a number of discrete and interconnected value-creating activities, such as operating a sales force, or after-sale service, engaging in manufacturing or design activities, or technology development. Conversely, these activities have points of connection with the activities of suppliers, channels and customers. The value chain provides a framework for identifying all these activities and analysing how they affect a company's relative cost position, and the value delivered to buyers. A business is profitable as long as the value it creates exceeds the cost of performing the value activities.

Information technology pervades the value chain because every activity involves the creation, processing and communication of information. With the internet, many physical activities have been virtualized to gain greater efficiencies or differentiation (see Porter, 2001). Mobilization is driven by a comparable logic. The internet virtualized physical activities, while creating new kinds of virtual activities. With an array of wireless technologies, most of these activities can be mobilized, while users can also deploy new kinds of mobile activities (see Figure 10.2).

Most obviously, mobile devices speed up the sales cycle. Mobilized customer relationship management, for instance, can cut out the normal series of media interactions required to complete a sale, because the transaction can all be done via the mobile instantly. By the same token, it can assist customer service departments and call centres to notify customers of potential problems, such as flight delays (see, for example, Stone and Foss, 2001).

During the past few years, customers have identified many qualitative benefits of mobilization in a wide variety of industries, vertical industries and job roles. In health care, mobilization allows better availability of information, such as quick access to medical reference documents. In financial services, mobility can support real-time processing of financial applications and shorter loan processing times. In many industries, mobilization enables services professionals to stay current on the road by notifications of market conditions and news wires. In education, mobility can storage large data eliminating the need to carry around bulk and weight. In manufacturing, it provides accurate and up-to-date centralized data for reliable analysis, more available real-time data to improve job scheduling, as well as improved data input quality with integrated bar code scanning. In real estate, mobility can offer more efficient access to the latest inventory in multiple listing services. In hospitality, it can support wireless transfer of food and drink orders to different locations, as well as up-to-the-minute reporting of rooms that have been cleaned for new guests. In retail and distribution, mobilization enables

Firm Infrastructure
- Mobile financial and ERP systems, including legal and government information, investor relations (information delivery, alerts)
- Voice-to-data conversions: mobile forms-based applications, to multi-function devices, multimedia cellular and wireless broadband
- Mobile services: rich voice (incl. imaging, videoconferencing), internet (plus intranet/extranet), messaging (LBS, SMS, MMS) and content (information, entertainment, transactions, database)
- Access to e-mails, personal information management, network security

Human Resource Management
- Mobile activities in recruiting, hiring, training, development and compensation, incl. mobile time and expense reporting
- Mobile sharing and distribution of company information
- Mobile services via HRM: voice guidance, messaging (MMS, LBS, SMS, via pull and/or push), internet (eg, downloading, footnote links, interstitials, etc) and infotainment (incl. distributed knowledge directories)

Technology Development
- Mobile efforts to improve products, processes and services
- Mobile teams, distributed collaborative product design across locations and among multiple value-system participants
- Real-time access by R&D to mobile sales and service information

Procurement
- Mobile input purchases used in the firm's value chain, including raw materials, suppliers and other consumable items as well as assets
- Mobile demand planning and fulfilment
- Other mobile linkages of inventory, and forecasting systems with suppliers and/or buyers
- Mobile procurement via markets, exchanges, auctions, and buyer-seller matching

Inbound Logistics	Operations	Outbound Logistics	Marketing & Sales	After-Sales Service
Mobile activities in receiving, storing and disseminating inputs to products/services	Mobile activities associated with transforming inputs into final products/services	Mobile activities associated with collecting, storing and distributing products/services to buyers	Mobile activities with means for buyers to purchase products/services and inducing them to do so, incl. advertising, promotion, sales force, channels, pricing	Mobile activities associated with providing service to enhance or maintain the value of product/services
• Mobile scheduling, shipping, warehouse/demand management and planning, advanced planning and scheduling across the company and its suppliers • Mobile distribution across the company of real-time inbound and in-progress inventory data	• Mobile information exchange, scheduling and decision making in inhouse plants, contract assemblers, and components suppliers • Mobile available-to-promise and capable-to-promise information to sales force and channels	• Mobile order processing and scheduling • Mobile delivery vehicle operation • Mobile forms of customer-tailored agreements and contracts • Mobile customer/channel access to product development and distribution status • Mobile channel management, incl. information exchange, contract warranty claims, contract management (versioning, process control)	• Mobile sales channels, eg, websites, marketplaces • Mobile access to customer information, product catalogues, dynamic pricing, inventory, quotes, order entry • Mobile product/service configurators • Mobile push/pull advertising • Mobile customer feedback, incl. mobile surveys, opt-in/opt-out marketing, and promotion response tracking	• Mobile support of customer service reps (incl. voice guidance, SMS, MMS, LBS, e-mail, billing, co-browse, chat, VoIP, video streaming) • Mobile customer self-service via portals and mobile service request processing, incl. updates, alerts and notifications to billing, shipping etc • Mobile field service access to customer account review, availability and ordering, work-order updates, service parts management

Mobile supply-chain management | True real-time access to information across primary activities | Mobile customer-relationship management

Figure 10.2 Mobility and the value chain

increased efficiency through location-based services for drivers and immediately transmitted wireless orders for same-day delivery (see Dedo 2004, and other industry observers).

These and many other examples of mobilization can be studied more systematically with the value chain framework of value chain.

Support activities

Every firm can be depicted as a collection of activities that are performed to design, produce, market, deliver and support its products, processes and services. These activities can be divided broadly into support and primary activities. In any industry, support activities can be divided into several generic categories, including firm infrastructure, human resource management, technology development and procurement.

Firm infrastructure

Unlike other support activities, infrastructure typically supports the entire chain, not individual activities. Often viewed only as 'overhead', this activity may be a powerful source of strategic advantage, particularly through smart use of management information technology. Firm infrastructure comprises general management, planning, finance, accounting, legal and government affairs. The transition from voice to data enables the conversion of physical paper-based activities to digitized forms-based applications. These are typical infrastructure conversions, which also support process engineering efforts. Examples include reducing operational costs, data collection time, improving customer response times and shortening the cycle time.

Increasing investigative efficiency nationwide

Credit Saison, one of Japan's major credit card companies, decided to use i-mode to streamline its investigation processes. Before using NTT DoCoMo's service, documents and reports were exchanged between branch offices in paper form via fax or delivery service. The process took a week in city areas and up to a month in remote areas. Now investigators working at 13 branches across Japan can access the corporate server to retrieve data and send reports to headquarters via their i-mode phones. With the i-mode service, Credit Saison has cut the investigation time in city areas to just three days, significantly improving business and adding differentiation from competitors. i-mode's easy-to-operate terminals have also reduced training time for new employees.[1]

Human resource management

Human resource management includes activities involved in the recruiting, hiring, training, development and compensation of all types of personnel.

From laptops to pocket PCs

Headquartered in New York City, Ray & Berndtson is the world's seventh largest retained executive search firm. Much of the work of its executive search professionals involves checking e-mail and using a custom contact management system that tracks more than 300,000 candidates. Laptops had become costly tools for these tasks. Instead of an estimated US $800,000 required to replace high-end laptops, the firm purchased pocket PCs (iPAQ) by Compaq. This approach resulted in a decrease of about 50 per cent from the capital acquisition budget. The solution enabled a high level of integration and synchronization with the enterprise, easy-to-learn development tools, and economical wireless capabilities.[2]

Technology development

Every value activity embodies technology, from tacit knowledge to process equipment. This category comprises a range of activities that can broadly be grouped into efforts to improve products, processes and services.

Lower development and maintenance costs

Dollar Rent A Car is one of the world's largest car rental agencies, which operates in more than 400 locations in 26 countries, including 250 locations and a fleet of 75,000 cars in the United States, along with a significant presence in Australia, Canada, the Caribbean and Latin America. By providing partners with direct, secure access into its reservation system, Dollar was able to cost-effectively open up another sales channel that has provided millions of additional rate requests and thousands of new reservations per year, equating to millions of dollars in additional revenue. For Dollar, a key benefit of this capability was the relatively low cost of acquisition for new reservations.[3]

Procurement

Procurement comprises the function of purchasing inputs used in the firm's value chain, including raw materials, suppliers and other consumable items as well as assets, such as machinery, office equipment and buildings. These are typically present in every value activity.

RFID versus bar codes

In rudimentary forms, radio frequency identification (RFID) has been around since the 1980s and has been widely used to identify vehicles and track livestock.[4] RFID's advantages over older technologies such as bar codes include a read capability that does not depend on contact or line of sight and a speed of reading that is less than 100 milliseconds. In 2003, SAP, Intel and a host of partners launched a working laboratory supermarket in Germany to test RFID. In the oil industry, BP had already begun to put RFID project opportunities into practice in some 32,000 retail sites around the world. RFID tags are poised to become the most far-reaching wireless technology since the cell phone.

Worldwide revenues from RFID tags are expected to jump from US $300 million in 2004 to US $2.8 billion in 2009. During this period, the technology will appear in many industries with significant impact on the efficiency of business processes (In-Stat/MDR, 2005).

Primary activities

In any industry, there are five generic categories of primary activities. These can be divided into a number of distinct activities that depend on the particular industry and firm strategy.

Inbound logistics

These are activities associated with receiving, storing and disseminating inputs to the product, including material handling, warehousing, inventory control, vehicle scheduling and returns to suppliers.

Inspecting inbound aircraft and sea vessels

US Customs Officers use pocket PCs when inspecting inbound aircraft and sea vessels at more than 300 international air and sea ports of entry, fighting to halt the smuggling of narcotics into the United States. Customs officials at Miami International Airport needed to make the time officers spend in the field conducting inspections more efficient while increasing the accuracy of data collected. The results include saving almost one work week per month and reducing errors by 80 per cent through automation and digitization. Access to critical information enables better-informed, timelier decisions and quicker action.[5]

Operations

These activities are associated with transforming inputs into the final product form, such as machining, packaging, assembly, equipment maintenance, testing, printing and facility operations.

A transportation and rail network

CSX Transportation is a railroad freight carrier that owns and operates the largest rail network in the eastern United States. With mobility, it hoped to improve the efficiency of its railroad operations and communication with the railroad conductors on its freight trains. With touch-screen mobile PCs running Microsoft Windows CE.net, Qualcomm created an on-board work order management system to keep 200 rail conductors in constant contact with workflow progress reports and freight scheduling updates. It eliminated the reworking and handling of manual data, thereby increasing workforce productivity, uniform job reporting and data accuracy. At the same time, the time lag in delivery reporting to customers was cut by two-thirds.[6]

Distribution

These activities are associated with collecting, storing and physically distributing the product to buyers, including finished goods warehousing, material handling, delivery vehicle operation, order processing and scheduling.

Information and order entry

Egmont Entertainment is Scandinavia's leading distributor of films for cinema, television and video as well as electronic games. Its field sales people employ pocket PCs to receive information and enter orders while at retailer outlets, enabling them to visit 20 per cent more customers per day. Automating about 50 per cent of all orders enabled Egmont to redeploy most of its call centre staff to provide improved customer service. The distributor found the user training costs to be minimal and the mobile solution maintenance costs to be low.[7]

Marketing and sales

These activities are associated with providing a means by which buyers can purchase the product and inducing them to do so, including advertising, promotion, sales force, quoting, channel selection, channel relations and pricing.

Manufacturing sales force automation

Coca-Cola Corp. obtained a portable selling tool to support its field sales force – the people who go out and prospect for new locations and customers for vending machines. This solution automated the collection of information about sales calls, customers and prospects. It was based on a US $500 handheld device, which supported the specific user's tasks that would have been done on a US $4,000 PC. This savings was associated with over 80 salespeople. The ability to point and click through the wizard windows of Visual CE enabled the application almost to develop itself. Radio buttons and drop-down menus tend to be quicker to access and manipulate while mobile than working with a keyboard and mouse on a laptop. The new approach was also good for mobile worker morale.[8]

Service

These are activities associated with providing service to enhance or maintain the value of the product, such as installation, repair, training, parts supply and product adjustment.

Greater accuracy and efficiency in order processing

Corochan has a chain of more than 600 croquette franchise stores throughout Japan. Prior to using i-mode, each store manager had to place a supply order to the headquarters via fax twice a day. This meant a rush at headquarters, mistakes in data translation into the main system, and forwarding the inaccuracies to suppliers. As the company introduced the i-mode ordering system, the user-friendly system allows store managers to place orders, send sales reports and time-card data to headquarters from anywhere via their mobile phones. Corochan is now able to process orders, compile data from stores with fewer mistakes and with greater efficiency, and can also view the sales status of each store more readily, allowing it to formulate more effective sales strategies.[9]

The examples above underscore the role of mobilization potential in differentiating value activities, reducing costs and providing new venues for innovation. This potential can create strategic advantage by providing companies with new ways to outperform their rivals. In addition to the transformation of value activities, mobility is changing competitive forces and thereby altering industry structure.

MOBILITY AND COMPETITIVE STRATEGY

Like the internet, mobility has created new industries, including location-based services. But as has been the case with the internet, its greatest impact may be in reconfiguring existing industries. The relative effect of mobilization is likely to be most intense in industries with high mobile information intensity, with a large mobile workforce, or in firms with value activities that are relatively easy to mobilize. Each industry is different, and each is affected by mobility in different ways. However, there are some broad mobility trends that seem to affect many industries (see Figure 10.3).

In thinking about mobility and economic value, it is useful to draw a distinction between the uses of mobility (such as offering mobile services, mobile commerce or trading) and mobile technologies, which can be deployed across many uses. Mobile technology providers (mobile vendors, operators, IT enablers, content providers and consumer electronics firms) can prosper for a time irrespective of whether the uses of mobility are profitable. But unless the uses generate sustainable revenues or savings in excess of their cost of deployment, the opportunity for technology providers will dissipate as companies conclude that further investment is not economically sound.

Industry rivalry

Whether old or new, the attractiveness of an industry is determined by the underlying forces of competition: the intensity of rivalry among existing competitors, the bargaining power of suppliers and buyers, the threat of substitutes, as well as the entry barriers for new competitors. Collectively, these forces determine how the economic value created by any product, process or service is divided between industry firms, their customers, suppliers, distributors, substitutes and complements, as well as potential new entrants (Porter, 1980).

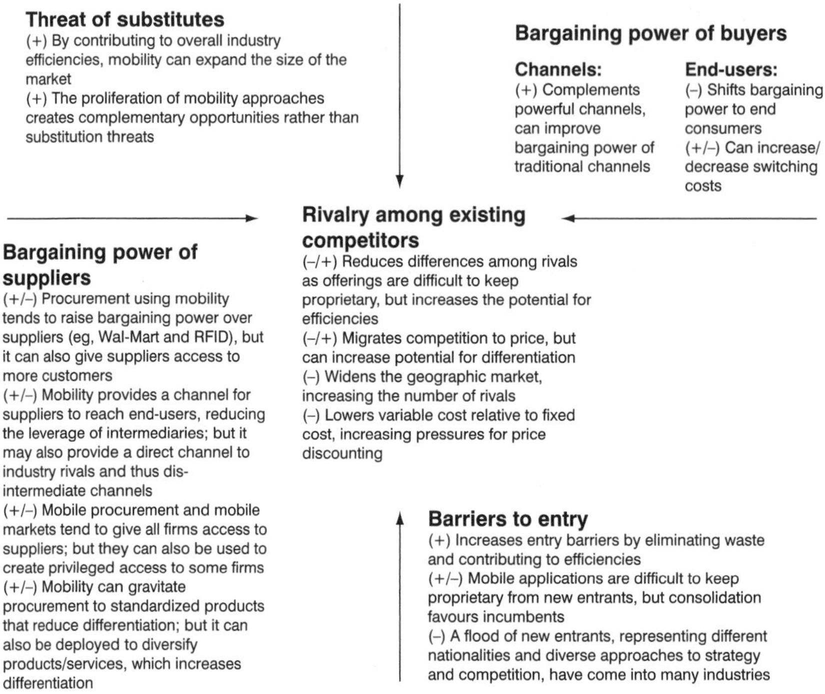

Threat of substitutes
(+) By contributing to overall industry efficiencies, mobility can expand the size of the market
(+) The proliferation of mobility approaches creates complementary opportunities rather than substitution threats

Bargaining power of buyers

Channels:
(+) Complements powerful channels, can improve bargaining power of traditional channels

End-users:
(−) Shifts bargaining power to end consumers
(+/−) Can increase/ decrease switching costs

Rivalry among existing competitors
(−/+) Reduces differences among rivals as offerings are difficult to keep proprietary, but increases the potential for efficiencies
(−/+) Migrates competition to price, but can increase potential for differentiation
(−) Widens the geographic market, increasing the number of rivals
(−) Lowers variable cost relative to fixed cost, increasing pressures for price discounting

Bargaining power of suppliers
(+/−) Procurement using mobility tends to raise bargaining power over suppliers (eg, Wal-Mart and RFID), but it can also give suppliers access to more customers
(+/−) Mobility provides a channel for suppliers to reach end-users, reducing the leverage of intermediaries; but it may also provide a direct channel to industry rivals and thus dis-intermediate channels
(+/−) Mobile procurement and mobile markets tend to give all firms access to suppliers; but they can also be used to create privileged access to some firms
(+/−) Mobility can gravitate procurement to standardized products that reduce differentiation; but it can also be deployed to diversify products/services, which increases differentiation

Barriers to entry
(+) Increases entry barriers by eliminating waste and contributing to efficiencies
(+/−) Mobile applications are difficult to keep proprietary from new entrants, but consolidation favours incumbents
(−) A flood of new entrants, representing different nationalities and diverse approaches to strategy and competition, have come into many industries

Figure 10.3   How mobility influences industry forces

The intensity of industry competition is driven by several interacting forces. Mobility can affect all of them. In industries with few firms and maturing growth, mobility tends to add to concentration and balance, and at least initially to fixed costs. It reduces differences among rivals, as offerings are difficult to keep proprietary, but it can also provide new ways for firms to differentiate, through product differences and, over time, brand identity. It can reinforce migrating competition to price, but also increases the potential for efficiencies. It may widen the geographic market, increasing the number of rivals and competitive intensity. It tends to lower variable cost relative to fixed cost, increasing pressures for price discounting. The challenge is to deploy mobile devices in order to increase switching costs, which can contribute to entry barriers.

Threat of substitutes

At the broadest level, all industry firms compete with industries producing substitute products and services. Substitutes that deserve the greatest attention are those that can pose a threat with relative price performance, through switching costs or buyer propensity to substitute. In many emerging markets, mobile devices serve as substitutes for fixed-line phones and networks. After all, mobile services are getting closer to price parity, can boost switching costs, and provide significant inducements by empowering people. In advanced markets, health services abound with examples of device substitution rivalries as hospitals, doctors and nurses are testing various mobile devices, including smart phones, web tablets, notebooks and communicators.

From the standpoint of the users, the mobile impact can be relatively positive. By contributing to overall industry efficiencies, mobility can expand the size of the market. Moreover, the proliferation of mobility approaches creates complementary opportunities rather than substitution threats.

Threat of entry

Average industry profitability is shaped by existing and potential rivals. Resting on irreversible resource commitments, entry barriers serve to prevent an influx of firms into an industry whenever profits, adjusted for the cost of capital, rise above zero. In the early days of the internet boom, many industry incumbents were concerned for attackers, challengers and the threat of entry. With mobilization, this concern has not been paramount.

Because of the successive waves of innovation and the subsequent dominance of large incumbents, new entrants tend to be small IT and mobile firms focusing on complementary technologies, products and services. In most cases, these start-ups and challengers pose little threat to industry leaders, with their scale economies, established brand identities, capital requirements and access to distribution. If anything, the new entrants tend to be cooperators that merely reinforce and solidify the relationships between various industry players. While new mobile entrants have come into many industries, this situation prevails on the user side as well. Mobility tends to increase entry barriers by eliminating waste and contributing to efficiencies. Mobile applications are often difficult to keep proprietary from new entrants, but consolidation favours incumbents.

Bargaining power of suppliers

Suppliers can exert bargaining power over participants in an industry by threatening to raise prices or reduce the quality of purchased goods and services. Along with other drivers, mobility tends to contribute to rather than disrupt general industry conditions. Accordingly, it may contribute to supplier concentration if suppliers are more concentrated than the industry they are selling to; if the suppliers' offerings are vital input to the buyers; and if these offerings are differentiated or come with substantial switching costs. These trends tend to be Janus-faced. Procurement using mobility may raise bargaining power over suppliers, but it can also give suppliers access to more customers. Mobility provides a channel for suppliers to reach end-users, reducing the leverage of intermediaries; but it also offers a direct channel to industry rivals. Mobile procurement and mobile markets tend to give all firms equal access to suppliers, but they also gravitate procurement to standardized products that reduce differentiation.

Bargaining power of buyers

Extending the internet migration from the physical to the virtual, mobility shifts bargaining power from computers that people use to people that use computers. It empowers producers and users, not just their desktops. This is the idea of 'intelligence everywhere' (Motorola) or 'connecting people' (Nokia). With mobility, the buyers may acquire substantial bargaining leverage, especially when they are concentrated, account for high volume, have lower switching costs relative to the firm than vice versa, possess information and have access to substitute offerings. Similar developments involve buyers' price sensitivity. As relative differences between offerings have declined, product differences and brand identity, and differences in quality and performance, are no longer as critical as they used to be for buyers. It is the very convenience of the mobile device that makes possible its extraordinary reach; but this reach is compromised by its small size and emotional intimacy. With aggressive deployment of push campaigns, firms risk alienating their customers, which carriers will pay as churn.

Mobility tends to complement powerful channels (Wal-Mart's RFID initiatives), but it can also improve bargaining power over traditional channels. By the same token, it may shift bargaining power to end consumers. And while it increases switching costs, it may underscore opportunity costs.

The value system

The impact of mobility can be assessed from the standpoint of individual firms (value chains) and the industry wherein they compete (industry forces). But all value chains are embedded in a larger stream of activities, the value system.

From wholesale to retail

The value system includes industry participants such as suppliers, channels and buyers. Suppliers, for instance, have value chains (upstream value) that create and deliver the purchased inputs used in a firm's chain. Similarly, many products and services pass through the value chains of channels (channel value) on their way to the buyer. Each of these participants performs additional activities that affect the buyer, while influencing the firm's own activities. Eventually, the technology, product or service becomes part of its buyer's value chain. The ultimate basis for differentiation is the role of the company's offering in the buyer's value chain, which determines buyer needs.[10]

During the past century, bargaining power in many industries has shifted from wholesalers to manufacturers to retailers (Chandler, 1977, 1990). In the past, the mobile vendors in the wireless business were best positioned to 'listen to the markets'. With the transition from voice to data, the operators are closest to the customers. The friction over co-branding between vendors and operators reflects not only operators' efforts at differentiation but also shifts of bargaining power in the value system, from upstream toward downstream activities. The models of leading mobile operators are no longer telecom giants, such as the historical AT&T, but globalizing retail powerhouses, such as Wal-Mart, and global brand marketers like Disney.

Cooperation and complementarities

With the laissez-faire internet, new start-ups could be launched with relative ease, whereas the evolution of the mobile business has been quite different. The mobile value system is based on complex systems and novel technologies, which are specializing and globalizing. No single strategic group can dominate the system. The smooth functioning of the whole requires cooperation and complementarities rather than destructive rivalry and substitution – intermediation, not disintermediation. With new start-ups and challengers, these trends underscore the importance of cooperative business models, as exemplified by the winning business models of carriers such as NTT DoCoMo, Vodafone, Verizon Wireless and SK Telecom.

Indeed, the mobile value system, suggests Takeshi Natsuno, the founder of i-mode, can be projected as an industry-wide value chain:

> These relationships can also be understood as a value chain, including sophisticated mobile phones that are easy to operate. A telecommunications network links those phones. Gateway servers connect the network to the Internet. Portals allow subscribers to easily find the content they like. A business model supports the distribution of that content. These relationships are held together by a value chain that delivers great user satisfaction. From the subscribers' perspective, it is the content that gives i-mode its value.[11]

Currently, the ringtone service is the most successful example of the intertwined value system:

> In order to deliver ringtones to subscribers, it is not sufficient to have a content provider make the melodies available on its server. Manufacturers must produce mobile phones, which have been designed to play back melodies. A telecom provider must set up a network to distribute them. There must be agreements on fee collection and authorization, and so forth. Only then can the subscriber hear the opening bars and personalize his or her phone. These elements – content, phones, networks, servers, portals marketing and billing – form a system. If one is missing, the ringtone service won't exist. And the same applies to other services. So it's this ecosystem that's critical to generate value.[12]

With mobility, most trends tend to be complementary, but they may come with a price. Like the explosion of the bar code, the future prospects of new mobile technologies, as well as products and services enabled by them, such as RFID, may be characterized by increasing concentration, reduced cost of managing variety in a retail network, and the shift of power in the value system toward retailers.

MOBILITY, BUSINESS MODELS AND STRATEGY

Today, the terms 'strategic advantage' and 'business model' are used almost interchangeably. In reality, they are quite different. Moreover, many observers and industry practitioners consider strategy dated in contemporary rivalry, which is often driven by the pursuit of speed and agility. In the past, business models were often evoked to justify the adoption of new and unproven technologies rather than effective business models.

Sources of business models

All new business models can be considered variations of the generic value chain underlying all businesses. These models are typically associated with upstream activities (design, manufacturing, purchasing) or with downstream activities (distribution, marketing, advertising, sales). By the same token, a new business model may focus on a new product or service for an unmet need (such as a traveller's cheque) or on a process innovation: that is, a way of making or distributing a proven offering.

Business modelling is not that different from the logic of scientific discovery. One starts with a hypothesis (tentative business model), which is tested in the marketplace and revised when or if necessary. When business models fail, it is because they fail the *conceptual test* (the story just does not make sense) or the *market test* (the numbers just do not add up). Sometimes the two go together (Magretta, 2002).

In the mobile business, WAP was a flawed concept *and* the numbers did not add up. Sometimes the two do not go together. The combination of phone and video has been around for decades, since the 1960s and AT&T's (fixed-line) videophone; but only around 2003–4 did mobile players come up with solutions (camera phones and video streaming) that might pass both the conceptual and the market tests. When the conceptual test fails, the business model is typically built on faulty assumptions about customer behaviour. In the WAP case, for instance, the mistake was the assumption that for the customers, services are secondary to technology. With i-Mode, NTT DoCoMo proved that the reverse was true: technology is secondary to value-added services.

Despite superficial similarities in service portfolios, the conceptual foundations of the two business models may imply quite different views on users, usage and pricing. Take, for instance, mobile service portfolios. The metaphors of the creators capture the difference. NTT DoCoMo provided a convenience store, Vodafone a branded department store. As Keiichi Enoki has commented:

> Think about department stores. You don't go there very often. But when you go, you spend a lot of money. Just the opposite is the convenience store. You don't buy lots of things. The variety is limited. But you go there every day. I thought that same concept could be applied to information. Mobile content is inferior to

other media in terms of speed and screen size. But in terms of ease of use and convenience, it's far superior... For i-mode to sell well, it's indispensable that people carry it around anytime and anywhere and use it conveniently. I don't want to do anything to damage these benefits.[13]

However, i-mode exploded in Japan, but did not initially pick up in Europe. The reason, says Thomas Geitner, Vodafone's chief technology officer, is the very same metaphor 'because you're asking an inexperienced customer to pay an entry fee to a store without knowing what's inside':

Our view of the store is that we're running a branded supermarket where we offer our content providers the shelf space. Vodafone Live! is the brand, and we've got a capability to build things, which they don't have. Our concept poses a low entry barrier to the consumer, or no barrier at all. Second, our concept does not make a difference between a convenience store and a supermarket because in the end content means many different things to different customers. One wants news, another wants ringtones, the third wants still something else. But they can all buy in our store.[14]

In terms of these two different paradigms, the arrival of the 3G capabilities made little difference. The differences between these two business models were conceptual, not empirical.

Sources of competitive advantage

In the aftermath of the internet impact on many industries, it has become all the more important for individual companies to set themselves apart from the rest. To be more profitable than the average performers, they must achieve a sustainable competitive advantage: by operating at a lower cost, by commanding a premium price, or by combining the two. These advantages can be achieved in two basic ways, operational effectiveness and strategy.

Operational effectiveness

Through operational effectiveness, a company can do the same things that competitors do, but do them better. With operational effectiveness, a company can exploit better wireless technologies or a more effective mobile sales force. Augmenting the internet, mobility can serve as a powerful productivity tool to enhance operational effectiveness. If the internet has facilitated the exchange of real-time information and thereby brought about improvements throughout the value chain, mobility essentially frees these gains from the constraints of location by empowering people.

Mobilizing firms

Since the early 2000s, many companies have begun to mobilize. It requires understanding users, assessing timing, aligning mobility as well as training and piloting.

Understanding users

First, it is vital to understand the value activities of the firm, the competitive characteristics of the industry, and the employee mobile profile. The success of mobility depends in part on how well employees can integrate mobile tools and functions into their daily work style. 'Enterprise mobility is defined by addressing unique user needs,' says Mary McDowell, Nokia's chief of enterprise solutions. The objectives of business decision makers (ROI, customer responsiveness, productivity, competitive position) and chief information officers (security, manageability, scalability) may differ, but all employees need to have 'access to information wherever, whenever' (McDowell, 2004).

Assessing timing

To reap the full benefits of mobility, companies must assess the degree of the technology maturity and the readiness of the market to accept new products and services. Technology innovation and marketing innovation do not provide an automatic guarantee of a profitable business. In the US automobile industry, more than 100 firms entered and participated in the business for a period of five years or longer, beginning in 1894 and continuing through 1950. Still, the industry is dominated by only a handful of global giants. This logic has played out in many technology-intensive industries, including typewriters, television and television tubes, transistors, electronic calculators, integrated circuits, Winchester disk drives and supercomputers (Utterback, 1996: 23–55).

Aligning mobility

With mobility, the promise is in the reach and the immediacy of the new media. Unfortunately, the past of information technology experimentation is littered with examples of promises betrayed. 'In the euphoria over information technology and the Internet in the 1990s and early 2000s, customer relationship management took center stage,' comments Michael E Porter. 'Unfortunately, the results fell far short of expectations. In fact, they have been downright disappointing' (Porter, 2004). Mobility – just like CRM and other enabling technologies – is not an end in and of itself. It is an instrument for company strategy. Adoption is not enough; mobility must be aligned with strategy.

Train and pilot

User training is essential to ensure that employees make the most of available technology and solutions, while pilot implementations will help the business understand how it can optimize its return on investment. In the 1990s, many firms insulated their internet groups. If it is true that 'small markets don't solve the growth needs of large companies', large established firms succeed 'by giving responsibility to commercialize the disruptive technology to an organization whose size matched the size of the targeted market' (Christensen, 1997: xxv).

The point, however, is to *integrate* these experiments within the organization. Since mobility tends to add value across the company, it should be trained and piloted across the organization: with business owners seeking to boost performance; with IT managers in need of secure, manageable systems; and with mobile professionals who want better on-the-move work tools and practices.

In both virtualization and mobilization, companies are achieving operational effectiveness, which is necessary to compete but not sufficient to win the competition.

Strategic positioning

Through strategic positioning, a company can do things differently from competitors, in a way that delivers a unique type of value to customers. In both cases, the achievement can utilize any value activity or myriad forms of value activities. With strategic positioning, a company may use mobility, among other things, to provide a different array of services, or different customer relationship arrangements.

Like the internet, mobility shapes operational effectiveness and strategic positioning in different ways. It provides companies with new ways to achieve operational advantages, but it also makes it harder for them to sustain those advantages. Similarly, it offers companies new opportunities for achieving strategic positioning, yet it makes it harder for them to sustain such advantages.

All firms can mobilize; but only a few know how to mobilize *strategically*. To establish and retain a distinctive strategic positioning, a company must follow the principles of strategic positioning (Porter 2001). It must have the *right goal*; superior long-term return on investment. Fast adoption of mobility may generate short-term pioneer advantages, but not necessarily economic value. The latter requires customers who are willing to pay a price for a product or service that exceeds the cost of producing it.

Embracing mobility is not a strategy. It is only through strategy that a company can deliver a *value proposition* that differs from those that rivals can offer. It is this proposition that provides continuity of direction. Strategic positioning also needs to be reflected in a *distinctive value chain*. A company must reject some features, services or activities to be unique at others. Strategy involves making *choices* throughout the value chain that are interdependent. Competitors can copy one activity, product feature or service aspect fairly easily, but it is more difficult to duplicate the whole system of competing. After all, strategy involves difficult *tradeoffs*. That makes it harder to imitate.

During the past two decades, it has become harder to sustain operational advantages. That makes strategic positioning all the more important - but all the more difficult to execute.

Notes

CHAPTER 1: GLOBALIZATION

1 This section draws from Steinbock (2002).

2 Critical country markets correspond to what Jeannet has termed 'must win' markets. See Jeannet, 2000: 92–93.

3 Certain cultural commonalities were reflected in mobile preferences, as well. For instance, the majority of consumers preferred pen-based handwriting input (51 per cent), instead of pinyin (37 per cent), key-stroke input (9 per cent) or traditional English input (2 per cent). Various sources; input preferences from Color Test – Synovate, September 2003.

4 When the GSM networks were first launched in Russia, that figure amounted to almost US $80 per month. By mid-2004 the ARPU of Russia's leading cellular operators was around US $15. The government experts believe that ARPU will fall to US $10–12 per month; the minimum level at which cellular operators could still make a profit.

CHAPTER 2: INNOVATION

1 On the mobile evolution, see Steinbock (2002).

2 The author's interview with Sean Maloney, EVP, General Manager, Intel Communications Group, Intel Corp, 31 April 2004.

3 See Foster (1986), Utterback (1994), Christensen (1997).

4 On marketing concept, see Kotler (2003), Chapter 1.

5   The author's interview with Sean Maloney, EVP, General Manager, Intel Communications Group, Intel Corp, 31 April 2004.

6   Utterback (1994). Utterback's discussion focuses on the issues of dominant product innovation.

7   For an early view on the drivers of new services, see De Brentani (1991).

8   For an early view on new service development, see Easingwood (1986).

9   For an early view on service positioning amid change, see Shostack (1987).

10 On the first two challenges, see Jones *et al* (1994) and Schneider and Bowen (1995).

11 On the difference of service marketing, see Berry (1980) and Thomas, (1978).

12 On new product development in services, see Cooper and Edgett (1999).

13 On service portfolio management, see Cooper, Edgett and Kleinschmidt (1998).

CHAPTER 3: SERVICE PIONEERS

1   Following the shift from analog to digital, NTT DoCoMo pioneered the development of non-voice mobile communications with DoPa, Japan's first 'packet' communications service.

2   On Ohboshi and NTT DoCoMo's strategy, see Steinbock (2002), Chapter 6.

3   A variant of TDMA, PDC is a proprietary standard used only in Japan.

4   Natsuno (2000: 1–7). And later this S-curve would be replaced by the third one, which represents dynamic content, or mobile media.

5   Unless otherwise stated, all quotes in this section are based on the author's interview with Takeshi Natsuno, managing director, multimedia services, NTT DoCoMo, Inc on 5 May 2004. Prior to NTT DoCoMo, Natsuno held positions in a Japanese utility, a leading internet venture, and Boston Consulting Group.

6   In the mobile business, applications enable services, which comprise a portfolio of choices offered to users, who might be charged for them separately or accept a bundle. Services are visible to users, applications are not; they serve as prime differentiators between service providers.

7   On DoCoMo's success, see eg Ratliff (2002) and Moon (2002).

8   Even in April 2004, NTT DoCoMo boasted 56 per cent market share, twice that of its rival, KDDI Corp. But in the previous 11 months this rival managed to sign up 2.4 million new subscribers, against DoCoMo's 1.6 million. KDDI's success has come in the sort of advanced data services that were supposed to be DoCoMo's speciality.

9   DoCoMo employs PDC, a variant of the TDMA standard used only in Japan, as opposed to GSM in Europe and Asia, or CDMA and another version of TDMA in North America.

10 On service marketing and seasonal demand, see Shugan and Radas (2000).

11 Internet survey by Sanwa Research Institute, Internetcom, and Infoplant (as of March 2002).

12 Unless otherwise stated, all quotes in this section are from the author's interview with Thomas Geitner, CTO, Vodafone Group, 7 July 2004.

13 'What we saw was Nokia surreptitiously inserting technologies into handsets like Nokia Smart Messaging that allowed content providers to deliver content directly to a handset, without the operators being involved in spending a lot of money to facilitate the market.'

CHAPTER 4: SERVICE INNOVATION

1   Taylor (2003). Strategy Analytics disputed the often cited figure for global adult entertainment revenues of US $20 billion, and believes it to be closer to the US $4 billion mark, of which only around US $500 million will be generated online. That is less than half of the value of the ringtones market in Western Europe in 2002.

2   In September 2004, the Taiwan-based Bestis Technologies bought the film rights to *Outside The Fortress Besieged*, a 4,200-character, 60-chapter novel that has been sent out to cellphone subscribers in short instalments. The film will consist of 30 to 40 segments and should be able to be viewed on cellphones.

3   Presence is the dynamic user profile, which allows users to create their own content and share it with others. By the same token, it can raise security and privacy concerns. See Nokia (2002a).

4   In the United States, legislation requires that all mobiles sold in the US can be positioned in case of emergency. Consequently, the US FCC mandates for E-911 services, and the equivalent EU requirement for E-112, have a substantial impact on the positioning technology adopted by mobile network operators.

5   Strategy Analytics (2003). Because of privacy and security concerns, the use of LBS in business markets has not proceeded without controversy, as evidenced by the early use of GPS in the United States (Forelle, 2004).

6   These requirements (particularly the form of subscriber consent) differ in the United States, Europe and Japan (Ackerman, Kempf and Miki, 2003).

7   These categories were driven by three initial objectives: to employ content categories that would facilitate the migration of these categories to mobile; to design the content portfolio in the resemblance of popular internet services; and to recruit the kind of service providers (such as banks) that would attract others.

8   Reuters (2004). Ringtone prices vary widely by region, with SK Telecom, South Korea's largest mobile carrier, charging the equivalent of 20 cents while Britain's Vodafone charges roughly US $2.75.

9   For an early discussion on mobile e-commerce, see Kalakota (2002).

10 Technologies enable services, but technical success is not identical with commercial viability. In Japan, NTT DoCoMo has invested in LBS, but as the primary objective is to boost user traffic, these have been embedded with the basic service categories.

11 The author's interview with Kurt Sillen, VP, Mobility World, Telefonaktiebolaget LM Ericsson, April 14, 2004.

CHAPTER 5: CONTENT SERVICES

1   In the past few years, Java technology has established itself as the leading third-party application development platform for downloadable mass-market applications for mobile devices (Nokia, 2003a).

2   A new online payment service called DoCommerce, for example, enabled both 2G and 3G SSL-compatible i-mode handset users to enjoy mobile shopping and pay online with credit cards.

3   Unless otherwise stated, all quotes in this section are based on the author's interview with Takeshi Natsuno, managing director, multimedia services, NTT DoCoMo, on 5 May 2004.

4   In order to facilitate this business, it must be possible to verify that the device has received and installed a media object before a payment trans-action is included in the billing system (Nokia, 2004c).

5   In person-to-person (P2P) video messaging, the video is recorded and then sent to another person. In content-to-person (C2P) video messaging, the video clip derives from a commercial service on a pull or subscription push basis. In the latter case digital rights management (DRM) issues become central. Just as the available memory capacity of the mobile device determines the storage potential, DRM defines the usage rules for commercial content.

6   Shosteck (2002b). The Nokia 2003 MMS study demonstrated similar trends in Asia, Europe and the United States. Rich media – including video – was not as much affected by price changes as less rich media.

7 For instance, the European DVB-T standard and the Japanese ISDB-T (Integrated Services or IP Datacast, or IP Datacast, Digital Broadcasting – Terrestrial) standard.

8 For more information, see DVB – Digital Video Broadcast at http://www.dvb.org

9 In September 2004, Motorola, NEC, Nokia, Siemens and Sony Ericsson announced their cooperation in mobile broadcast services, under Open Mobile Alliance (OMA). The charter of the work is to specify the enablers needed to bring broadcast services to mobile devices and to open up the market for new exciting mobile services and terminals.

10 CD-burning software maker Roxio later purchased the bankrupt Napster's assets for about US $5 million. It coupled Napster with pressplay and relaunched the brand as an online service that let users legally download music from its library for 99 cents a song.

11 The case was settled and YourMobile obtained licences for ringtones from EMI and three other publishing representatives.

12 The agreement for EMI Music Publishing's catalogue would be used for custom downloadable ringtones. Nokia provided a service to mobile users, whereby they could download additional ringtones for their mobile phones. EMI Music Publishing licensed the use of ringtones to Nokia on a non-exclusive worldwide basis. The initial service contained well-known songs, television and film themes. These were later coupled with additional famous titles. Ringtones could also be provided for promotional purposes and sponsored.

13 Unless otherwise stated, all Jopling quotations are from the author's interview with Keith Jopling, Director of Market Research, IFPI, 11 May 2004.

14 The author's interview with Christa Haussler, Vice President, New Technology, BMG Entertainment, April 27, 2004.

15 The service allowed users to choose from among 10,000 songs on six websites and download them on to 3G mobile phones for a few hundred yen, the equivalent of several dollars each. KDDI signed up 20 record labels and opened the service to all interested content providers (KDDI, 14 October 2004).

CHAPTER 6: MOBILE MEDIA AND ENTERTAINMENT

1 The objective of the Content Management License Administrator (CMLA), for instance, was to promote new digital rights management (DRM) specification from industry group the Open Mobile Alliance (OMA), as well as the formation of a new licensing body led by Intel, Nokia, Panasonic and Samsung that will promote the technology.

2　On the mobile value chain, see Steinbock (2002). On the mobile enter-tainment value chain, see Smorodinsky (2002) and Booz, Allen & Hamilton and Mobile Entertainment Analyst (2003).

3　Publishers/aggregators fund application or product development through advances against royalties, staged or one-time payments, or other revenue models. Portals or web communities that gather and sell member-generated content also fit into this category. Example companies include Digital Bridges, JAMDAT, Aspiro and the wireless divisions of Sega and THQ.

4　On the rise of basic cable and CNN, see Steinbock (1995), especially Chapter 5.

5　Unless otherwise stated, all quotations in this section are from the author's interview with Mitch Lazar, vice president, wireless and emerging tech-nology, TBS International, 4 March 2004.

6　Some 35 operators in 50 countries distribute CNN Mobile in SMS, WAP, HTML and Compact HTML.

7　In 1979, Milton Bradley released a hand-held programmable unit, the Microvision, which incorporated a built-in LED screen. On the history and evolution of videogames, see Kent 2001, Paavilainen 2003, Bellows 2003.

8　The first hand-held game console with interchangeable cartridges was the Milton Bradley Microvision (1979).

9　As 3G licence auctions swept across Europe, Nintendo of Japan released the Mobile Adapter GB, which was compatible with the Game Boy Advance.

10　Source: the author's interview with Takeshi Natsuno, Managing Director, multimedia services, NTT DoCoMo Inc, 5 May 2004.

11　Data transmission already accounted for about 20 per cent of DoCoMo's total revenue, and 17 per cent of all content accessed over its internet service was games. See NTT DoCoMo annual reports. Compare Dvorak (2004).

12　Same sources. Worldwide games sales estimate from the Informa Media Group, a London-based media and telecommunications research firm.

13　The Informa Media Group has predicted that the mobile games segment of the industry will grow from only tens of millions of dollars in revenue in 2001 to more than US $3.6 billion in 2006. Ovum Research expects mobile games revenue to reach US $4.4 billion by 2006.

14　These projections are from Strategy Analytics, Arc Group and Informa Media Group respectively.

15 Built for active and hardcore gamers, N-Gage was the first mobile and connected game deck to feature online high-quality 3D multiplayer gameplay over Bluetooth wireless technology and GPRS. It offered unique online games services and a growing games catalogue from the leading game publishers.

16 Unless otherwise stated, all quotations in this section are from the author's interview with Larry Shapiro, EVP business development and operations, Walt Disney Internet Group, 12 April 2004.

17 The theme of the keynote speech by Larry Shapiro at the iWireless World conference. Quoted in Hollywood Reporter (2003).

18 See http://www.disneymobile.com. The site will provide consumers with information regarding Disney Mobile content offerings and purchases as well as product demonstrations. It can be accessed directly from the homepage of Disney.com, the leading family entertainment site. Samsung became the exclusively featured handset provider on DisneyMobile.com.

CHAPTER 7: 'DEVICE FORMERLY KNOWN AS CELLPHONE'

1 The author's interview with Geoffrey Frost, chief marketing officer, Motorola Inc, 30 June 2004.

2 The author's interview with Martin Cooper, executive chairman and co-founder, ArrayComm Inc, 29 April 2004.

3 On mass marketing and segmentation, see Tedlow (1990) and Sloan (1963), especially Chapter 4.

4 Quotes in this section are from the author's interview with Frank Nuovo, chief designer and vice president, Nokia Design, Nokia Corp., 1 March and 11 May 2004.

5 On the broad principles of segmentation, see Kotler (2003, Ch 9); on segmentation, and mobile market research, see Steuernagel (1999); Steinbock (2003a); and studies by the Arc Group, Gartner, Informa Telecoms & Media, Shosteck Group, and In-Stat.

6 On the Newton project and early smart phone visions, see Steinbock (2002: chs 13–14).

7 The author's interview with Ed Suwanjindar, lead product manager, Microsoft Mobile and Embedded Division, 8 April 2004.

8 These devices tend to differ in terms of features such as voice communications, size and clarity of colour screens, weight, battery life, computing power, as well as a variety of input choices such as keypads, pens, touch pads and speech recognition.

9   Over time, this segment is expected to move toward embedded connectivity. Additionally, industrial PDAs are designed to endure more challenging conditions. Many of these more rugged variants are used for remote data collection.

10 In Japan, where camera phones were launched in 2000, some 10 per cent of the pictures are printed. That could translate to 3 billion camera phone pictures by 2006, or US $500 million in revenues for photo-service providers. See Reinhardt *et al* (2004).

11 On functional, image and experiential brands, see for example Tybout and Carpenter (2003: ch 4).

12 An actual waterproof wristwatch, the Wristomo also offers the reduced power consumption of the PHS system rather than PDC, and offers a range of functions in addition to voice communications in the form of Paldio mail, access to mobile internet and location-based web pages, and PC synchronization. The ultra-modern mobile features e-mail and web access. The US $300 product sold out of its 1,000 unit inventory in 20 minutes when released.

CHAPTER 8: MOBILE MARKETING AND CONSUMER BEHAVIOUR

1   According to industry observers, in the past the mobile marketing business has benefited from soaring demand, not from sophisticated marketing capabilities. See Steuernagel (1999).

2   Turchetti quotations from the author's interview with David Turchetti, CEO, 21 Communications, 30 April 2004.

3   Take, for instance, Enpocket's Zingo, which was among the first to employ a location-based taxi hailing service using GPS and mobile triangulation technologies.

4   These databases contain far more information than just customer mailing lists. In consumer services, for instance, the ideal customer database contains information on the user's past purchases, demographics (age, income, family members, birthdays), psychographics (activities, interests and opinions), mediagraphics (preferred media), and other useful information.

5   The author's interview with Ami Hasan, Partner and Creative Director, Hasan & Partners, 23 March 2004.

6   'For ninety years marketers have relied on one form of advertising almost exclusively,' argues Seth Godin. 'I call it Interruption Marketing. Interruption, because the key to each and every ad is to interrupt what the viewers are doing in order to get them to think about something else' (Godin, 1999: 25).

7   Ho (2004), based on the Yankee Group survey of 5,510 Americans over the age of 18.

8   Quotations from the author's interview with Brian Levin on 17 June 2004.

9   Peppers and Rogers (1993: 4–5). On the context, see Steinbock (2000). On the mobile applications, see Newell and Lemon (2001), Lamont (2001), Bayne (2002).

10 Quotations from the author's interviews with Anssi Vanjoki, EVP, Nokia Multimedia, June 2003 and 23 March 2004.

11 These ideas arrived in the US technology sector around the 1970s and 1980s, when they were first conceptualized in the corporate markets (Regis McKenna), and later, in the early 1990s, in mass consumer markets (Geofrey A Moore). See Steinbock (2000: ch 3). On adopter categorization in business markets, see McKenna (1991). On the restatement of these categories in mass consumer markets, see Moore (1991).

12 On technology, segmentation and lifestyle, see Forrester Research (1998, 1999) and Modahl (2000).

13 In 1999, Nokia suggested that the operator could consider targeting the users in three waves. At first, the service offering could be targeted for business high flyers and youth trendsetters in order to stimulate interest in multimedia services. After the initial phase of the transition, Nokia recommended progressively paying more attention to other opinion leader segments. See Nokia (2000).

CHAPTER 9: MOBILE BUSINESS SERVICES

1   The author's interview with Takeshi Natsuno, Managing Director, Multimedia Services, NTT DoCoMo, Inc, 5 May 2004.

2   On the Medtronic case, see http://www.nttdocomo.com/corebiz/imode/forbiz/

3   On the AFLAC case, see http://www.nttdocomo.com/corebiz/foma/forbiz/

4   Quotes from the author's interview with Thomas Geitner, CTO, Vodafone Group, 7 July 2004.

5   The site provides full interoperability between GMACCM's lenders partners, sourcing a projected US $6–8 billion in loans annually. On the case of GMACCM (1 January 2002), see http://www.microsoft.com/windowsmobile/resources/casestudies/CaseStudy.asp?CaseStudyID=13371.

6   On the case of the Kudos Restaurant & Wine Bar, see http://www.microsoft.com/australia/business/casestudy/studies/kudos.aspx

7   For organizations concerned about moving from a single function to a multi-function device, pocket PCs can be configured so that nonessential applications may be locked down and employees have access only to work-related functionality.

8   On the Itoki case see http://www.nttdocomo.com/corebiz/foma/forbiz/

9   On the Otsuka Shokai case, see http://www.nttdocomo.com/corebiz/foma/forbiz/

10 See http://www.qualcomm.com/qwbs/solutions/flt_mgt_overview.shtml

11 On NTT DoCoMo's i-Appli, see http://www.nttdocomo.com/corebiz/imode/services/iappli.html

12 On the Holston Medical Group case, see http://www.allscripts.com/ahcs/sol_testimonials2.htm#2

13 Total implementation cost (including software, hardware, consulting and internal personnel) can run as high as 2–3 per cent of a company's revenues (US $100 million for a US $5 billion company) (Austin *et al*, 2003).

14 Virtual private networking (VPN, based on the Secure Sockets Layer (SSL) or the IP Security (IPSec) standards, or both, can today be fully supported for corporate mobile users (Nokia, 2004d).

15 Nor should operators ignore employees based in a single location; even if their mobility needs are low, their mobile service usage needs may be relatively high.

CHAPTER 10: STRATEGY AND MOBILITY

1   On the Credit Saison case, see NTT DoCoMo's website, http://www.nttdocomo.com

2   On the Ray & Berndtson case, see http://www.microsoft.com/mobile/enterprise/casestudies/CaseStudy.asp?CaseStudyID=13303

3   On the case of Dollar Rent A Car Systems (August 12, 2002), see http://www.microsoft.com/resources/casestudies/CaseStudy.asp?CaseStudyID=11626

4   A basic system consists of an antenna or sensor, a transceiver with decoder and a transponder tag that is electronically programmed with unique data.

5   On the US Customs case, see http://www.microsoft.com/resources/casestudies/casestudy.asp?casestudyid=13634

6   On the CSX Transportation case, see http://www.qualcomm.com/enterprise/alist_csx.html

7 On Egmont Entertainment case, see http://www.microsoft.com/mobile/enterprise/casestudies/CaseStudy.asp?CaseStudyID=13322

8 On the Coca-Cola Corp. case, see http://www.mobileplanet.com/askexperts/solutions/syware_case10.asp

9 On the Corochan Co. Ltd. case, see http://www.nttdocomo.com/corebiz/imode/forbiz/

10 On generic value systems, see Porter (1985: 34); on wireless value systems, see Steinbock (2002).

11 The author's interview with Takeshi Natsuno, managing director, multimedia services, NTT DoCoMo, 5 May 2004. See also Natsuno (2002).

12 The author's interview with Takeshi Natsuno, managing director, multimedia services, NTT DoCoMo, 5 May 2004. See also Natsuno (2002).

13 Quoted in Kridel (2000). This paradigm is critical to the i-mode business model, as noted by Gaver and Cusumano (2002: 224–25).

14 Source: the author's interview with Thomas Geitner, Chief Technology Officer, Vodafone Group, 7 July 2004.

References

Ackerman, L, Kempf, J and Miki, T (2003) *Wireless Location Privacy: A report on law and policy in the United States, the European Union, and Japan*, DoCoMo USA Labs, 28 October

Ankeny, J (2002) Thomas Dolby Robertson: beatnik – cutting edge, *Wireless Review*, March

Ankeny, J (2003) The new sound of music, *Wireless Review*, 1 Nov

Austin, R D, Cotteleer, M, Austin, R D and Escalle, C X (2003) *Enterprise Resource Planning: Technology note*, Harvard Business School Case Study, 9–699–020, Rev 14 March

Barnes, J G *et al* (2000) Self-service and technology, in *Handbook of Services Marketing and Management*, ed T A Swartz and D Iacobucci, pp 89–102, Sage, Thousand Oaks, Calif

Bartlett, C A and Ghoshal, S (2000) Going global: lessons from late movers, *Harvard Business Review*, March

Bayne, K M (2002) *Marketing without Wires*, Wiley, New York

Bellows, M (2003) A short history of wireless games, *Mobile Entertainment Analyst*, 26 June

Bensche, J M and Ritter, J C (2003) The emerging wireless value chain and capital market perceptions, in *Competition for the Mobile Internet*, ed D Steinbock and E Noam, Kluwer, Boston, Mass

Berry, L L (1980) Services marketing is different, *Business*, May–June, pp 24–30

Booz, Allen & Hamilton and Mobile Entertainment Analyst (2003) *Future Mobile Entertainment Scenarios*, MEF White Paper, March

Brown, K A (1992) *Critical Connection*, Motorola University Press, Rolling Meadows

Budde, N (2000) Wireless internet news: another challenge for newspaper publishers, speech at Online Information 2000 Conference, London, 7 December

Budden, R and Burt, T (2003) Brand is a big issue, *Financial Times*, 22 December

Carat Interactive (2002) *The Future of Wireless Marketing*, White Paper, Carat Interactive

Chandler, A D Jr (1977) *Visible Hand*, Harvard University Press, Boston, Mass

Chandler, A D Jr (1990) *Scale and Scope*, Harvard University Press, Boston, Mass

Charny, B (2001) Net porn loses its wires, CNET Newscom, 16 March

Christensen, C M (1997) *The Innovator's Dilemma*, Harvard Business School Press, Boston, Mass

CNN (2001) Vodafone sells shares to firm its J-Phone grip, CNN, 2 May

Cooper, R G and Edgett, S J (1999) *Product Development for the Service Sector*, Perseus Books, Cambridge, Mass

Cooper, R G, Edgett, S J and Kleinschmidt, E J (1998) *Portfolio Management for New Products*, Perseus Books, Reading, Mass

Cellular Telecommunications Industry Association (CTIA) (1994) *Building the Wireless Future*, CTIA, Washington, DC

Dabholkar, P A (2000) Technology in service delivery, in *Handbook of Services Marketing and Management*, ed T A Swar and D Iacobucci, pp 103–10, Sage, Thousand Oaks, Calif

Davenport, T H (1998) Putting the enterprise into the enterprise system, *Harvard Business Review*, July–August

De Brentani, U (1991) Success factors in developing new business services, *European Journal of Marketing* 25 (2), pp 33–59

Dedo, D (2004) *The Return on Your Mobility Investment: Enterprise opportunities for Windows mobile-based pocket PCs and smartphones*, White Paper, Microsoft Corp, April [Online] http://wwwmicrosoftcom/windowsmobile/resources/whitepapers/mobilityROImspx

Dickie, M (2004) No longer taking China for granted, *Financial Times*, 23 August

Diercks, R (2003) Vertical markets: where everything old is new again, *Wireless Internet Magazine*, 15 May

Downton, P (2003) Taking more music, to more people in more ways, Presentation, NMIC, 30 October

Dvorak, P (2004) Cell games go ka-ching!, *Wall Street Journal*, 23 April 23, p B1

Easingwood, C J (1986) New product development for service companies, *Journal of Product Innovation Management*, **4**, pp 265–75

E-Letter (2002) 10 tips to effectively target the lucrative tween market, packaged facts, E-Letter, November

Ellsworth, B (2004) In Latin America, a cellular need, *New York Times*, 26 May

Ericsson (2004) *Mobile Multimedia: The next step in richer communication*, White Paper, Ericsson, March

Etoh, M (2003) *Trends in Mobile Multimedia and Networks*, DoCoMo Communications Laboratories USA [Online] http://wwwdocomolabs-usacom

Eurotechnology Japan KK (2004) Camera phones: disruptive innovation for imaging, *Eurotechnology Japan KK*, 14 Jan

Fong, M (2004) Don't tell the kids: computer games can make you rich, *Wall Street Journal*, 21 May, p A1

Forelle, C (2004) On the road again, but now the boss is sitting beside you, *Wall Street Journal*, 14 May, p A1

Forrester Research (1998) *Technographics(tm) Explained*, Forrester Research, January

Forrester Research (1999) *Applying Technographics*, Forrester Research, April

Foster, R (1986) *Innovation*, Summit, New York

Franchi, L (2001) *Worldwide Java Adoption Report*, helloNetwork, November

Frost, G (2003) ECOMOTO: brand momentum, Motorola, 29 July

Fukumoto, M and Tonomura, Y (1999), 'Whisper: A Wristwatch Style Wearable Handset', CHI99 Conference Proceedings, pp 112–19, Pittsburgh, May 1999

Garrard, G A (1998) *Cellular Communications: Worldwide market development*, Artech House, Boston, Mass

Gates, B (2003) Remarks by Bill Gates, Chairman and Chief Software Architect, Microsoft Corp, ITU Telecom World 2003, Geneva, Switzerland,13 October

Gaver, A and Cusumano, M A (2002) *Platform Leadership*, Harvard Business School Press, Boston, Mass

Gelenbe, P (2003a) *Science Fiction or Reality*, Flytxt, November

Gelenbe, P (2003b) *The Mobile Marketing Value Chain*, Flyxt, 7 October

Gibson, S W (1987) *Cellular Mobile Radiotelephones*, Prentice-Hall, Englewood Cliffs, NJ

Gilmore, F and Dumont, S (2003) China mobile: preparing to capitalize on its customer base, in *Brand Warriors China*, Profile, London

Glazer, R (2000) Smart services, in *Handbook of Services Marketing and Management*, ed T A Swartz and D Iacobucci, pp 409–18, Sage, Thousand Oaks, Calif

Godin, S (1999) *Permission Marketing*, Simon & Schuster, New York

Grönroos, C (1997) Value-driven relational marketing: from products to resources and competencies, *Journal of Marketing Management*, **13** (5), pp 407–19

Guyon, J (1999) Next up for cell phones: weaving a wireless web, *Fortune*, 25 October

Hinchcliffe, A (2002) *SMS TV Forecasts 2002–2007*, visiongain, 20 July

Ho, C H (2004) For more advertisers, the medium is the text message, *Wall Street Journal*, 2 August

Hollywood Reporter (2003) Disney surveying mobile frontier, *Hollywood Reporter*, 5 August

Honeycutt, J (2004) *Windows XP Professional, Windows Mobile 2003, and Office Professional Edition 2003 for a Mobile Workforce*, Microsoft, March

IFPI (2004) *Online Music Report*, International Federation of the Phonographic Industry, London

In-Stat/MDR (2004a) 118 million 3G wireless subscribers in China by 2008, Press release, In-Stat/MDR, 15 June

In-Stat/MDR (2004b) Growth returning to worldwide mobile subscriber market, Press release, In-Stat/MDR, 28 July

In-Stat/MDR (2004c) Research points to natural demand for mobile video, News release, In-Stat/MDR, 24 May

In-Stat/MDR (2004d) *Personal Video Recorders Expand Their Reach*, In-Stat/MDR, April

In-Stat/MDR (2005) RFID Tag Market to Approach $3 billion in 2009, *In-Stat/MDR*, 12 January

InfoSync World (2003) Walt Disney goes wireless, *InfoSync World*, 16 December

Intel (2004) *Empowering the Healthcare Industry – and Its Own Employees – with Wireless Productivity*, Intel Business Center Case Study

Jardin, X (2004) Life, liberty and pursuit of porn, *Wired News*, 19 February

Jeannet, J-P (2000) *Managing with a Global Mindset*, Pearson, London

Jeannet, J-P and Hennessey, H D (1998) *Global Marketing Strategies*, 4th edn, Houghton Mifflin, New York

Jones, T O, Heskett, J L, Loveman, G W, Sasser, W E Jr and Schlesinger, L A (1994) Putting the service profit chain to work, *Harvard Business Review*, **72**, March–April, pp 164–74

Jupiter (2002) News release, Jupiter, January

Kaiser, A (1999) Express yourself: why phone makers offer something special for you, *Wall Street Journal*, 1 October

Kalakota, R (2002) *M-Business: The race to mobility*, McGraw-Hill, New York

Kalakota, R (2004) Mobile enterprise applications, Intel/SAP Executive Brief, January

Karjalainen, U (2003) Nokia in China, President/Corporate SVP, Nokia China, Beijing, 11 November

Kent, S L (2001) *The Ultimate History of Video Games*, Prima, New York

Kotler, P (1984) Design: a powerful but neglected strategic tool, *Journal of Business Strategy*, Fall, pp 16–21

Kotler, P (2003) *A Framework for Marketing Management*, 2nd edn, Prentice-Hall, Upper Saddle River, NJ

Kridel, T (2000) I-opener, *Wireless Review*, 1 October, pp 22–28

Kunii, I with Baker, S (2000) Amazing DoCoMo, *Business Week*, 17 January

Lamont, D (2001) *Conquering the Wireless World*, Capstone, Oxford

Lazar, M (2003) Speech, Nokia Mobile Internet Conference, 29 October

Levitt, T (1960) Marketing myopia, *Harvard Business Review*, July–August, pp 45–56

Levitt, T (1980) Marketing success through differentiation – of anything, *Harvard Business Review*, January/February

Levitt, T (1981) Marketing intangible products and product intangibles, *Harvard Business Review*, May–June

Levitt, T (1986) *The Marketing Imagination*, Free Press, New York

Lewis, M (2001) Introduction: the invisible revolution, in *Next: The future just happened*, Norton, New York

Lindholm, C and Keinonen, T (2003) *Mobile usability: how Nokia changed the face of the mobile phone*, McGraw-Hill, New York

Lorenz, C (1986) *The Design Dimension*, Blackwell, New York

Magretta, J (2002) Why business models matter, *Harvard Business Review*, May

Marek, S (2003) India: wireless hotbed set for explosive growth, *Wireless Week*, 1 November

McDowell, M (2004) Enterprise solutions, Nokia Capital Market Days, 5 November

McKenna, R (1991) *Relationship Marketing*, Addison-Wesley, Reading, Mass

McLindon, A (2001) Music industry cracks down on ringtones, *electricnewsnet*, 5 Nov

Menn, J (2004) How Microsoft got smart about phones, *Los Angeles Times*, 4 April

Meurling, J and Jeans, R (1997) *The Ugly Duckling: Mobile phones from Ericsson – putting people on speaking terms*, Ericsson, Stockholm

Mobile Marketing Association (MMA) (2003) *MMA Code for Responsible Mobile Marketing: A code of conduct and guidelines to best practice*, MMA, December

Modahl, M (2000) *Now or Never*, HarperCollins, New York

Moon, Y (2002) *NTT DoCoMo: Marketing i-mode*, Harvard Business School Case Study, 0–502–031, Rev 17 July

Moore, G A (1991) *Crossing the Chasm*, HarperBusiness, New York

Moore, G A (1995) *Inside the Tornado*, HarperBusiness, New York

Moore, G E (1965) Cramming more components onto integrated circuits, *Electronics* **38** (8), 19 April

Motorola (2001) *Intelligence Everywhere*, Motorola

Motorola (2003) Motorola celebrates 20-year anniversary of the world's first commercial portable cellular phone, News release, 6 March

Natsuno, T (2000) *i-Mode Strategy* (English version (2003) Wiley, Hoboken, NJ)

Natsuno, T (2002) *The i-mode Wireless Ecosystem*, (English version (2003) Wiley, Hoboken, NJ)

Nester, K and Lyall, K (2003) Mobile Marketing: A Primer Report, *FirstPartner*, September

Newell, F and Lemon, K (2001) *Wireless Rules*, McGraw-Hill, New York

Nokia (1999) *Nokia Annual and Interim Reports 1999*, 22 April

Nokia (2000) *Make Money with 3G Services*, White Paper, Nokia

Nokia (2001a) *Instant Messaging goes Mobile*, White Paper, Nokia Mobile Software Unit, Nokia

Nokia (2001b) *Mobile Phone as a Personal Trusted Device*, Report, Technology & Services, Nokia, August

Nokia (2002a) *Staying in Touch with Presence*, White Paper, Nokia

Nokia (2002b) *Multimedia Streaming*, White Paper, Nokia

Nokia (2003a) *Java[!tm!] Technology Enables Exciting Downloading Services for Mobile Users*, White Paper, October

Nokia (2003b) *Next Generation Mobile Browsing*, White Paper, Nokia

Nokia (2003c) Nokia Imagewear products, unique displays of personality, PressRelease, 25 September

Nokia (2003d) *Nokia for Business: Meeting the mobility and service needs of employees*, White Paper, Nokia Networks, October

Nokia (2004a) *Connecting Mobile Consumers and Merchants*, White Paper, Nokia

Nokia (2004b) *Push to Talk over Cellular – Real-time always-on voice service*, White Paper, Nokia

Nokia (2004c) *Reliable Content Download to Boost User Experience*, White Paper, Nokia

Nokia (2004d) *The Anytime Anyplace World*, White Paper, Nokia for Business

NTT DoCoMo (2003) *Annual Report 2003*, NTT DoCoMo

NTT DoCoMo (2004a) *Videophone Communication that Deepens Bonds Between Parents and Children*, Report, NTT DoCoMo, July

NTT DoCoMo (2004b) NTT DoCoMo introduces revolutionary mobile wallet service with first P506iC i-mode Smart-Card Handset, Press release, 7 July

NTT DoCoMo (2004c) *The i-mode Effect*, Report, NTT DoCoMo, February

NTT DoCoMo (2004d) *Size and Weight Reduction of Progressively Higher Function Mobile Phones*, Report, NTT DoCoMo, June

OECD (1999) *World Telecommunication Development Report 1999: Mobile cellular*, OECD, Paris

Ohmae, K (1985) *Triad Power: The coming shape of global competition*, Free Press, New York

Ollila, J (2004) Nokia Today – Towards the mobile world, speech at Nokia Annual General Meeting, 25 March

Ollila, J and Ala-Pietilä, P (1999) Letter to our shareholders, *Nokia Annual Report*, pp 6–7

Ollila, J and Ala-Pietilä, P (2000) Letter to our shareholders: making best execution an asset, *Nokia Annual Report*, pp 6–7

Paavilainen, J (2003) *Mobile Games*, Pearson, Boston, Mass

Pachter, M and Woo, E (2004) *The Definition of Insanity: Why the next console cycle will start off with a whimper*, Wedbush Morgan Securities, June

Parker, G (2004) Vodafone's Japan unit taps rival for new CEO, *Wall Street Journal*, 17 August, p B1

Peppers, D and Rogers, M (1993) *The One-to-One Future*, Doubleday / Currency, New York

Petrakis, H M (1965) *The Founder's Touch: The life of Paul Galvin of Motorola*, Motorola University Press / JC Ferguson Publishing Press, Chicago

Poropudas, T (2004) Russians bought 17 million phones in 2003, IDC, Newsrucom, MosNews, 2 May

Porter, M E (1980) *Competitive Strategy*, Free Press, New York

Porter, M E (1985) *Competitive Advantage*, Free Press, New York

Porter, M E (2001) Strategy and the internet, *Harvard Business Review*, March

Porter, M E (2004) Foreword, in *CRM Unplugged*, ed P Bligh and D Turk, Wiley, Hoboken, NJ

Pringle, D (2004a) After long peace, wireless operator stirs up industry, *Wall Street Journal*, 12 Nov, p A1

Pringle, D (2004b) Symbian grabs bigger market share, *Wall Street Journal*, 3 August

Raeghi, A J and Calder, B J (2002) Using interaction maps to create brand experiences and relationships, in *Kellogg on Integrated Marketing*, ed D Iacobucci and B Calder, Wiley, New York

Ratliff, J M (2002) NTT DoCoMo and its i-mode success, *California Management Review*, 44 (3) Spring

Raugust, K (2004) *The Licensing Business Handbook*, 5th edn, EPM, New York

RCR Wireless News (2004) Walt Disney Internet Group plans 3D wireless games, RCR Wireless News, 22 March

Register (2000) Steve Ballmers vision for the future of mankind, *The Register*, 20 April

Reinhardt, A, Tashiro, H and Elgin, B (2004) The camphone revolution, *Business Week*, 12 April

Reuters (2004) Ring tones bringing in big bucks, Reuters, 13 January

Rocks, D (2004) Japan: making 3G look as slow as smoke signals, *Business Week*, 15 November

Rohwer, J (2000) Today, Tokyo; tomorrow, the world, *Fortune*, 18 September

Ryan, B and Gross, N C (1943) The diffusion of hybrid seed corn in two Iowa communities, *Rural Sociology*, **8**, pp 15–24

Sapsford, J (2004) As cash fades, America becomes a plastic nation, *Wall Street Journal*, 23 July, p A1

Schmidt, B (2003) *Customer Experience Management*, Wiley, New York

Schneider, B and Bowen, D E (1995) *Winning the Service Game*, Harvard Business School Press, Boston, Mass

Schultz, D E, Tannenbaum, S I and Lauterborn, R F (1994) *The New Marketing Paradigm: Integrated marketing communications*, NTC Business Books, Lincolnwood, Ill

Shalit, R (2002) Lord of the ring, *M-Pulse Magazine*, November

Shiller, R J (2000) *Irrational Exuberance*, Broadway Books, New York

Shostack, G L (1987) Service positioning through structural change, *Journal of Marketing*, **51**, January, pp 34–43

Shosteck (2002a) Finding new value in mobile wallets, *Shosteck Group*, **55**, May

Shosteck (2002b) Travels to Asia – a skeptic's addiction to new services, *Shosteck Group*, July

Shosteck (2003) Mobile virtual network operators (MVNOs) – a new look at a growing phenomenon, Email Briefing, **70**, Shosteck Group, August

Shugan, S M and Radas, S (2000) Services and seasonal demand, in *Handbook of Services Marketing and Management*, ed T A Swartz and D Iacobucci, pp 147–70, Sage, Thousand Oaks, Calif

Siegel, J (2002) *Stocks for the Long Run*, 3rd edn, McGraw-Hill, New York

Sloan, A P Jr (1990) *My Years with General Motors*, Doubleday, New York (originally published 1963)

Smith, E and Wingfield, N (2004) Online music is ringing up sales with outtakes, mixes, *Wall Street Journal*, 1 April

Smorodinsky, R (ed) (2002) *Mobile Entertainment: A value chain analysis*, Mobile Entertainment Forum (MEF) Commercial Task Force, Global Communications Interactive

Statistical Abstract of the United States (2003), US Government [annual]

Steinbock, D (1995) *Triumph and Erosion in the American Media and Entertainment Industries*, Quorum, Westport, Conn

Steinbock, D (2000) *The Birth of Internet Marketing Communications*, Quorum, Westport, Conn

Steinbock, D (2001) *The Nokia Revolution*, Amacom, New York

Steinbock, D (2002) *Wireless Horizon*, Amacom, New York

Steinbock, D (2003a) Globalization of wireless markets, in *Competition for the Mobile Internet*, ed D Steinbock and E Noam, Kluwer, Boston

Steinbock, D (2003b) Toward a mobile information society: globalization of wireless technology and market evolution, *Georgetown Journal of International Affairs*, Summer/Fall

Steinbock, D (2003c) Twin drivers and irrational exuberance: markets, the internet and mobility, *International Journal of Media Management*, **5** (2)

Steinbock, D (2004), Got Mobile, Go Global, *European Business Forum*, Issue 17, Spring

Steuernagel, R A (1999) *Wireless Marketing*, Wiley, New York

Stone, A (1998) Playing the cellular boom: Nokia vs Ericsson, *Business Week*, 10 August

Stone, M, Bond, A and Blake, E (2003) *The Definitive Guide to Interactive and Direct Marketing*, Pearson-FT, 2003

Stone, M and Foss, M (2001) *Successful Customer Relationship Marketing*, Kogan Page, London

Strategy Analytics (2003) *Location Based Services: Strategic outlook for mobile operators and solutions vendors*, Strategy Analytics, March

Strother, N (2004) Boom times for India's wireless market, In-Stat/MDR, June

Swartz, T A and Iacobucci, D (2000) *Handbook of Services Marketing and Management*, Sage, Thousand Oaks, Calif

Taylor, P (2003) Wireless porn opportunity limited to $1 billion in 2008, *Insight*, Strategy Analytics, 16 April

Tedlow, R S (1990) *The Story of Mass Marketing in America*, Basic Books, New York

Thomas, D R (1978) Strategy is different in service business, *Harvard Business Review* **56** (4), pp 158–65

Tybout, A M and Carpenter, G S (2003) Creating and managing brands, in *Kellogg on Marketing*, ed D Iacobucci, Wiley, New York

UMTS Forum (2002) 3G – portals: a call for open standards, Position Paper No 3, UMTS Forum, Feb

UNCTAD (2004) *World Investment Report 2004: The shift towards services*, UNCTAD, New York

Utterback, J M (1996) *Mastering the Dynamics of Innovation*, Harvard Business School Press, Boston, Mass

Vodafone (2004) *Annual Report 2004*, Vodafone Group

Waldman, A (2004) What India's upset vote reveals: the high tech is skin deep, *New York Times*, 15 May

Webster, F E Jr (1994) Executing the new marketing concept, *Marketing Management*, **3** (1), pp 9–18

Zafirovski , M (2004) Motonext: operating in an era of convergence, paper at Sanford C Bersteins Annual Strategic Decisions Conference, 2 June

Index